Dark History
Season One

Ben Cutmore

Copyright © 2021 Ben Cutmore

Cover design by Jessica Deare

Logo Design by Courtney Donkersteeg

All rights reserved.

darkhistories.com

ISBN: 979-8-5246-8563-6

For my mum and dad, whose patience is pretty incredible to be honest.

Contents

Episode 1 - Jack the Ripper: A History — 1

Episode 2 - The Enfield Poltergeist Story — 15

Episode 3 - Burke & Hare: The Westport Murders — 21

Episode 4 - The Dyatlov Pass Incident — 27

Episode 5 - Tamam Shud: The Somerton Man Mystery — 38

Episode 6 - Zombies: A True Story of Haitian Voodoo — 45

Episode 7 - Charles Walton: The Pitchfork Murder — 53

Episode 8 - Hagley Wood: Who Put Bella in the Wych Elm — 60

Episode 9 - Eilean-Mor: The Missing Lighthouse Keepers — 68

Episode 10 - The Devil's Footprints of 1885 — 77

Episode 11 - Vampires: From Myth to Murder — 87

Episode 12 - The Fire From Within: Spontaneous Human Combustion — 100

Episode 13 - The Clapham Woods Mystery: Satanism & The Occult — 109

Episode 14 - The Hinterkaifeck Murders — 122

Episode 15 - Terri Hoffman & The Black Lords — 136

Episode 16 - Peter Stumpp, The Werewolf of Bedburg — 158

Dark Histories: Season One

Episode 17 - The Pimlico Poisoning 170

Episode 18 - The Second Life of Omm Sety 186

Episode 19 - Joshua Maddux: The Boy In The Chimney

Episode 20 - Krampus & Co. 207

Acknowledgements

Number one on the list would have to be Howard Hughes. I listened to his radio show back when I was in college and later, his podcast long before Dark Histories was ever a thing and it was mostly through his show that I got the idea to start a podcast in the first place. Thanks also to Hally, who has been a constant source of support throughout and has helped me to handle some of the aspects of running a podcast that I find particularly challenging, like basic organisational skills. Thanks to Jessica for illustrating the covers for all of the Dark Histories books and not killing me in the process. I'd also like to thank all the listeners to the show over the years. I know it sounds a bit cheesy, but I honestly have always felt that making a podcast is a communal effort and reading all the emails, messages and general feedback. All the banter on Discord. All the abuse from Amanda during live streams and all the Instagram comments, episode suggestions and especially the Christmas Campfire submissions from everyone has been a true motivational drive for me over these past few years. I have told the story once or twice before, but when I started the podcast it was as a distraction from some pretty wild anxiety issues that I was suffering at the time, so to have been able to get through it together with a community of people has been invaluable. Truly thank you for all the support, in every form.

Preface

Looking back on Season One brings mixed feelings for me, until I was preparing the scripts for this book, I hadn't dared to retread the old episodes for several years and it was completed with no small measure of cringing as I resisted the urge to rewrite each episode entirely. When I began the podcast, it was actually as a YouTube channel and each episode was a series of short, 5 minute long videos, with the total of all episodes aiming for between 20-30 minutes. Compared to the most recent episodes where I aim for 45 minutes to an hour and often overshoot, they were very different in ambition and scope. It was with Episode 6 that I realised that perhaps YouTube wasn't the best medium and put the episodes together, releasing them as a podcast. When I look back now, there is so much I would do differently, so much I would add to each episode, the glaring difference in historical context being one of the main things that stand out to me, but they are what they are. Season One is still full of great mysteries, some of the best, in fact and the core of what makes Dark Histories what it is, is still in place. I was still making episodes with the number one priority to stick to the facts, cross check my sources, giving each the weight they deserve and research as deep as my ability would allow. See, there is that word, ability. In making the first couple of seasons really, I found it very much to be a process of learning in public, learning to write, learning to record, edit and produce an episode from start to finish and one step at a time, incrementally, things slowly climbed in quality. The same goes for my equipment too. Back in this season, I was using an old drum mic with an earth problem that meant it would buzz and hum at random intervals. I found fixing it was a matter of giving it a trusty whack. I learnt about and became more aware of the recording environment too, and midway through the season I moved from recording in my echoey lounge, to my far more sound insulated bedroom, opening the wardrobe to allow my clothes to absorb the reflections, a trick I still use now. Writing this midway through Season Five, I still feel I'm learning, nothing has changed in that respect at all, but with this book, I can see quite clearly how far the podcast has come. I hope as you read back through these old episodes you can find as much enjoyment in them as I had making them and enjoy seeing the progression episode to episode, season to season.

Episode 1 - Jack the Ripper: A History

Whitechapel, East London. Home to one of England's most renowned and evasive serial killers of all time, Jack the Ripper. We explore these murders from the shocking beginning, to the brutal and mysterious end.

1888, Victorian England

In 1888 England was ruled by Queen Victoria. The British Empire was in full swing and London was the largest capital city in the world. East London however, did not reflect this period's supposed prosperity. It was a densely populated area, where the residents lived in poverty, amongst the highest crime rates and with little future prospects. Whole families were often residing in just one room. Whitechapel, a district of East London, had the highest crime and death rates of the city. It was also home to much of the immigrant communities, leading to high racial tensions, exacerbated by high unemployment and overcrowding. There were many law abiding and hard working citizens, however, there were also many slums and ghettos full of drunken violence and crime.

For the poorest, housing came in the form of lodgings, or 'bunkhouses'. These were large buildings where people could rent a bed for the night, or if they couldn't afford that, could sleep standing up propped up by a rope. Many of the bunkhouses were crumbling, upkeep was often overlooked by the landlords and the roads and alleyways around the bunkhouses were often dark, winding and full of squalor. The East End could certainly be a pretty grim place, full of anxiety and fear, poverty and crime.

Many women who had found themselves on hard times, found themselves pushed into prostitution to fund their beds in the bunkhouses. These were women of an East End underclass who were poor, desperate and struggling. It was these working women that would become the focus of a murderer who arose in Whitechapel during four months in 1888, causing fear among England's populace with a brutal series of murders. Jack the Ripper.

Though there are five canonical, or, accepted victims of Jack the Ripper, there are theories that his murders may have escalated in brutality and that some earlier attacks may be attributed to him. These attacks have been debated for years, some debunked and others still open to interpretation. Considering the violence of the time, there are many possible victims that could have been Jack's early attacks, we will focus on just two murders prior to the canonical five, as whether or not they were Ripper killings, the first marks a landmark in the history of the Ripper case and the second is classed by many to be the likeliest non-canonical victim and stands tall as the subject of many heated debates.

3rd April, 1888 - Emma Smith

Emma Smith suffered a brutal attack on the night of 3rd April 1888. She survived the initial attack and finally, through coercion from two women from her lodging house, made it to the London hospital on Whitechapel Road. She spoke to the doctors there and explained that she had been beaten and robbed by a gang of men. Emma Smith died later that morning, on the 4th April. Her story of being attacked by a gang of men is largely accepted, therefore it's unlikely it was a Ripper attack, however, her death marks a landmark in the Ripper case as it saw the opening of the Whitechapel murders file by the police. This file would later encompass the Ripper Killings.

7th August, 1888 - Martha Tabram

Martha Tabram was a prostitute in her late thirties. During the late hours of August 6th, she was working with her friend Mary Anne Connely. They had picked up two soldiers and then split up, presumably to "get to business". Her body was later found in the early hours of the morning of the 7th by John Saunders Reeves who was on his way to work. She was found sprawled out on the landing of the Georges Yard buildings, arms and hands by her sides and legs open. She had been brutally stabbed thirty-nine times.

The soldier in this story would be the natural first suspect, however, despite a lineup, neither soldier was ever identified. Two other witnesses had passed by the scene at earlier times of the night and hot not seen Martha's body, though this may be attributed to the darkness of the buildings themselves being that there was no lighting, it could be argued that perhaps she was not killed by the soldier at all, but rather a different client from later in the night. Further arguments state that her body was found close to the Ripper heartland and that her wounds were concentrated in much the same areas of the body of the later Ripper victims, though her throat was not cut. Several of the detectives and important police figures who worked on the Ripper case themselves, considered Martha Tabram to be the first Ripper victim, leaving it open to many still today to be the most likely non-canon attack to have been by the Ripper himself.

The brutality of the murder shocked East London, though this was just the beginning of what was to be a bloody and gruesome four months for Whitechapel.

31st August, 1888 - Mary Anne Nichols

Mary Anne Nichols was a small woman in her mid to early forties. She had lived a colourful life, had been married for twenty-four years and had had five children. After many separations, she finally left her husband for good in 1881 and began living as a prostitute. She had turned to drink and was an alcoholic, moving from workhouse to workhouse throughout London. After landing a job as a maid, she stole clothing from her employers and took flight back to the workhouses she had been so familiar with.

In the early hours of August 31st, she had met her fellow prostitute, Emily Holland walking through Whitechapel Street, on the corner of Osborne Road, just a stone's throw away from the scene of earlier attack victim Emma Smith. She was apparently drunk and having some trouble supporting herself without the aid of the walls and told Emily she had had her doss money three times that day, but drank it all away. Ominously, she then told Emily that she would "soon be back" before disappearing down Whitechapel Street and into the night.

At 3:45am, Mary Anne Nichols' body was discovered by Charles Cross on Buck's Row whilst he was on his way to work. Upon seeing the body, he called to his friend across the street, the two observed her and believed that she was possibly still breathing. They arranged her skirt to "allow her some decency" and agreed to tell the first police officer they saw about their discovery and continued their walk to work. On Bakers Row, they met PC Jonas Mizen and told the officer of their grim discovery. Meanwhile, PC John Neill had also discovered the body whilst walking his beat. He signalled to PC John Thain who joined him and the duo was soon joined by Mizen. PC Thain went to a nearby house to call on the local doctor Rees Ralph Lewellyn who returned to Mary Anne Nichols body with PC Thain, but pronounced her dead at the scene, though only by minutes.

Mary Anne Nicholls' body was found in a busy industrial area of Whitechapel. On one side of the street were warehouses and factories and on the other, terraced houses belonging to tradesmen. Her body lay below one of the windows of the houses, though when questioned, the residents claimed to have not heard any disturbances. She had minimal possessions, a comb, white pocket handkerchief and a piece of broken mirror. Doctor Lewellyn was in no doubt that she was killed where she lay, on the street of Buck's Row, her blood running into the gutter by her side.

At the inquest, her wounds were described. She had several bruises to her face and several cuts across her abdomen, along with three or four deeper cuts running downwards from her abdomen. She also had had her throat cut, causing two brutal wounds from her left ear to below her chin which had severed all tissue down to her vertebrae.

Mary Anne Nicholls was well known and well liked in Whitechapel, her friends knew her affectionately as Polly and were moved to tears when identifying her body. Her father, ex-husband and eldest son paid for her funeral and she was buried in a polished Elm coffin in the City of London Cemetery. The Ripper had given London a taste of what was to come, Mary Anne Nicholls was poor and had no valuables to steal. Her killing was violent and senseless and it would not be long before he would strike again.

8th September, 1888 - Annie Chapman

In the days following Mary Anne Nicholls' murder, the press and local residents of Whitechapel had begun to panic, attributing the murder to that of a madman who had been able to vanish amongst the morning foot-traffic. Fear was creeping in.

Annie Chapman was forty-seven years old. She was petite, standing only five feet tall. She had married and had three children, though her youngest had died at the age of only twelve of meningitis. She had separated from her husband in 1885, though reasons are uncertain, it is likely that both husband and wife were heavily into drink at the time. She received an allowance from her ex-husband, though after his death in 1886 she took to prostitution to make her living. She resided at Crossinghams lodging house in Spitalfields and was seemingly in something of a stable relationship with a man named Edward Stanley who often paid for her bed in Crossinghams.

On the morning of the 8th September, Annie Chapman was seen several times in the kitchen of her lodging house. She was drinking beer with Frederick Stevens, another lodger, around midnight. She then appeared to go to bed, however, it is likely that she had in fact left as she was seen later returning eating a baked potato by John Evans, the night watchman. He had been sent to collect her lodging money, which she did not have. Annie went to see Donovan, the house manager, to explain that she had no money for her bed but told him not to worry, for "I'll soon be back" and asked for her bed to be kept for her. John Evans watched her leave and turn towards Spitalfields market around 1:30am.

At 5:30am, Annie was seen talking to a man at Hanbury Street by Elizabeth long. The man had his back towards Elizabeth who stated she heard him ask Annie "will you?" to which Annie replied "yes".

Annies body was found at 6:00am laying in the backyard of 29 Hanbury Street by a resident who lived on the third floor with his family. Upon discovering the body he alerted three men on Hanbury Street and then went to Commercial Street police station. Annies attacker had used a sharp knife to cut her throat, the wound was jagged and appeared to reach right around her neck. There was blood on the ground by her head and smeared on the fence directly behind her. The murderer had then gone on to cut her abdomen clean open. Her intestines were removed and placed by her shoulder, her uterus, upper parts of her vagina and two thirds of her bladder had also been removed but no trace of these parts were left at the scene. Doctor George Bagster Phillips, upon describing Annie's body at the inquest later, remarked that her wounds could not have been done in such a way through surgery without taking the better part of an hour. These comments would later light the fire of debate that Jack the Ripper was a skilled surgeon or butcher, or at least someone who was well trained with a knife and possessing some anatomical knowledge, though this is something which is still debated today.

Annies possessions were a small piece of muslin, a comb and some pills. It was later discovered that she was dying either from tuberculosis or syphilis, and had been suffering for some time prior to her murder. Her funeral was held in secrecy by her closest family, so that only her relatives attended to avoid public attention. With Annie's death, the press had gone into overdrive reporting the murder with extreme language and gruesome imagery. They published outlandish theories and criticised the police. Panic had struck Whitechapel following the second murder. The nightmare of the Ripper had begun.

As panic and fear swept through East London, a new inspector was drafted in to take care of matters on the ground. Frederick Abberline. He was well respected and one aspect of his appointment was thought to be to stabilise the public perception of the police at the time. There were many accusations, suspects and even arrests, the most famous being a man nicknamed "Leather Apron", though he provided an alibi for the murders and was released by the police. Almost three weeks passed before Jack would resurface, this time giving himself a name which would become infamous the world over for over a hundred years.

30th September, 1888 - Elizabeth Stride

Elizabeth Stride was a forty-five year old Swedish woman. She had moved to London in 1866 and by 1888, was living in the lodging houses on Flower and Dean Street in Whitechapel, working as an occasional prostitute.

On the night of 30th September, Elizabeth Stride was seen several times with men of varying descriptions, though it is the testimony of Israel Schwartz that is the most intriguing. He claims to have seen Elizabeth Stride at 12:45am with a man around thirty years of age, five foot five inches tall with fresh complexion, dark hair and a small brown moustache. He was dressed in an overcoat and an old felt black hat with a wide brim. The man had stopped to talk to Stride in the gateway of Dutfield's Yard and the two began to quarrel. The man pulled her into the street and threw her onto the ground. Schwartz crossed the street, thinking he was avoiding a domestic argument and not wanting to become involved. There was a second man lighting his pipe on this side of the street and the attacker called out, apparently to this second man "Lipski". Schwartz believed he was being followed by the second man so ran away from the scene until the second man did not follow.

At 1:00am, Louis Diemschutz entered Dutfield's Yard on his pony and cart. His pony refused to enter the yard and although he could not see anything, as the yard was pitch black, Diemschutz thought that perhaps something was blocking the path. Using his whip, he probed the ground ahead of him and came into contact with a woman's body. Assuming she was either drunk or asleep, he entered the working mans club at the back of the yard to get some help. Upon returning with Isaac Kozebrodsky and Morris Eagle, the three men discovered that she was dead. It was the body of Elizabeth Stride. She was lying on the ground, head against the wall of the yard with her throat cut. Upon arrival of the police and doctor Blackwell, the doctor noted that her body was still warm and judged that by the severity of the cut to her throat, she would have bled to death in around one minute. Judging the timings, it is very likely that Israel Schwartz was the only man to have seen Jack the Ripper at the time of a murder. It is also very possible that Jack had been in the yard at the same time as Louis Deimshutz when he arrived, perhaps cutting his brutal killing short of any further mutilations.

The calling out of "LIpski" to the second man has caused much debate as to whether or not Jack the Ripper was Jewish, or perhaps worked with an accomplice in his murders. However, Inspector Abberline himself did not suspect the second man to be an accomplice at all and suggested that the murderer was not calling out to him, rather than to Schwartz himself, hoping he would flee. A year previous, a Jewish man named Lipski had been hung for the murder of a woman and the name Lipski had become a common insult used towards Jewish people at the time. Indeed, upon questioning, Schwartz could not be sure to whom the man was addressing. It appears however, that despite these close calls, Jack was not finished for the night. Rather than fear of capture, he was perhaps frustrated that his work had been cut short.

The Same Night - Catherine Eddowes

At almost the exact same moment that the body of Elizabeth Stride was discovered in Dutfield's Yard, Catherine Eddowes was being released from Bishopsgate police station. Catherine Eddowes was a prostitute who had been arrested earlier that night for being drunk and disorderly but had sobered up enough for the on duty police officer to release her. She left the police station with a simple farewell: "good night old cock".

Catherine Eddowes was forty-six years old. She had been, if not married, in a stable relationship and had had three children prior to her arrival in 1881 to the workhouses of Flower and Dean Street. She was not known as a prostitute and was thought to have been in a relationship with a man named John Kelly. Nor was she an alcoholic, though it had been noted that she would occasionally fall to drink. Apparently the 30th September, 1888, was one such night.

At 1:30am PC Edward Watkins walked through Mitre Square on his beat and noticed nothing of any significance. Upon his return at 1:45am however, he saw the body of Catherine Eddowes, lying on her back in a pool of blood and with her clothes pulled up above her waist. Catherine Eddowes had had her throat cut severing her arteries, being the cause of her death, this was, however, not the full-extent of her injuries. Her intestines had been removed and placed over her right shoulder, a two foot long piece had been detached and placed on the left hand side of her body. Her earlobes had been cut off, her face mutilated, her eyelids, nose and cheeks all stabbed and sliced. Her abdomen had been cut completely open and many of her organs had been stabbed or cut through including her left kidney, which had been completely removed. All mutilations were done after her death. If Jack had been frustrated from being disturbed during his first murder, he certainly took it out on the poor woman here. Catherine Eddowes was buried in the City of London Cemetery on the 8th October, 1888.

Dear Boss

Following the night of the double murders, the police saw fit to release to the public a letter which they had received a few days prior on the 27th September. The letter was headed "Dear Boss" and has become famous in history, referred to simply as "the Dear Boss letter". It read:

"Dear Boss,

I keep on hearing the police have caught me, but they won't fix me just yet. I have laughed when they look so clever and talked about being on the right track. That joke about Leather Apron gave me real fits. I am down on whores and I shan't quit ripping them until I do get buckled. Grand work the last one was. I gave the lady no time to squeal. How can they catch me now? I love my work and want to start again. You'll soon hear of me with my funny little games. I saved some of the proper red stuff in a ginger beer bottle after the last job to write with but it went thick like glue and I can't use it, red ink is fit enough I hope HA HA! The next job I do I shall clip the lady's ears off and send to police officers just for jolly wouldn't you. Keep this letter back until I do some more work and then give it out straight. My knife is so nice and sharp, I want to get to work right away if I get chance. Good luck!

Yours truly,
Jack the Ripper

Don't mind me giving the trade name.

P.S Wasn't good enough to post this before I got all the red ink off my hands, curse it no luck yet. They say I'm a doctor now ha ha."

With the release of the letter, Jack the Ripper became a household name, both in England and America. As the press and public grew louder, the streets of Whitechapel fell quiet, though it wouldn't last long.

October 1888 - Calm Streets

The press and the public now had a name for the murderer of the Whitechapel victims: Jack the Ripper. The name captured the imaginations of the locals and several hoax letters were sent to both the press and police in the following weeks.Indeed, the authenticity of the Dear boss letter itself is still debated today. The second most likely authentic correspondence from Jack to the police came on a postcard, today named the "Saucy Jacky Postcard". It read:

"I was not codding Dear old Boss when I gave you the tip. You'll hear about Saucy Jackys work tomorrow, double event this time, number one squealed a bit couldn't finish straight off. Had not the time to get ears for police. Thanks for keeping last letter back 'til i got to work again,

Jack the Ripper"

The Saucy Jacky Postcard contains references to both the removal of Catherine Eddowes ears and the double murder before the details were described by the press, leading people to believe that this was a genuine correspondence, however, there are others who say that details could have been taken from the original Dear Boss letter and riffed with.

On October 16th, George Lusk, the president of the Whitechapel Vigilance Committee, was sent a small parcel. The Whitechapel Vigilance Committee was an organisation set up prior to the double murder by local business and tradesmen, their aim was to aid the police in their hunt for Jack the Ripper by supplementing police numbers in the area and raising money for a cash reward for information leading to Jack's capture. Inside the parcel was half of a human kidney preserved in wine. There was also an accompanying letter, famously sent "From Hell". It Read:

"From Hell,

Mr Lusk,

Sor, I sent you half the kidney I took from one woman and preserved it for you. The other piece I fried and ate, it was very nice. I may send you the bloody knife that took it out if you only wait a while longer,

Signed,

Catch me when you can Mr Lusk"

Upon medical examination, the kidney was found to be very close to the one removed from Catherine Eddowes, though the results were inconclusive. This parcel and letter is another of the letters which is still debated until this day, though the inclusion of the kidney sets it apart from other possible hoaxes.

There were other letters, so many in fact, that the police became inundated. The month fell quiet and no more murders led people to return to their lives as usual. October passed by without incident on the streets of Whitechapel.

9th November, 1888 - Mary Kelly

Mary Kelly was twenty-five years old. She was raised in Wales by a decent family and had a good education. She was married at the age of sixteen, though two years later her husband was killed in an explosion. She arrived in London in 1884, aged twenty-one. She was well liked around Whitechapel and seemed to be clear of most of the troubles of the area, though at times could be drunk and have a temper. She rented a room in Miller's Court in the Spitalfields area and lived with an unemployed fish porter named Joseph Barnet. Due to falling on hard times financially, she had taken to prostitution to pay the rent.

In October, Mary Kelly had invited a homeless prostitute to stay with them in their room and after an argument, Joseph Barnet decided that he had had enough and moved out. At 2am on the morning of November 9th, Mary Kelly met a man named George Hutchinson on Flower and Dean Street and asked if she could borrow some money. He declined and Mary Kelly replied that "I must go and find some money". George Hutchinson saw Mary approached by a man and the pair walked off together towards Mary's room in Miller's Court. The pair stopped outside her room and George heard her tell the man she was with "Alright my dear, come along, you will be comfortable". The pair kissed and walked into Miller's Court. George Hutchinson described the man as being around five foot six inches tall, thirty-five or thirty-six years old, pale complexion, a slight moustache turned up at the corners, dark hair, dark eyes and bushy eyebrows, he is, according to Hutchinson, of Jewish appearance. The man was wearing a soft felt hat pulled down over his eyes, a long dark coat trimmed in Astrican, a white collar with a black necktie fixed with a horseshoe pin, wearing dark spats over light button over boots, a massive gold chain in his waistcoat with a large seal and red stone hanging from it.

At 10:45am Mary Kelly's landlord, John McCarthy, sent his assistant, Thomas Bowyer, to Mary Kelly's room to collect overdue rent. Upon knocking and receiving no answer, he stepped around to the window, put his hand inside through a broken pane, smashed earlier during a drunken quarrel between Mary Kelly and Joseph Barnet, and pulled aside the curtain. Inside he saw blood on the bed and ran back to tell McCarthy of the scene. Both men headed back to the room and upon looking through the window himself, McCarthy confirmed that inside lay the mutilated body of Mary Kelly.

McCarthy later told journalists:

"The sight that we saw I cannot drive away from my mind. It looked more like the work of a devil than that of a man. I had heard a great deal about the Whitechapel murders, but I declare to God, I had never expected to see a sight such as this. The whole scene is more than I can describe. I hope I may never see a sight such as this again."

Mary Kelly was laying naked on her bed. Her right arm had been partially detached. All the skin from her abdomen and left leg had been removed and placed on the bedside table. All organs along with both of her breasts had been removed and placed around her body. Her uterus and kidneys along with one breast were under her head. The other breast was by her right foot. The liver was placed between her feet, the intestines were placed by the right side of her body and the spleen by the left. Her face had suffered such mutilation that she was beyond recognition, with parts of her nose, cheeks, eyebrows and ears removed. The cause of her death had been a cut through her neck that had been so deep that it went down to her vertebrae, the bones themselves notched from the blade.

Mary Kelly's body was buried in St. Patrick's Roman Catholic Cemetery, Leytonstone on the morning of 19th November, 1888.

Though there were several murders at later dates around Whitechapel, some attributed to Jack the Ripper by the press, the police never suspected another murder to be his handiwork. He had disappeared as he always had done after a murder. With one final, gruesome killing, he was gone. Still today, 129 years later he remains the mystery he was in 1888.

Suspects

There have been several hundred suspects as to who might have been the Ripper over the years. Was he a medical man possessing skill with a blade and anatomical knowledge? Or perhaps a butcher or a crazed man driven insane by Syphilis? Or perhaps just an ordinary man who had frenzied, blood fuelled outbursts? The names have come and gone, adding to a long list. We'll take a look at two of the contemporary suspects, highly suspected by the Whitechapel police at the time and two more modern suspects.

Jacob Levy

Jacob Levy had lived his whole life in the Whitechapel area. He was thirty-two years old at the time of the Whitechapel Murders in 1888, working as a butcher and lived in Middlesex Street with his wife and children. He had a history of violence and mental instability. In 1886, he was sentenced to twelve months in prison for stealing meat from another butcher. His own wife remarked about him that:

"He feels that if he is not restrained he will do some violence to someone. He complains about hearing strange noises, cries for no reason, feels compelled to do acts which his conscience cannot stand and has a conscious of a feeling of exaltation."

She also mentioned that he does not sleep at nights and wanders around aimlessly for hours. Jacob Levy was committed to City of London Lunatic asylum in 1890 and died due to complications from Syphilis in 1891, suggesting that he very likely had some liaisons with prostitutes during his life. Working as a butcher, Levy would have been both knowledgeable of anatomy and skilled with a knife, both things which were remarked upon during the murders. The police themselves heavily suspected a man who worked on Butchers Row. Inspector Robert Sagar said of this man:

"We watched him carefully, there was no doubt that this man was insane and after a time, his friends thought it advisable to have him removed to a private asylum. After he was removed, there was no more Ripper atrocities."

One of the witnesses, a Mr Joseph Levy who saw Catherine Eddowes with a man on the night of her death, was later reported on as follows:

"Mr Levy is absolutely obstinate and refuses to give the slightest information, leaving one to infer that he knows something, but that he is afraid to be called upon in the inquest."

It is possible that Joseph Levy was Jacob Levy's cousin, at the least, he was also a butcher and worked a few doors down from Jacob. Was he aware of Jacob Levy's involvement, but not willing to let on, due to familial ties or close working relations?

Aaron Kosminski

Aaron Kosminski was the man believed to be, by several high ranking police officials at the time, one of the strongest suspects, however, many of their accounts do not tally with the man himself, nor indeed with each other. Dates, behaviours and mix ups seem to be prevalent in all the official accounts of him as a suspect. This has led people to question whether or not they all speak of the same man in the first place, and thus, create great doubt that he is a strong suspect at all. Regardless, with the high ranking police naming him outright, he requires some research.

Aaron was born in Russia or Poland and moved to London around 1881. He was twenty-four years old in 1888 and lived in Whitechapel. By the later period of the 1880's he was thought to have been suffering from Schizophrenia, was delusional and paranoid. He believed that he was spoken to by a higher power, refused to wash and ate food dropped as litter by others due to his paranoia of being fed. He was eventually committed to Colney Hatch Lunatic Asylum in 1891. In 1894 he was transferred to Levinstone Asylum where he died in 1919. During his time in the asylum, he was never known as being violent.

Interestingly, in 2014, Kosminski was named by author Russell Edwards as definitively the Ripper. Edwards came to his conclusions through modern DNA evidence which is documented in his book "Naming Jack the Ripper". The book has fascinating scientific details and the DNA extraction methods are interesting, however the book's conclusions are hotly debated and largely unaccepted as a whole. We eagerly await the peer review of the latest DNA work, but until then he remains a suspect with a rather muddled back story.

Montague John Druitt

Montague John Druitt was the number one suspect of Inspector Melville Macnaghten, a police officer from Scotland yard who was involved with the Whitechapel Murders file from 1889 until 1891.

Druitt was a barrister and assistant schoolmaster in Blackheath. According to Macnaghten's description, he was:

"A doctor of about forty-one years of age and of fairly good family, who disappeared at the time of the Miller's Court murder and whose body was found floating in the Thames on the 31st December. The body was thought to have been in the water for a month or more. From private information, I have little doubt that his own family suspected this man of being the Whitechapel Murderer. He was said to have been sexually insane."

Macnaghten believed that Druitt had killed himself due to his brain giving way to insanity after the murder of Mary Kelly on November 9th, however, there are some discrepancies with what Macnaghten states about Druitt and the facts. Firstly, he was thirty-one, not forty-one years old. He was a barrister and a schoolmaster, not a doctor and thirdly he had committed suicide by jumping into the Thames more than three weeks after the murder of Mary kelly, in all likelihood due to him losing his position in both of his jobs. Inspector Abberline himself stated about Druitt:

"I know all about that story, but what does it amount to? Simply this, soon after the last murder in Whitechapel the body of a young barrister was found in the Thames, but there was absolutely nothing beyond the fact at the time to incriminate him."

We are then left with just Macnaughton's words and little solid evidence. Still he remains high on the list of suspects today, simply due to these suspicions of Macnaghten, which are difficult to ignore.

Hyam Hyams

Hyam Hyams was thirty-three years old in 1888. He lived at 29 Mitre Street, Whitechapel, with his wife and two children. In December of 1888, he was arrested by police and taken to Whitechapel workhouse infirmary suffering from delirium tremens. He spent the next few years in and out of asylums, usually forcibly taken by the police after violent outbursts, until in 1889, he was taken to Colney Hatch asylum after being arrested for attacking his wife with a knife. He lived out his days there until his death in 1913. During his time at Colney Hatch, he was described as being violent, threatening, noisy and destructive, once even stabbing a member of staff in the neck with a makeshift knife.

Interestingly, it is the confusion and mixups of the high ranking police reports concerning earlier suspect Aaron Kosminski that place Hyam Hyams into the frame. Many of the statements made about Kosminski that miss the mark ring true for Hyams. They stated that Kosminski was committed to Colney Hatch in the spring of 1889, only he wasn't taken in until 1891, Hyams however, was admitted in April 1889. They claimed the suspect Kosminski to be violent against women, which didn't seem to be true according to records, however Hyams was. Had time taken toll and names between suspects become confused?

There are many other suspects in the case of Jack the Ripper. Whether or not the real murderer will ever be found is just as much a mystery as the man himself. There is a strong community of amateur researchers and people who have given their whole lives researching the Ripper murders and new details are continuously coming to light. Perhaps one day the mystery will be solved for good.

Episode 2 - The Enfield Poltergeist Story

In 1977, a family living in a small semi detached house in Enfield, a quiet suburb of London, was subject to a series of violent paranormal disturbances which lasted for an entire year. Levitations, moving objects, overturned furniture and channeled voices were all witnessed by more than 30 people, including residents, journalists, neighbours and Police officers. Today we look at the story of the Enfield Poltergeist.

1977, 284 Green Street, Enfield, London

47 year old Peggy Hodgson lived at 284 Green Street, Enfield, with her four children, Margaret aged 13, Janet aged 12, Billy aged 7 and John aged 11, who was rarely at home, as he boarded at school and returned only for holidays and some weekends. Peggy was a divorcee, a quiet but strong woman, she was working hard to keep her family afloat during difficult financial times.

31st August, 1977

On the 31st of August at around 9:30 PM, Janet and John were in bed when they heard a shuffling sound. Mrs Hodgson came into their room to tell them to quiet down, the night before the children had complained that their beds were shaking up and down and Peggy was a little tired of them playing around at night, rather than sleeping. Janet complained that the chair in their bedroom was making the noise, slightly irritated, she removed the chair from the room and took it downstairs. Upon returning to the children's room, she turned out the light and the shuffling sound started again. She turned the light back on and it stopped immediately. The children were in their beds, apparently not moving. She turned the lights off once again, and once again, the shuffling sound could be heard. Mrs Hodgson explained the sound as if "someone was walking across the room wearing slippers". Then came the knocking. As they listened, a chest of drawers by the bedroom door slid out into the room, around 18 inches from its usual position against the wall. They stood in the quiet room, all staring at the chest. Mrs Hodgson pushed it back against the wall and once again, it slid back out, into the room. She tried to push it back again, but this time, it would not budge. Panicked, she took the kids out of the house and over to their neighbours. Vic, 'Peggy next door' and their 20 year old son Gary Nottingham were close friends of the Hodgsons. They explained their predicament and the Nottinghams naturally dismissed the story, but agreed to come and have a listen to see if they could hear anything. The knocking continued, and this time, the Nottinghams heard it too. Vic stated that he thought it sounded as if the knocks were following him around the house. At a loss, they called the police. WPC Heeps and PC Hyams arrived around 1am. WPC Heeps testified to the investigation later, detailing their visit to the house as follows:

"On Thursday 1st September 1977 at approximately 1am, I was on duty in my capacity as a policewoman, when I received a radio message to 284, Green St, Enfield. I went to this address where I found a number of people standing in the living room. I was told by the occupier of this house that strange things had been happening during the last few nights and that they believed that the house was haunted. Myself and another PC entered the living room of the house and the occupier switched off the lights. Almost immediately I heard the sound of knocking on the wall that backs onto the next door neighbour's house. There were four distinct taps on the wall and then silence. About two minutes later I heard more tapping, but this time it was coming from a different wall, again it was a distinctive peal of four taps. The PC and the neighbours checked the walls, attic and pipes, but could find nothing to explain the knockings."

"The PC and the neighbours all went into the kitchen to check the refrigerator pipes, etc., leaving the family and myself in the living room. The lights in the living room were switched off again and within a few minutes the eldest son pointed to a chair which was standing next to the sofa. I looked at the chair and noticed that it was wobbling slightly from side to side, I then saw the chair slide across the floor towards the kitchen wall. It moved approximately 3-4 feet and then came to rest."

"At no time did it appear to leave the floor. I checked the chair but could find nothing to explain how it had moved. The lights were switched back on. Nothing else happened that night although we have later reports of disturbances at this address."

With nothing more that they could do, the police left the house, leaving the Hodgson family to make camp in their lounge, where they would all sleep for the next several days.

September 1977

Over the next few days, lego and glass marbles began being thrown around the house. This was witnessed by both the Hodgson and Nottingham family. Vic Nottingham's father, upon picking up one of the thrown marbles from the floor noted that it was burning hot. On the 4th September, feeling unsure of who to contact next, Mrs Nottingham called the Daily Mirror, a national newspaper, hoping to gain some help through the press.

Journalist Douglas Bence and photographer Graham Morris visited the house the following day and witnessed the Lego blocks flying around the room, one hit Graham Morris in the forehead, which apparently caused bruising that lasted for several days. They returned to the newspaper convinced there was a story in the house and senior reporter George Fallows and photographer David Thorpe visited on September 7th. Fallows sympathised with Mrs Hodgson and upon hearing the knocking for himself, contacted the Society for Psychical Research on behalf of the family.

Society for Psychical Research

The Society for Psychical Research is one of the oldest paranormal investigative bodies in the world. Set up in London in 1882, by a group of scientists, philosophers and other academics, it was the first scientific organisation to ever examine claims of psychic and paranormal phenomena. It's mission statement was "to approach these varied problems without prejudice or prepossession of any kind, and in the same spirit of exact and unimpassioned inquiry which has enabled science to solve so many problems, once not less obscure nor less hotly debated." Although not without its critics, it has remained until today as one of the most legitimate research bodies into such activity and still funds various research papers around the world. In 1977, the society had a new member, Maurice Grosse. Grosse was keen to embark on his first investigation and soon got his chance at Enfield.

October 1977

By October, the moving and throwing of objects had now been continuing for some weeks. Soft furnishings, cutlery and any household object that wasn't nailed down had become the focus of the disturbances and were routinely disrupting various rooms in the house. On one night, the investigators cleared all objects that could be moved from Janet's room as a sort of experiment. Guy Lyon Playfair reported that after some time, they heard 'a tremendous vibrating noise' coming from the now empty room. "It was as if someone was drilling a great big hole," he said. He went into the room to find the fireplace torn out from the wall.

"It was one of those old Victorian cast iron fires that must have weighed 60lb. The children couldn't have ripped it out of the wall, but in any case they weren't there."

The pipes to supply the fireplace had been ripped clean in half.

Although Morris Grosse and Guy Lyon Playfair were convinced by this point, many members of the Society for Psychical Research were not so quick to believe. Many thought it was simply the girls playing tricks to gain attention. In later years Janet admitted to sometimes "messing about" but claims that they only played small tricks and none of the major events were hoaxes. Indeed Morris Grosse has said the same, explaining that at times the girls would play up to the events, but were always simple tricks and always caught out quickly.

November 1977

By November, Maurice Grosse had noted that the knocking sounds around the house had seemed to become intelligent and decided to ask it questions. They started simply, requesting the perpetrator to knock once for no, twice for yes. Upon asking if it was dead, it replied by knocking 53 times.

As November passed, Janet's behaviour was getting more and more erratic and at times she had become very unsettled. The words possession were not used, but Maurice Grosse went as far as to say that "She seemed to be taken over". On the night of November 26th a doctor had to be called to the house due to Janet's wild behaviour and injected her with 10mg of Valium. This was enough to put Janet to sleep, however half an hour later, the investigators heard a loud crash coming from upstairs and upon checking on the girls, found Janet on top of a dresser, still asleep, kneeling on a wide clock radio. Apparently having been thrown 14 feet across the room.

As part of the investigation, cameras were set up in the girls room which could be remotely operated and take bursts of photos every 4 seconds. The images documented from these cameras showed several strange happenings in the room. The first was a pillow, appearing to twist around in mid air, thrown by no one. The second was a curtain, appearing to twist around by itself, though no windows were open. The most extreme photos however, were apparently images of Janet herself, levitating in the air, being thrown from her bed. Janet described the events as such:

"The levitation was scary, because you didn't know where you were going to land. I remember a curtain being wound around my neck, I was screaming, I thought I was going to die."

December 1977

On December 10th of 1977, the intelligence of the disturbance progressed further, this time going as far as manifesting a voice. Janet began emitting a gravelly, growling and barking sound along with whistles. The investigators theorised that if it could bark and whistle, could it perhaps talk? Through questioning, it gradually formed a voice, a low guttural growl with which the investigators would hold many conversations over the coming months. Janet described it as "Like someone standing behind me putting their hand on my neck".

The investigators recorded the interviews with this voice and one crucial recording, during an interview by both investigators, the voice refers to itself as a man by the name of Bill.

Months later, Grosse was contacted by a man by the name of Terry Wilkins. Terry's father had lived in the Hodgson's home prior to the family. He had, Terry confirmed, died of a hemorrhage in his favorite chair on the first floor. His father's name was Bill.

The investigators claim to have later put water in Janet's mouth and covered it with a strip of tape, though the voice still spoke. John Hasted, a physicist at London's Birkbeck College, carried out an experiment together with Adrian Fourcin, a phonetics expert at University College, London. Tests with a laryngograph indicated that the voice was using Janet's false vocal folds, not by the larynx as in usual speech. If a person was to talk using their false vocal folds for any period of time, they would usually suffer from a sore throat at best, with the danger of long term injury very real. Janet however, would talk to investigators in this voice for hours on end, and later, upon returning to her normal voice would suffer no adverse effect at all.

The end

The disturbances continued in much the same vein until in July 1978, Janet was admitted to Maudsley Hospital for extensive psychiatric testing. Two months later she was given a clean bill of health, with no signs of tourettes or epilepsy or any other illness which could partially explain some of the events from the past months. Upon her return home, the disturbances seemed to calm down. Almost as quickly as they had begun, the strange happenings of the Hodgson home had finally ceased. Today, 40 years on, The enfield case remains as Britain's most famous haunting and though has had extensive criticism, has never been fully debunked.

Episode 3 - Burke & Hare: The Westport Murders

During the early 1800s, medical education was taking great strides in anatomy. Edinburgh was a central influence on the teaching of anatomy to enhance surgical understanding, however, in order to best teach anatomical knowledge, it was essential for lecturers to procure cadavers, dead bodies that they could dissect during practical lectures. The demand was far outstripping supply. Enter two men, William Burke and William Hare.

Edinburgh, Scotland: The 1820s

In the early 19th Century, Edinburgh was a leading city in the charge to bring Anatomy to the world as a proper science. Alexander Monro, John Bell, John Goodsir and Robert Knox were surgeons that all taught in Edinburgh, all of whom were central to the development of science around the globe. Due to the nature of the lectures, human bodies were needed for dissections and demonstrations, however, Scottish law stated that only bodies of prisoners, suicide victims and Orphans could be used for such a purpose. This naturally led to something of a shortage and there were some that sought to take advantage of this by robbing graves and selling the bodies, which were fetching a price as high as £10, several months wages for a skilled workman. Grave robbing could be seen as a lucrative business for the enterprising individual, who was willing to bend the law. The legal parameters of the time stated that disturbing a grave and taking belongings from the deceased was punishable by law, however, taking the body itself was not an offence, as it did not technically belong to anyone.

By the 1820s, Graverobbing had become so widespread that citizens held a protest in the streets of Edinburgh. To deter graverobbers, people could hire slabs of stone to place on top of a grave for a period of time allowing the body to decompose, making it useless as an anatomical subject and therefore worthless to the graverobbers. Watchtowers were built in cemeteries, manned by guards and iron bars were installed over graves. The wealthiest could even hire private guards to sit and watch over a specific grave.

William Burke

William Burke was born in 1792, in County Tyrone, Ireland. He had a comfortable upbringing and a good education. He joined the army as a teenager, later marrying a fellow Irish woman. He attempted to settle down, however, after a family argument pertaining to land ownership in 1818, he fled from his wife and moved to Scotland, where he remarried a prostitute named Helen McDougal. By 1827, they were settled in Edinburgh and Burke was working as a Cobbler earning a decent living.

William Hare

William Hare was born in Ireland around the turn of the century. Little is known about his early life, however, he is thought to have been illiterate, suggesting a poor background. He wound up moving to Edinburgh in the mid-1820s and worked as a coal man's assistant. He lodged in the house of a married couple and began having an affair with the wife, Margaret Logue. Upon detection of the affair, he was thrown out by the husband, however, he died soon after, whereby Hare swiftly moved back in and he and Margaret ran the lodging house as husband and wife.

In 1827, Hare went to Midlothian to work on the harvest, where he met Burke. The two men promptly became friends, likely due to their shared Irish backgrounds. After returning to Edinburgh they remained close, earning a reputation around the area for heavy drinking and loud behaviour.

29th November, 1827

On the 29th Of November, 1827, one of Hares' tenants, an old army pensioner who went by the name of 'Old Donald' died of dropsy. Unfortunately for Hare, the man owed £4 in back rent and upon mentioning this to Burke, the pair came up with the plan to sell his body to recoup Hares financial loss. After Old Donald's body was laid into his coffin, Burke and Hare removed it, hid it under the bed and filled the coffin with wood bark. They resealed the body and it was later collected and buried, with no one any the wiser. Burke and Hare then took the body to Edinburgh University, where a student directed them to speak with Surgeon Robert Knox.

Robert Knox

Robert Knox was an army physician, serving in the Battle of Waterloo in 1815 and during the Cape Front War in South Africa. After his military career, he settled in Edinburgh, became a member of the Royal College of Surgeons of Edinburgh and began teaching anatomy lectures, twice a day, advertising a full demonstration on fresh anatomical subjects for each lecture.

Robert Knox bought the body of 'Old Donald ' for £7, 10s. As Burke and Hare were leaving, one of Knox's assistants reportedly told the men that they "would be glad to see them again, when they have another to dispose of."

A New Opportunity

In January of 1828, Burke saw a fresh opportunity presented to him by another lodger in his house. This tenant, named Joseph had become ill and so Burke and Hare, sensing another quick profit, saw fit to help him along a little. They fed Joseph whiskey and then whilst Burke laid across his chest, Hare suffocated Joseph with a pillow. This left the body in good condition for the anatomists and they promptly delivered Joseph's body to Robert Knox, who paid them £10 for the corpse.

What followed was a flurry of murders as the two men sensed there was good money to be made in the business of killing.

In February of 1828, Burke and Hare met Abigail Simpson walking the streets late at night, she was an old pensioner who came to Edinburgh to sell salt. She was drunk and the pair invited her to stay at Hares house, where they gave her more alcohol and then promptly suffocated her. They put her body in an old tea chest and sold it to Robert Knox for £10.

An English travelling salesman of matches and tinder was next, he was lodging at Hares house when he fell ill with Jaundice and so, he simply had to go. He too was suffocated and his body sold to Knox for £10.

With their new found wealth, Burke and Hare spent with abandon and their opulence was becoming a talking point. They explained away any rumours by telling people they had inherited money, which people seemed to accept. However, with their increased spending, they had to increase their earnings.

In April, Burke met two women, Mary Paterson and Janet Brown, prostitutes from the Canongate area of Edinburgh. He took them home and drank whiskey with them, Mary Patterson fell asleep and McDougal, seeing Janet

Brown talking with Burke, accused him of having an affair. An argument ensued and Janet Brown left the house. Burke and Hare smothered Mary Paterson in her sleep and upon Janet's return to collect her friend, was told that she had already left for Glasgow with a travelling Salesman. The pair took Mary's body to Knox and sold it for £8. One of Knox's assistants, however, thought he recognised the woman, probably having been a client of hers in the past and inquired how the men had come across the body. Burke explained this away, saying that she had drunk herself to death and they had purchased her body from "an old woman in Canongate". This was apparently enough to satisfy the surgeons.

Throughout May, Burke and Hare killed Mrs Haldane, another lodger. She had become drunk and fallen asleep in the stable. She was suffocated and sold to Knox, as was her daughter, who later, after drinking with Burke, fell asleep and was suffocated, fetching £8 from Knox. Shortly after, an unnamed old woman, another lodger, another drinking party with Burke, became another suffocation and £10 earnt.

Effie, a beggar-woman who scavenged from bins and tips and in the past had sold scraps of leather to Burke, was coaxed into the house with whiskey where she was quickly dispatched and sold.

Burke and Hare were becoming confident in their business and when they met with a drunk woman who was being helped home by a police officer, Burke offered to take her home. The officer thankfully passed her over to the care of the men, who instead took them to Burke's house, killed her and sold her to Knox for a further £10.

In June, Burke and Hare killed two lodgers, an old woman and her grandson. The trusty tea chest that they had used to transport the bodies to Knox was not big enough to accommodate both bodies, and so they stuffed them inside a barrel, called a porter and had him help them to transport it to Knox, who bought both bodies for £8 each.

At the end of June, the pair took a well deserved holiday. Burke and his wife McDougal travelled to Falkirk to visit family. Hare was short on cash, however, upon their return, Burke noticed that he had new clothes. He suspected Hare had been working alone and confirmed as such with Knox, who told Burke that Hare had sold a body for £8. This led to a rift in the partnership, however by September, Mrs Ostler, a washerwoman, visited Hares house to do laundry. The pair got her drunk on whiskey and suffocated her, selling her body to Knox for £10.

Their previous falling out was now water under the bridge, and in October, the pair killed a local, mentally disabled beggar, James Wilson. He was well known in the area as "Daft Jamie" and had club feet and a facial disfigurement. They kept his snuff-box and snuff spoon and sold the body to Knox. However, being well known and having unique disfigurements, many of the assistants thought they knew of the boy. Knox denied the boy's identity as daft Jamie and promptly removed his head and feet prior to the dissection.

A Fatal Mistake

On the 31st of October, Burke lured an old Irish woman named Margaret Docherty into the lodging house by telling her that his mother was also a Docherty from the same area of Ireland. Burke, Hare and their wives got drunk with the woman and paid two of the other lodgers, Ann and James Gray, to sleep elsewhere for the night, on the pretence that they would be drinking until late and they didn't want to inconvenience them. They Murdered Margaret Docherty and left her body in a pile of hay at the end of the bed. The Grays returned early the next morning and became suspicious when the men would not allow Ann to look for her clothing around the room that Margaret Docherty's body now lay. Later that evening, when they were left alone, the Grays searched the hay and found Margaret's body and rushed out to tell the police. Burke's wife, McDougal met them en-route to the police station and offered them £10 a week for their silence, however they refused and made their report. Meanwhile, Burke and Hare took the body to Knox and sold it for a final £10. The next day, the police visited Knox, identified the body of Margaret and promptly arrested Burke, Hare and both of their wives.

As You Sow, So Shall You Reap

Upon searching the homes of Burke and Hare, items of clothing of victims were found as were the snuff-box and snuff spoon of Jamie Wilson. Due to lack of bodies or evidence, however, many of the murders had little to no evidence on which to convict the men. Hare was promised Immunity if he confessed to the murders, which would also include his wife's safety from prosecution. He gave a full confession, implicating Both him and Burke in the murder of Mary Docherty, Mary Patterson and James Wilson.

On Christmas day of 1828, Burke was found Guilty as charged, with the penalty being the sentence of death by hanging. Helen Mcdougal was given a verdict of not proven, so avoided any prosecution.

Helen McDougal was released from jail on the 26th December 1828. She was driven from Edinburgh by a ravenous public, however, and she made sail to

Australia, where she died in a house fire in 1868.

Margaret Hare, despite having immunity from prosecution, was held in Jail for her safety. She was released on 19th January 1829, where she fled to Ireland and was not heard from again.

William Burke was hanged on the 28th January 1829. His body was taken to Edinburgh University, where it was dissected as part of an anatomy lecture. Later, his skeleton was preserved and put on display, where it remains to this very day.

William Hare was released from prison on the 5th February 1829. He fled to London, where he was rumoured to live as a beggar on the streets until his death, though there were reliable sightings that placed him in Carlisle, alive and well.

Dr Robert Knox was not charged nor prosecuted for his part in the murders, he was cleared of any complicity during an inquiry, which agreed that he had no knowledge of murder whilst procuring the subjects for his lectures. Public opinion was against him, however, and so eventually, was professional. He was eventually shunned by his peers and moved to London, where he held a medical practice in Hackney until his death in 1862.

Up the close and doon the stair,
But and Ben' wi' Burke and Hare.
Burke's the butcher,
Hare's the thief,
Knox the boy that buys the beef.

- 19th century Edinburgh rhyme

Episode 4 - The Dyatlov Pass Incident

In 1959, a group of 9 experienced Russian ski hikers trekking through the Ural Mountains were the victims of an unexplained disaster that left no survivors. Eerily, the area of the incident was called Kholat-Syakhl, or in English, The mountain of the dead. To this day there is still no concrete explanation for what happened to the party, however, theories range from an avalanche to secret military testing, from UFOs to an animal attack and things stranger still. Though sensationalised over the years to bolster certain claims, the story at its core still remains a compelling mystery.

Sverdlovsk Oblast, Russia. 1959

In 1959, Soviet Russia was a vast, sprawling landscape, from the city of Moscow to the snow-capped mountains of Siberia. Many people were interested in exploring the wilderness, for sport and adventure. Known as ski tourism, trekking on skis through challenging terrain was a popular pastime amongst many young people. A group of hikers, formed of students and graduates of Ural Polytechnic Institute, were planning one such trip in January of 1959. The groups' main goal was to reach the mountain of Ortorten, amongst the Ural Mountains on the Siberian border. Although the mountains were a gentle climb, the weather would average -15C and the planned trail was described as category 3, the most difficult to traverse, demanding a very high level of fitness. All members of the group were well experienced and qualified to take on the route however, and the atmosphere as they stepped onto the train that would take them North from Sverdlovsk was relaxed and easy going, prepared for the adventure ahead.

The Group

The trekking group was 10 strong, 8 men and 2 women. All but one of them were students or graduates of Ural Polytechnic Institute.

Igor Dyatlov was the leader of the group, he was 23 years old, a radio enthusiast and studying engineering. A keen inventor, he had built a radio and portable stove for hikers and carried the stove on the trip. He was reportedly dating Zinaida Kolmogorova, another student on the expedition.

Alexander Kolevatov was 24 years old and a student of nuclear physics. He had transferred to Ural Polytechnic Institute in his second year from the All Union Polytechnical Institute. Prior to joining Ural Polytechnic Institute, he had worked for a secret soviet institute whose purpose was to supervise the Soviet nuclear industry.

Alexander Zolotaryov was the only member not affiliated with the university. He was 38 years old, a hiking instructor and WW2 veteran. He joined the team in order to add points to his degree, allowing him to gain the rank of Master instructor.

Yuri Krivonishchenko was 23 years old. He was a construction and hydraulics student and the joker of the group. He played the mandolin and took it on many hikes, including this one.

Lyudmila Dubinina was 20 years old. She was the youngest of the group, a dedicated communist studying economics. On a previous hike, she had been accidentally shot by a fellow hiker who was cleaning his gun.

Nikolay Thibault-Brignoles was 23 years old. He was a graduate of Ural Polytechnic Institute, where he had studied civil construction. The son of a French communist, he was born in a concentration camp for political prisoners. He was often noted to be taking care of other hikers on previous trips and had promised his parents that this would be his last expedition.

Rustem Slobodin was 23 years old and another graduate, he was born in Moscow to an affluent family and had studied Mechanical Engineering.

Yuri Doroshenko was 21 years old. He was a radio engineering student. He had gained infamy around the university for having charged down a giant bear with nothing but a geologist's hammer on a previous camping trip. He was previously in a relationship with Zinaida Kolmogorova, who was now dating Igor Dyatlov, though kept good relationships with both.

Zinaida Kolmogorova was 22 years old. She was a radio engineering student. She was outgoing and lively, well-liked around the school. On a previous trip, she had been bitten by a viper but continued regardless.

Yuri Yudin was 21 years old, he was an economics student and suffered from rheumatism. An infliction he would become thankful for, as we shall soon see.

23rd-31st January, 1959 - Into the wild

On the 23rd January, the group left Sverdlovsk and travelled some 200 miles North by train to the city of Ivdel, arriving at midnight on the 25th January. They stayed the night before they travelled by truck further north to the Northern frontier town of Vizhal, where they arrived at 4:30 pm and again stayed the night and prepared to begin their trek towards Ortorten the next day, the 27th January. Before leaving, Igor Dyatlov agreed with the sports club that the group would send a telegram confirming their safe return to Vizhal no later than February 12th. They borrowed horses for the first leg of the trek that would take them to an abandoned geologist's village. They stayed the night in the abandoned village, however, Yuri Yudin fell ill and after collecting a few minerals for the university the next morning, he left the group and returned to Vizhal. This turn of events makes Yuri Yudin the only surviving member of the expedition. The group is now 9, 7 men and 2 women.

The group continued to travel along the river until the 31st January, the cold weather dropped to -24C at night and they estimated their travel time to be around 1 mile per hour. On the 31st of January, they left the river and made for the base of the Kolat-Syakhl mountain, the local indigenous tribe, The Mansi, having named it after it's lack of wildlife and poor foraging as "The Mountain of the Dead". In a diary that the group was collectively keeping, the final entry is written,

"Wind is not strong, snow cover is 1,22 m. Tired and exhausted, we started the preparations for the night. Not enough firewood. Frail damp firs. We started fire with logs, too tired to dig a fire pit. We had supper right in the tent. It's warm. It is hard to imagine such a comfort somewhere on the ridge, with a piercing wind, hundreds of kilometers away from human settlements."

1st February, 1959 - Mountain of the Dead

The group left the camp base late on the 1st February, leaving some of their gear behind on a raised platform that they could collect on their return trip. They walked just 2 and a half miles before setting up camp on the slopes of

Kholat-Syakhl, just 10 miles from their destination of Ortorten. Around 6 or 7pm they ate dinner. Tired but in good spirits, they prepared to sleep for the night. They were not to be seen alive again.

20th February, 1959 - Search & Rescue

As the days passed, the 12th of February came and went. Despite Igor Dyatlovs promise to telegram the school no later than the 12th, deadlines for returns were frequently missed on such trips and so no one had any reason for undue concern. There had been reports of heavy snowstorms around the area they were known to be trekking, and most assumed the group had taken shelter for several days, delaying their trip. Dyatlov himself had told Yuri Yudin before he left the group to return to Vizhal that he expected the return to be later than the 12th. And so it was that no one paid much mind to the group's silence until the 20th February, when members of the expedition's family insisted to the local head of the communist party that they needed to send out a search team. The first groups sent out were student and teacher volunteers led by the head of the military department of the Ural Polytechnic Institute, Colonel Georgy Semenovich Ortyukov. They had little luck on their own and the military became involved with the search a few days later. On the 25th February, a ski trail was finally found and presumed to be that of Dyatlov's group.

26th February, 1959

They followed up the ski trail and the next day, the 26th February, the search and rescue crews discovered the tents of Dyatlov's group on the slopes of Kholat-Syakhl. The tents were found ripped and torn, with gaping holes in their sides. Upon investigation, they concluded that the tents had been cut open from the inside. The tents contained all of the group's belongings, including money, clothing and boots. They found footprints leading away from the tents that seemed to show people walking barefoot in a calm and orderly manner. Outside of the tent they found a pair of skis sticking out of the snow, an ice pick and Igor Dyatlovs jacket. They also found Dyatlov's flashlight and upon turning it on, found that it was in working condition.

The following day, the 27th February, search & rescue teams followed the barefoot trails leading down the mountainside towards the edge of a forested area and found the remains of a small fire below a large cedar tree. The tree branches were all torn off upwards of 15 feet from the ground. Later forensic investigation of the tree found traces of skin embedded in the tree bark. Near the fire, they found the two bodies of Yuri Doroshenko and Yuri Krivonischenko. Both had no footwear, Doroshenko was wearing a short sleeved shirt and shorts, along with socks on both feet, whilst Krivonischenko was found wearing a long sleeved shirt, underwear and only one sock on his left foot. Soon after the search team discovered three more bodies between the cedar and the tent, those of Igor Dyatlov, Zinaida Kolmogorova and Rustem Slobodin.

Dyatlov was found dressed, but without shoes, wearing one woolen sock and one cotton sock, his fists were clenched in front of his chest . Zinaida was better dressed, wearing several sweaters and three pairs of socks, though again, had no footwear and Rustem Slobodin, also better dressed, wore several layers of clothing and one felt boot on his right foot. It was to be several months before the rest of the bodies were found, once the thaw had set in and the snow began to melt.

4th May 1959

Once the snow had melted, the search and rescue team finally uncovered the lost 4 bodies from the Dyatlov expedition. They were found under four metres of snow, in a ravine 75 metres further into the woods from the cedar tree. Alexander Zolotaryov, Nikolay Thibeaux-Brignolles, Alexander Kolevatov and Ludmila Dubinina bodies were all well dressed and found in an improvised, man made shelter. Alexander Zolotaryov was found wearing a hat, scarf, several layers of clothing as well as leather handmade shoes. He had a pen in one hand and a notepad in the other. Curiously, he had a camera under his clothing. Though the film was water damaged, it was his second camera and Yuri Yedin later mentioned that no one seemed to have any knowledge of the cameras existence on the trip. Nikolai Thibeaux-Brignolles wore a hat, scarf, several layers of clothing and felt shoes. Alexander Kolevatov had no hat or shoes, however he had several pairs of socks and several layers of clothing. Lyudmila Dubinanas was wearing two sweaters, one of which belonged to Krivonischenko, one of the expedition members found dead by the cedar tree. She had apparently improvised footwear by cutting a sweater into halves and wrapped them around her feet, although only the half on her left foot remained.

The Investigation

The investigation into the deaths concluded that they had all died 6-8 hours after their last meal, around 11:30-1:30 am. Had all left the tents of their own accord and no other people had been around the site. There were no survivors, six of the members had died of hypothermia, whilst three had suffered fatal injuries, though they were not inflicted by another human being. Many of the injuries, including all of the hypothermia victims, were reportedly received during 'agony of death'. The investigation's conclusions however, did not tell even half of the story.

The Autopsy Reports

The autopsy reports of the nine bodies make grim reading. Not simple hypothermia victims. In contrast, many of the bodies had severe wounds and there were many strange details that were not sufficiently commented on during the autopsy reports.

Yuri Doroshenkos underwear was badly ripped. He had livor mortis spots on the back of his neck, which were not consistent with the way in which his body was found. This meant that his body had to have been moved after his death. The hair on the right side of his head was burnt and he had blood on his ears, nose and lips . He had upwards of 10 various bruises and abrasions throughout his body, including shoulders, armpit, arms and legs.
His right cheek was covered in a grey foam coming from his open mouth, suggesting a force of some kind upon his chest. Cause of death was listed as Hypothermia.

Yuri Krivonishchenko's body had several bruises and abrasions, along with bruises on his head. He had apparently chewed off part of the back of his right hand. Cause of death was listed as hypothermia.

Igor Dyatlovs body had bruises and abrasions on his face, ankles and knees as well as bruises on the backs of his hand and knuckles. Cause of death was listed as hypothermia. Zinaida Kologorovas body had several bruises and abrasions on her face, missing skin on the back of her right hand and a 29cm long, bright red bruise on the lumbar region of the right side of her torso. Cause of death was listed as hypothermia.

Rustem Slobodins body had bruises and abrasions on his face, haemorrhages of his temporal muscles on his head, blood from his nose, bruises on the backs of his hands and knuckles and a fracture of the frontal bone of his skull. Cause of death was listed as hypothermia.

Alexander Zolotaryovs body was found with eyeballs missing, missing soft tissue around his left brow, with bone exposed, an open wound on the right side of his skull and ribs 2,3,4,5 and 6 on the right side were broken. Cause of death was listed as fatal injuries.

Nicolas Thibeaux-Brignollels body had multiple skull fractures, centring around the temporal region but extending around his skull and a haemorrhage on his right forearm. Cause of death was listed as fatal injuries.

Alexander Kolevatovs body had a lack of soft tissue around his eyes, with his skull exposed, a broken nose, an open wound behind his left ear, and a deformed neck. Cause of death was listed as hypothermia.

Ludmila Dubininas body had missing soft tissue around the nose, eyes and cheeks, damaged tissue around the left temporal bone, missing eyeballs, broken and flattened nose, missing tongue. Her right side ribs 2,3, 4 and 5 were broken and on the left, 2,3,4,5,6 and 7 ribs were all broken. She had a massive haemorrhage in the heart's right atrium. She also had blood in her stomach, suggesting that her tongue was removed whilst she was still alive, though there is evidence that this was also caused by natural phenomena. Cause of death was listed as fatal injuries.

Curiouser & Curiouser

Many of the injuries could be attributed to animals scavenging, however, the presence of blood shows that they would have happened prior to death, not after. The bruises on several of the members' back of hands and knuckles are not consistent with falling, whereby you would expect the palms to be injured and the head and rib injuries are often extreme. The doctor who inspected the bodies said that the forces that caused the injuries exceeded that capable of another human and were equal to the effect of a car crash. Many of the doctors' reports showed higher than normal levels of radiation on many of the items of clothing. Strange details, such as Dyatlov's jacket being taken off outside of the tent, his flashlight, in working order discarded and cameras that were there going missing, whilst other cameras not known to be there showing up raise questions, aside from the largest question of all, what made the group leave their tent, in the dead of night in such a hurry as to have them all in various states of dress, cutting themselves out through the side of their tents and then would cause all of the injuries? The biggest clues were the rolls of film and diary found at the campsite allowing us to piece together the events leading up to the fateful night, and perhaps, in the case of the rolls of film, giving us clues as to what may have happened to the expedition. The official investigation's final conclusion was that "a compelling natural force" had caused the deaths, though for three years after the incident, the pass was closed to tourists. The inquest was wrapped up quietly and all files were sent to an archive, where they were only uncovered 31 years later, in 1990. So what did happen on the mountain of death that night?

Avalanche

One of the most obvious theories is that the pass suffered an avalanche, capturing the victims of the group in its wake. The avalanche caused injuries and panic amongst the victims and with the tents covered in Snow, explains why the tents were cut from the inside. It could also explain why the group retreated away from the tents, perhaps they moved in fear of a second avalanche. However, whilst almost the first logical step when considering the Dyatlov pass incident, an avalanche is not as likely as can be first assumed. The slope that the group camped on was not very steep, nor was it very tall. Modern analysis has shown that the location is not conducive to conditions that would lead to an avalanche. Furthermore, the footprints leading away from the tents suggest that the injuries suffered by the victims happened away from the camp, not in it. There are photos which show items of the group's gear stuck into the snow which are still standing 4 weeks later when the camp was discovered by the search team, along with the front of the tents. The group was also experienced and would likely have known that fleeing the tents, leaving all their clothing would have been far more dangerous than the threat of a second avalanche. All of this evidence, plus the fact that no snow drifts were noted mean that an avalanche was quite an unlikely culprit.

Mansi

The local indigenous Mansi tribes form the basis for one theory that was common at the time of the event. There was a Mansi encampment to the northeast of the pass and a Mansi trail led past the Dyatlov's groups camp, just 200 metres away. Many people suggested that the Mansi were well versed in the mountains and would have known how to hunt and then cover their tracks in the mountains. Some claimed that the Mansi would not have taken lightly to people encroaching on to their territory, whilst others claimed that the mountains were a spiritual ground and the group camping on the slope would have caused offence, leading to conflict. Much of this, however, has been put down to the misunderstanding of the Mansi people, the mountain, in fact, was not a spiritual ground at all and the Mansi religion did not hold ground like this sacred in the first place, nor did the Mansi have any problem with people trekking through the mountains. One Mansi testified during the investigation that

"Everyone goes to this mountain: Russian men and women and Mansi. There is no special prohibition to hike the mountain."

There are other factors that go against this theory, the Mansi actually volunteered and helped in the search and rescue teams. There was a considerable sum of money found amongst the possessions as well as alcohol, which was often used as currency amongst the Mansi and was perhaps even more valuable than the money itself. If it was a Mansi attack, why would they have left such valuables? In fact, the Mansi did not even have any precedent of attacking people. There was one story of a Mansi attacking a Russian woman during the 1930s, but it was akin to that of urban legend and may well be attributed to suspicion of indigenous tribes people by some Russians of the time.

Military Testing

One of the longest standing and often touted theories is that the expedition fell victim to secret military testing of some sort, either rockets, chemical weapons or developmental weaponry that either exploded and caused the injuries from force or could have poisoned them or scared them sufficiently to induce panic. Yuri Yudin himself was commonly a proponent of this theory, who saw evidence amongst the recovered possessions that there were items of clothing that he didn't think belonged to the group. Foremost were items used to wrap around the feet that were common military issue and he stated none of the team owned them. Many of the items of clothing found were noted to have been tested for radiation, an unusual test to have been made in the first place, however, it was found that they were in fact radiated, showing they had come into contact with some form of radiation. There were rumours that there was a secret military base nearby to the pass and the Soviets had tested rockets in the Northern Ural mountains before. Furthermore, there were reports from geologists staying in Ivdel that on the night of the incident, lights were observed in the sky over the direction of the pass. One fascinating aspect of this theory pertains to the camera found on Alexander Zolotaryovs body. Though the film was water damaged, the images were processed and seem to show what some speculate were lights in the sky. Possibly of planes and possibly of an explosion. Lev Ivanov, the man in charge of the investigation also claimed later on that during the search, they noticed that the tops of many trees had been burnt and that he was forced by the KGB to remove any mention of lights in the sky from the report given by various Mansi witnesses.

This theory, however, doesn't explain why only some of the members had such forceful injuries. The radiation on the clothing, though present, was later found to be inconsequential and there were no positive results from toxicology testing on the bodies. Further, there is no evidence that shows testing of weapons over the pass, though naturally, this doesn't discount secret tests that might have taken place.

UFO

Following on from the military testing theory, the logical leap for some is that UFOs or aliens could have been the cause. Much of the same evidence for the military testing is sighted as proof, the burnt trees, the reports of lights in the sky, Zolotaryovs photos etc. However, one other piece of information used to bolster the theory comes from testimony of Lev Ivanov, the leader of the investigation. As we heard in the previous theory, he was the man who testified that the tops of the trees had been burnt and that he was forced to remove mentions of light in the sky from the reports. Shortly after the incident, he became unusually fascinated by UFO phenomena. Throughout the 1960s, he made several requests to the KGB archives for information on UFO sightings. This is peculiar in itself, given that this man held a high legal position and at the time, UFO phenomena were regarded as a pseudo-religious interest in an ideologically atheist Soviet Russia. Was it all just one man's leap in curious logic, or was he onto something with this theory, did he know more than others, given his position in the investigation? The obvious flaw with this theory is that it is all speculation, there is, of course, no solid evidence that UFOs or aliens were to blame for the incident, but the testimonies from Ivanov are fascinating.

Yeti

One of the more bizarre theories involves a Yeti coming across the group's camp and frightening them out of their tents, where it then savaged them. The severity of the injuries and the doctors claim that they could not have been caused by another human are used to bolster this theory. There is perhaps one other piece of evidence and that is in Frame 17 of the photos taken from Nikolay Thibault-Brignoles camera. The image shows a figure in the background that many have claimed was a yeti stalking the group. In reality, it is likely that it was simply another member of the group. There is no other evidence that any animal attacked them, let alone a yeti, such as prints in the snow or any other animal tracks. This also doesn't explain why only some of the members had such injuries whilst others closer to the camp were relatively unscathed in comparison.

KGB Agents

Theorised by Alexei Ratikin, it is posited that one or more of the team could have been KGB agents looking to meet with CIA agents to deliver samples of radioactive clothing to the spies and take photos of them. This theory suggests that the expedition was cover for their mission, however, the meeting went wrong and fighting ensued. Evidence put forward to bolster the theory is mainly centred around the backgrounds of certain members who had worked in secret Soviet institutes prior to the trip. Alexander Zolotaryov is the main contender for KGB spy, being that he was considerably older than the rest of the group, unknown to them and had a military career as well as a secret Soviet posting prior to the trip. He also had a camera that was found on his body which Yuri Yedin stated was not known to the group. It's also known that at least one camera that the group was using later went missing. Whilst this all sounds far-fetched, remember that this was the height of the cold war and certainly we now have evidence and concrete proof of much more bizarre events that happened between the KGB and CIA during this era. However, this theory has been roundly debunked by family and friends of members of the expedition, as well as many research groups who flatly deny any evidence to support it.

Infrasound

New research suggests that a rare weather phenomenon may have caused the expedition members to flee in irrational fear. The general theory goes that in certain circumstances, wind can hit certain elements of terrain creating a series of vortices, known as a Karman Vortex Street. This would create infrasound, vibrations which produce sound below the range of human hearing that is known to create panic, anxiety, difficulties with breathing and nausea. Perhaps it's possible that this panic would have driven the expedition out of their tent and into the cold night. These phenomena are widely reported in similar conditions to those of Dyatlov pass, amongst many other peaks and it has been suggested that the peak of the mountain could have created such vortices, the sound then carrying down through the pass. The main proponent of this theory was Donnie Eichar, who spent five years researching the incident and came to the conclusion of infrasound causing the event, stating that it is the only logical explanation for the events .

Conclusions

Despite all the theories, we are still left with something of an unexplained mystery. Much can be explained, but we are still left with many unanswered questions. No one theory can wrap up all events that took place and due to lack of any witnesses, it will likely stay that way, barring any great future revelations or undiscovered documents coming to light. Many of the 'concrete' theories have sensationalised certain aspects of the evidence that were simply not true and the reality is, that we are left with a genuine unsolved mystery, one which will probably unlikely ever be solved.

Episode 5 - Tamám Shud: The Somerton Man Mystery

In 1948, a man of around 45 years of age was found dead on Somerton Beach, on the outskirts of Adelaide, Australia. Sitting up as if staring out to sea, he was a man that, until this day, has no name and no cause of death. In 2013, new layers of intrigue were added, spurring renewed interest in the case, but the story of the Somerton man still remains a mystery. In this episode, we detail the case of what's often called simply, Tamám Shud.

Somerton, Australia. Tuesday 30th November, 1948

On the morning of Tuesday 30th November, a man arrived, presumably by train, in Adelaide train station. He bought a ticket to Henley Beach station, one of only three tickets sold for that particular train that morning. At around 11am, he checked a brown suitcase into the cloakroom and instead of taking the train he had a ticket for, he decided to catch a bus from opposite the station to St Leonards, in Somerton.

At 7:15 pm, John B. Lyons and his wife, Helen Lyons were walking by the beach and saw a man, lying against the seawall, his feet crossed. He raised his arm, before letting it fall limply.

At 7:30 pm, Gordon Strapps and Olive Neill taking an evening walk along the beach stop on a bench. Just below them, propped up against the sea wall, they notice a man, apparently asleep. They joke that he could be dead. The sun was setting and mosquitoes were in the air, and yet he showed no sign of movement for the thirty minutes they were there, however, the pair concede that it is more likely that he is a drunk and decide not to investigate any further.

Wednesday 1st December 1948

At around 5:30 am, Neil Day and Horrie Patching, two jockeys taking an early morning walk with their horse along the Beach noticed a man sitting down, propped up against the sea wall wearing an overcoat. They thought it strange that he was wearing an overcoat on such a nice morning, however, walked on by. At 6 am, as they returned and passed the man, they decided to stop and check if he was okay, far from okay, however, they found that the man was dead. Jack Lyons and Arthur Lee arrived on the beach from an early morning swim and saw the jockeys standing by the body and went to check on the commotion. Unsure of what they should do, Jack Lyons told the jockeys to leave it to them, and they contacted the police. Jack Lyons observed that the body was wearing dry clothes, with his mouth and eyes closed. There was no disturbance of sand and no debris or personal items around the body. His expression was as if he was sleeping, with normal clothing, light stubble, and his feet crossed. At 6:45am Constable John Moss arrived on the scene. He observed that the body was cold, damp and stiff. He had an unsmoked cigarette behind his ear, his left arm down by his side, right arm, palm upwards slightly out from his side and he had a smoked cigarette butt between his cheek and his lapel, presumably fallen from his mouth.

Upon inspecting the pockets of the body, he found a bus ticket, the unused train ticket to Henley Beach, two combs, one made of plastic and one from aluminium. He also found a packet of Juicy Fruit chewing gum, a box of matches and a pack of cigarettes containing cigarettes of a more expensive brand than the brand on the box. At 9:40am an ambulance arrived, took the body to the hospital and he was pronounced dead by Dr John Barley Bennet, with his time of death estimated by the state of his rigor mortis as being around 2am, earlier that morning. The Pathologist was cited as stating that the man was of "Britisher" appearance and thought to be aged about 40-45. He was in "top physical condition", 180 centimetres tall, with hazel eyes, fair to ginger-coloured hair, slightly grey around the temples, with broad shoulders and a narrow waist. He was dressed in a white shirt, red and blue tie, brown trousers, socks and shoes, a brown knitted pullover and fashionable grey and brown double-breasted jacket. All labels on his clothes had been removed, and he had no wallet. Upon further police investigation, it was found that his teeth did not match the dental records of any known living person in any databases, nor his fingerprints, which were circulated internationally, but received no positive identifications. This may all seem very strange and indeed at the time, the police found it to be unprecedented, but the mystery of the Somerton man was just beginning.

The Autopsy, 2nd December, 1948

The Autopsy was carried out the next morning. The coroner noted that there was no sign of violence and his heart was healthy. His organs were deeply congested with blood and mixed with the food in his stomach. His spleen was three times that of the normal human size, though it was noted that this could possibly be from a pre-existing illness. No sand was found in the man's nose or mouth, but there was sand found in his hair and he had small abrasions in between his knuckles which extended to the back of the right hand. Although the body had been found with his head propped up against the sea wall, large amounts of lividity (blood pooling) was found at the back of the head, suggesting that his body had spent some considerable time after dying with the head in a quite different position, the lividities concentration towards the back of his head and neck suggesting a spell of time lying on his back. Toxicology tests for poisons or toxins came back negative and no cause of death could be determined. The Coroner commented that he was quite sure that the man had not died a natural death and suspected poisoning of some kind, though the food found in his stomach, that of a pasty estimated to have been eaten at around 11 pm on the night of his death, was not the culprit.

As the police were yet to identify the body and had no leads with which to work, the body was embalmed for preservation on the 10th December. Over the next few weeks, there were many positive identifications of the Somerton man reported in the media, though they were all dismissed after further investigation by police. Hard facts go quiet on the Somerton man for a short time, but on the 14th January, workers at Adelaide train station discovered a brown suitcase checked into the cloakroom on the morning of the man's death.

The Suitcase, 14th January, 1949

The police checked the suitcase out of Adelaide station on the 14th January 1949. It was brown in colour, new and unlocked. Inside they found a dressing gown, a pair of slippers, some spare thread, four pairs of underpants, pajamas, shaving items, a light brown pair of trousers, an electrician's screwdriver, a table knife cut down into a short sharp instrument, a pair of scissors with sharpened points, a small square of zinc which was thought to have been used as a protective sheath for the knife and scissors and a stenciling brush.

Identification marks and tags had been removed from the clothing, however, a tie, laundry bag and singlet were stitched with the name "Keane" and "T. Keane". They also found three dry cleaning marks, though there were no men by the name of T. Keane reported missing in any English speaking country and no identification was made from the dry cleaning marks. The police did find, however, that the type of stitching in the jacket was that of a type only found in America and being as how the jacket was made to measure, there was a very high likelihood that he was an American man or had spent significant time in America .

At the inquest on the 21st June 1949, the result was left inconclusive. Speculation from the coroners of poisoning was noted. In particular, poisons Digitalis and Ouabain were both identified as being possible to kill a human and yet remain untraceable after death. A second doctor at the inquest, however, contradicted this statement. Dr Robert Cowan stated that

"I feel quite satisfied that if the death were caused by any common poison, my examination would have revealed its nature. If he did die from poison, I think it would have been a vary rare poison.... I think that the death is more likely to have been due to natural causes than poisoning."

An unnatural death was finally presumed, though cause was unknown and there was no identification of the victim. The inquest was adjourned Sine Die, a plaster cast of the dead man's head and shoulders was made for later attempts at identification and the body was finally buried, with the headstone marking the plot: "Here lies the unknown man who was found at Somerton beach".

The mystery of the man's body is buried in the earth, however, the true mystery is just beginning. Prior to the inquest, the coroner wrote to Sir John Cleland, professor of Pathology at the University of Adelaide, asking for assistance. A request he duly complied with. Upon his inspection of the body and the suitcase, Cleland made several key observations that the police had failed to note. Firstly, he found that the spare thread in the suitcase matched that of the clothing sewn into a repair of the lining of one of the pockets of the man's trousers and that the brand of thread was rare to be found in Australia, tying the two together conclusively. He also noted that the man's shoes were remarkably shiny and recently polished, commenting that he did not think the man would have walked on the beach much, if at all. Finally, he found one last piece of key evidence in the case. Rolled up and stashed in a small fob pocket in the man's waistband, was a small scrap of paper, torn from a larger page. There was print on one side that read simply "Tamám Shud". A Persian phrase meaning "Ended" or "Finished".

Tamám Shud

Public Library officials were called in to try to identify the printed text. They successfully identified it as the final phrase on the last page of a book known as 'The Rubaiyat of Omar Khayyam', a book of poems attributed to a Persian poet named Omar Khayyam and translated by Edward Fitzgerald. It was a reasonably popular book at the time, however it would soon be found that this particular page had been torn from a very specific, and rare copy. A photograph of the scrap of paper was released to the press and on 22nd July, 1949, a man went to the police with a copy of the Rubaiyat, printed in Christchurch, New Zealand in 1941, that he had found in the footwell of his car. There is some uncertainty as to the exact date the book was found, however, the man stated that he had left his car parked with the window open and found the book either on the day that the Somerton man's body was found or some weeks prior. Regardless of this precise date, the book he handed to the police had the back page missing, and after microscopic tests, was confirmed to be the same paper, with the tears matching that of the small strip found in the dead man's pocket. On the back page were faint indentations of handwriting along with two telephone numbers, one of a bank and one unlisted, which turned out to belong to a Nurse named Jessica Thomson. Jessica Thomson just so happened to live only 400 metres from where the body of the Somerton man was found.

Jessica Thomson

Jessica Thomson was contacted and interviewed by police. She claimed that she did not know the man, nor had any idea as to why he would be in her neighbourhood on the night of his death. Thomson stated that she had once owned a copy of the Rubaiyat of Omar Khayyam, but had given it away as a parting gift to a man named Alf Boxall, an army lieutenant serving during world war 2. For a while, the police speculated that Alf may be the identity of the dead man. Alf Boxall, however, was alive and well and presented himself and his copy of the book to police, quickly shutting down any further speculation. The police asked Jessica to see if she recognised the man from the plaster bust taken of the body, prior to its burial. Upon seeing the bust, she was reported to have looked down at the floor, flustered and though she might faint, refusing to look at the bust again. Despite this strange behaviour, she nonetheless held tight to her story that she did not know or recognise the man.

In later years, after her death, interviews with Jessica's relatives, including her daughter Kate Thomson were conducted. Kate told the interviewers that her mother had in fact known the identity of the man in the bust and that she had told her privately that she had lied to the police, and that the man's identity was known to people "on a level higher than the police". She also told of her mother's ability to speak Russian, though she refused to tell her daughter where or why she had learnt the language.

The Rubaiyat Code

The faint indentation of writing in the back of the copy of the Rubaiyat is yet one more puzzling aspect. On the final page were lines of text in capital letters. The second line is struck out and at first glance resembles a possible code. At the time, it was sent to both the Navy and Defence departments. Neither were successful at deciphering any meaning, stating that "there are insignificant symbols to provide a pattern" and that "the symbols could be a complete substitute code or the meaningless response to a disturbed mind". The final conclusion at the time was that "it was not possible to provide a satisfactory answer."

Modern analysis has been undertaken several times and although still undecipherable, conclusions state that the letters are unlikely to be random, the message is in English and it is likely that the Rubaiyat is a one-time-pad, but not a straight substitution one time pad, leading to it being incredibly complex and needing an exact same copy of the book to decipher it. After 60 years, the original has been destroyed, along with the suitcase and much other evidence, and no second copy of the book has ever been found.

Modern (in)Conclusions

The mystery of the Somerton man is multifaceted. Starting with the body, the conclusions about cause of death are initially problematic. One doctor at the time was convinced of poisoning, whilst another was adamant no poison was possible and this was backed up by the fact that all toxicology results showed no sign of poisons. Items around or on the body are equally confusing. All identification marks, labels and tags were removed from clothing, many of the articles were common in America rather than Australia, the aluminium comb, an item not made in Australia, but common for American soldiers during the war, his jacket with the American style stitching, juicy fruit gum and the thread which tied the man to the suitcase. All point to a man who was not an Australian national, or at the very least, a man who had travelled extensively.

Was his body dumped on the beach or did he die in situ? If he died there on the beach, what of the pooling of blood in the back of his head and neck? And what about his shoes, so clean, that it was reported he was unlikely to have been walking on the beach. And of course, there is the small fact that no record of the man's name, dental records or fingerprints exist.

After looking at the autopsy photos of the Somerton man, Doctor Maciej

Hennenberg noted that the man's ears had an unusual formation, whereby the top of his ear (the Cymba) was the same size as the bottom (the Cavum). This trait is known in only 1-2% of the Caucasian population. Derek Abbot, a professor at Adelaide University, later found that He also had Hypodontia of both his lateral incisors, a rare genetic feature present in only 2% of the population. Derek Abbot obtained a photograph of Jessica Thomsons eldest son, which clearly showed that he had not only Hypodontia, but also the same larger Cymba of the ear as the Somerton man. The chance that this is coincidence and that Jessica's eldest son was not the child of the Somerton man is estimated to be between one in 10-20 million.

In 2011, a woman contacted Maciej Henneberg with an ID card, issued by the United States to foreign seaman during WW2 that she had found in her father's possessions. The man on the ID card was named H C Reynolds and the photograph had several matching characteristics with the Somerton man, including a mole and the larger cymba of the ear. Hennenberg stated that "In a forensic case, this would allow him to make the statement positively identifying the Somerton man". The card was Issued to the man named H C Reynolds in 1918. He was 18 years old and his nationality was "British". Despite this official form of identification, no records relating to an 'H.C. Reynolds' have ever been found in British, American or Australian national archives.

So just who was the Somerton Man and what relationship did he have with Jessica Thomson? It seems highly likely that they had at least a personal relationship, but did they perhaps have a professional relationship too? Investigative work is continuing to this day in the hopes we may one day find out. The most often touted speculation lies on the possibility that he was a spy, possibly with Jessica too. This was, after all, the beginning of the cold war.

The code remains a mystery that may hold many answers as to exactly what his business was in Somerton in December 1948.

As for his death, that will likely always remain a mystery. It seems easy to point to poisoning as the likely answer, but if so, who, why and how? Was he poisoned on the beach or killed elsewhere and dumped and posed by the seawall? The questions are many and the answers few, making the Somerton man one of the most intriguing cases in our dark history.

Episode 6 - Zombies: A True Story of Haitian Voodoo

In 1980, A man walked into the marketplace of the Haitian town of L'Estere. He approached a woman and greeted her warmly, introducing himself by his boyhood nickname. The man and woman were in fact family, but the woman simply stared back at him in shock. As word spread throughout the marketplace of the man's arrival, panic and commotion began to stir the humid, Haitian air. The man's name was Clairvius Narcisse and he was well known in L'Estere. To his dismay, he found that his warm greeting was not returned. This should not have struck him as such a surprise, as Clairvius Narcisse had died and been buried in L'Estere cemetery 18 years prior.

Harvard University, 1982

In 1982, Wade Davis, now a professor of Anthropology at the University of British Columbia, was studying for a PhD in Ethnobotany at Harvard. He had travelled to far-flung reaches several times in support of his studies and had taken a particular interest in studying psychoactive plants used among the tribes people of the Americas.

In the Spring of 1982, he received a call from Professor Richard Evans Schultes, his professor at Harvard and a man who had travelled extensively himself to many of the remotest places on earth in the search of obscure plant knowledge . He had once lived in the Rainforest for 8 years, after taking a single semester leave. He had also been instrumental in fostering Davis' own exploratory urges, when in 1974, whilst studying at Harvard, Shultes had advised Davis on his first expedition into the South American rainforests. This time, he had something for Davis that would prove to be a little stranger. They arranged a meeting and when Davis arrived in Shultes' office, he asked Davis if he would be able to leave for the Caribbean country of Haiti within two weeks.

Shultes set Davis up with Dr Nathan Kline, a psychiatrist who had done exhaustive work in the field of psychopharmacology. Davis agreed to meet Kline, and two days later, in a Manhattan apartment, over drinks in thick, crystal glasses, Kline handed Davis the death certificate, dated the 2nd of March, 1962 of one Clairvius Narcisse .

Clairvius Narcisse

Clairvius Narcisse lived in the village of L'Estere, Haiti, where he was born in 1922. He had little responsibilities and had never settled to marry. He had nevertheless taken to several women around L'Estere, fathering children with multiple women, whilst side-stepping the responsibilities, both financial and parental. He owned several small plots of land, which he had inherited from his parents with which he farmed for profit and had made a secure living for himself. His sister told of how he had been able to afford a Tin Roof for his house before anyone else in the neighbourhood. Despite this, Narcisse had never been of much help to his family, preferring instead to keep his wealth to himself which had led to several disputes with his brothers in the past, both over his land, which by Napoleonic code, should have been divided amongst offspring after the parents death, but which Clairvius had kept to himself, and his money. His wealth was, in no small part, afforded to him due to his lack of familial and parental responsibilities. So the picture of Narcisse builds that he was a man of many enemies within the small market community of L'Estere.

On the night of 30th April, 1962. Clairvius Narcisse, then 40 years old, admitted himself to the hospital in Deschapelles at 9:45pm. Complaining of fevers, an aching body and spitting blood. Once in the hospital, his condition deteriorated rapidly. On the 2nd May, he was pronounced Dead by both a Haitian and American physician. Two of his sisters, Angelina and Marie Clare Narcisse witnessed the body, after which he was held in cold storage for 20 hours and then buried in the cemetery on May 3rd at 10am.

18 years later, he stumbled into L'Estere marketplace and approached his sister, Angelina. He used a boyhood nickname for himself, that which only his family had known and had not been used for decades. He claimed that one of his brothers had contracted a zombie ritual upon him in retaliation for one of the land disputes and that he had been resurrected from his grave shortly after his death, beaten, bound and taken away to work as a slave in the Northern region of Haiti with a group of other Zombies. There he worked the land, emotionless and cold for two years until the death of the master broke his spell. He stayed away from L' Estere for the next 16 years in fear of his

brother, but upon hearing of his death, chose to return. Angelina was not the picture of joy he may have hoped for. She recoiled from Clairvius, her eyes catching a scar on his cheek from where 18 years prior, a misplaced nail had caught his skin as his coffin lid had been hammered shut. She offered him money and told him to leave. For he was a dead man walking, his life departed and his flesh pulled from the ground by Haitian Voodoo.

Saint-Domingue, 1789

In 1789, Haiti was under colonial rule by the French Empire and named Saint-Domingue. It produced 40% of the sugar and 60% of the coffee that was consumed throughout all of Europe at the time. Known as "The pearl of the Antilles", it was one of the richest colonies in the world. Needless to say, it was built and supported on the back of black slavery and its estimated that the French Colonialists bought in around 790,000 African slaves between the years of 1783-1791. This accounted for one third of the entire Atlantic slave trade. These people, torn from their homes, bought the traditions of their homeland with them, one of which, despite French efforts to force Catholicism upon the slaves, was the religion of African Voodoo. It was in fact, a voodoo ceremony that would eventually lead to a revolution in 1791, when the spirit Ezili Dantor possessed a priestess and received a black pig as an offering. All those present pledged to fight for their freedom. In 1804, the slaves liberated themselves from French rule, fighting back Napoleon's armies to take Saint Domingue and declaring Independence. The Island was renamed Haiti, however in 1835, Voodoo became punishable by law, forcing it underground. As we have seen however, traditions die hard, and secret Voodoo societies would hold night-time rituals in secret Hounfour, away from the eyes of the ruling elite, priestesses thrashing wildly to rhythmical drums as they took in the spirits of the voodoo gods. They used voodoo to both protect and punish the people of the local communities, offering aid, or cautioning sickness, amongst the blood of animals and the heat of hot coals.

Port-au-Prince, Haiti, 1918

One of the first mentions of Zombies in western writing is in a book written by William Seabrook and published in 1929 titled "The magic Island". The section pertaining to zombies is short, but the story he tells goes as such:

In the spring of 1918, an American Sugar factory in Port-au-Prince ran by Hasco was having a busy season and needed to hire extra workers for the harvest. Whole families would register at the Hasco fields and at the end of the week, each member would be paid for their work. One morning a man named Ti Joseph and his wife Croyance showed up at Hasco with a pack of workers, all walking and standing as if in a daze. The registrar apparently likened them to cattle, with a vacant stare, but Ti Joseph explained that they were ignorant people from the mountains, unable to speak the local language. At the end of the week, he would collect the wages of each member, naturally keeping it for himself. Each night Ti and his wife would prepare meals for themselves and the workers, keeping the workers food separate and taking care to make sure that no meat or seasoning be mixed into the workers food.

At weekends, a nearby market town held a fete and the husband and wife would take turns to attend whilst the other stayed with the workers. Ti Joseph's wife, Croyance, however, felt sorry for the workers and wanting to see the procession for herself, decided one weekend to take them to the fete. She led the workers to the village and they sat, staring vacantly under the shade of a tree as the parade walked past. A peddler selling Tablettes, a sugar-based cookie with peanuts, passed Croyance, who bought some of the sweets for herself and also for the zombies. She did not realise, however, that the peanuts in the cookies had been salted prior to baking and upon tasting the salt, the dazed workers sprung up, panicked by their situation. They marched ceaselessly back to their home village, with Croyance unable to stop them, turned into the cemetery and each found a grave site that belonged to them, climbed down into the pits of the freshly ripped up soil and died again. For these workers were Zombies, under a voodoo spell of Ti Joseph. The locals of the village proceeded to take revenge on Ti Joseph and promptly cut off his head.

This story was told to William Seabrook by a Haitian man named Polynice. Seabrook didn't really believe it and indeed it sounds more like an urban legend than any truth, but Polynice swore blind that it was true and further promised Seabrook that he could show him a real-life zombie. Polynice took Seabrook to see an old woman named Lamercie, whom he knew to have men work for her that she had risen from the grave. When Seabrook came face to face with the zombies he found men with glazed looks in their eyes, he likened them to a dog he had once seen in a Histological laboratory in Columbia which had had its entire front brain removed. The men, as the dog in the lab, were alive, but emotionless, staring blankly into nothingness. Seabrook took one of the men's hands and greeted it "Bonjour compere", but Lamercie quickly intervened and told him to leave, Seabrook translated her words as "Negroes affairs are not for the whites". Seabrook felt that the men were probably mentally handicapped in some way, but Polynice continued to insist on his story of voodoo.

Seabrook spoke about his experience with Dr Antoine Villiers before he left Haiti. He told of the men he had seen and hypothesised about their handicaps as being a rational cause for their condition. Villiers agreed that this could be possible, but was not so sure, telling Seabrook there may be more truth in Polynice's stories than Seabrook would like to admit, he showed article 246 of the Haitian criminal code:

"It shall also be qualified as attempted murder the employment which may be made against any person of substances which, without causing actual death, produce a lethargic coma more or less prolonged. If, after the person had been buried, the act shall be considered murder no matter what result follows."

The implication to Seabrook was a simple one. What he had seen was common enough to require it to become a legally recognised criminal practice. This had a profound effect on Seabrook, for this was Haiti, where they practised voodoo and these were the walking dead.

Port-au-Prince, Haiti, 1982

Wade Davis had spent time before travelling to Haiti hypothesising on a rational explanation for the apparent zombification of Clairvius Narcisse. he had concluded that an African plant, Datura Stramonium, could have been used as the basis of a poison and could have been introduced to Haiti along with the African traditions. Datura Stramonium could be used in a concoction that, when rubbed on the skin, would have a variety of effects including hallucinations, delusions, confusion, disorientation and amnesia. In large doses, it could put a human into a numb stupor or even result in death.

When Davis arrived in Haiti, he first met with Max Beauvoir. Beauvoir was a renowned authority on Haitian voodoo and he warned Davis that he would be looking for the zombie poison for some time, as it was not a poison which made a zombie, but a Bokor, a voodoo priest. He invited him to witness one of his commercial voodoo ceremonies later that night. Davis obliged and duly spent the night enthralled as he watched a mambo, a voodoo priestess, trace out symbols on the ground to invoke spirits amongst prayer and drums.
An initiate of the temple, a Hounsis, thrashed about dancing wildly until the spirit arrived, possessing her, whereby she began to careen around the floor of the temple, chewed glass, sacrificed a dove by breaking its wings and biting its throat out. She then lay on a fire and danced whilst holding a red-hot coal in her mouth. When the drums stopped, the spirits left and Davis had been given a vivid introduction to Haitian Voodoo.

Davis next met with Clarvius Narcisse. Narcisse vividly told Davis of his experience of death, of lying in hospital, aware of his family next to him whilst he was presumed dead. Of being buried and of how a nail, hammered into the lid of the coffin had pierced his cheek, and of being called out of the ground by a voodoo priest, beaten, bound and taken away to work as a slave. He was conscious the entire time, but not living. He assured Davis that throughout the ordeal he was very much a dead man. Narcisse knew what he had become, but was powerless to stop it. "The Bokor had my soul" he said.

Davis spent the next day exploring Haiti and trying to find any trace of Datura Stramonium. He found none.

The Poison

Davis next stop was to meet with Marcel Pierre, a voodoo priest whom he was assured could create a zombie. He asked Pierre to create him a poison to turn a man into a zombie and after some haggling, Pierre agreed. Davis watched as Pierre ground various plants in a mortar, grated a human skull and added the shavings and finally added several sachets of coloured talc. He placed the green powder into a small glass bottle and Davis left, convinced that the powder in the bottle was worthless. He had not not noticed any of the ingredients to contain anything that could have psychoactive, nor physiological effects. He returned after ten days and confronted Pierre. He told him that his backers in America could pay him thousands upon thousands of pounds if the poison were real, for they were interested in its possible pharmaceutical uses and after a bit of bravado between the men, Marcel Pierre finally capitulated and agreed to make a zombie poison, this time for real.

Davis joined Pierre in collecting several of the ingredients. This time the ingredients were far more gruesome, but to Davis, far more promising and included digging the body of a three year old child from her grave. They worked by night and after they had rubbed an oily substance on their skin, Pierre crushed the head of the decaying corpse open with his hands and added it to a mortar already containing plants and the carcasses of a toad and large sea worm that had previously been placed inside a jar and buried in the ground until the creatures had "died from rage". Several fish that had been placed on a grill to burn were added and the whole thing was crushed into a powder, poured into glass jars, placed into the coffin with the corpse of the child and buried in the ground of Marcel Pierre's temple for three days. Davis had his poison. Before his return to America and quite coincidentally, whilst out walking, Davis stumbled upon a field of plants that he recognised. It was an entire field of Datura Stramonium.

After Davis returned to Harvard, he immediately sent his poison to the laboratory, along with specimens of the ingredients for toxicological analysis. His results were fascinating. He found that the plants all had physiological effects, leading to rashes, sores and skin irritations. The toad contained a multitude of poisons, but importantly all symptoms matched with the symptoms Clairvius Narcisse showed before his death. The sea worm made logical sense, as the toad would secrete more of its toxins if it felt threatened, so by placing the creatures together in a jar and burying them, they were not simply dying of rage, but the toad was being coerced into creating a hazardous amount of toxin before its death simply by the presence of the worm in the jar.

The real breakthrough came with the fish, however. The species used in the poison was blowfish or puffer. The poison of the blowfish, tetrodotoxin, is one of the most poisonous toxins known. Its effects included reduction of temperature, a prickling sensation leading to numbness, often giving the feeling of floating, paralysis and glassy eyes, eventually leading to a comatose state, however, full consciousness is retained until either the victim of the poison dies or recovers, depending on the dosage. This Davis hypothesised would not only explain why, upon speaking with Narcisse, he could remember everything about his "death" and his feeling of floating above the ground, but it could also perfectly explain how he could have, for all intents and purposes, appeared dead to the physicians in the hospital. He researched more into the puffer's poison and found several cases in history, especially in Japan where it's often eaten as a delicacy of people "dying" only to miraculously return to life on their way to the morgue.

The plants were used as an irritant, a way in which to create a sore and open wound which would allow the toxins to reach the bloodstream. It all fell into place so neatly.

So what of the Datura from his initial hypothesis? Although not in the main poison, Davis recalled his conversations with Narcisse and noted that upon being taken from his grave he was immediately beaten and bound by his voodoo graverobbers. Davis believes that Datura is used after the zombie poison, whilst the victim's psychological state is still frail, as a way to create a constant state of disorientation, effectively zombifying a victim for as long as the poison was used, maintaining a constant psychological stupor. This would also explain why, after the death of Narcisse's master, the zombies had been able to break free of their slavery as the effect of the drug, no longer being administered, wore off. But whilst all of this fieldwork provided a material basis for understanding zombification, voodoo has its own rules.

Voodoo

Now that Davis had a grasp on the practicalities of zombification, he was driven to understand the meaning and through his search discovered the Bizango, secret voodoo societies, that trace a lineage of rites and rituals descending from the hidden groups of escaped slaves during colonial French rule. These groups of men and women, enacting their cultural traditions in the mountains, would eventually form a militia that played a forefront role in the fighting of the rebellion. Now, these traditions survived as secret religious sects, meeting in shadowy temples during the black of night, submitting offerings into coffins lit by firelight as drums rattle and priests sing. The Bizango both protect their communities and enact measures of judgement. As Davis was told directly during his time in Haiti, The Bizango can be sweet as honey and bitter as bile. Clairvius Narcisse himself told Davis vaguely of a tribunal and judgement prior to his death and being pulled from his grave.

Zombification is something of a form of capital punishment from the Bizango. Narcisse knew he had wronged the community and understood his punishment in the context of voodoo. He accepted his fate as a zombie and as voodoo dictates, he had become the walking dead.

Episode 7 - Charles Walton: The Pitchfork Murder

On the night of February 14th, 1945. The body of Charles Walton was found on a farm in Lower Quinton, Warwickshire in England. His throat had been slashed open and the prongs of a pitchfork dug into the mud on either side of his neck, pinning the body to the ground. As leads on the case faded away, paranoia and superstition crept in, leading to theories of witchcraft and the occult, remnants of which linger still.

Charles Walton

Charles Walton was born on the 12th May 1870. In 1945 he was 74 years old, suffered from rheumatism and walked with the aid of 2 sticks. Despite this, however, he was still undertaking light work on the local farms of Lower Quinton. His life had been centred around the land, he had worked since a young man as a farm labourer and had earned the reputation of being a skilled horse trainer. His wife had died in 1927 and now, as a widower, he shared a rented cottage in the heart of Lower Quinton with his 33-year-old niece Edith Walton who he had adopted with his wife after his sister had died in 1915. Lower Quinton was a small, rural community with a population of just 493 and Charles was well known in the village. Though he was thought of as something of a loner and there were those that regarded him as an eccentric, whilst others viewed him with a mixture of suspicion and respect, he was generally popular among the locals. For the previous nine months, he had been working on a local farm known as The Firs, owned by Alfred Potter. Around 9am on the morning of February the 14th, Charles left his house to walk up to a field known as Hillground, part The Firs which rested on the slopes of an area locally known as Meon Hill. With a mind to trim the hedgerows, he left home with a pitchfork and slash hook - A long-handled, sickle-like instrument used for cutting and trimming foliage. As he passed through the churchyard, he was seen by two witnesses who were to be among the last people that would confidently record seeing him alive.

The Pitchfork Murder

At 6pm, Edith Walton returned to their cottage after her day's work to find it empty. Charles was usually home from work by 4pm and was a man of fierce habits, therefore, she found it to be unusual that he hadn't yet returned. Beginning to worry that Charles had fallen ill, Edith visited her neighbour, another agricultural worker named Harry Beasley. Together they walked up to the Firs farm and called in on Alfred Potter, the owner of the farm. Alfred confirmed that he had seen Charles earlier in the day cutting hedgerows up on Hillground and all three walked up to the field, torches in hand to see if they might find him.

Alfred took them to the spot he had seen Charles working earlier in the day and after a short search, the party came across the body of Charles Walton, lying on the ground near the hedgerows. The scene was a grisly one and it proved too much for Edith to bear, she began screaming loudly at the site of Charles' body and Harry Beasley attempted to pacify her and pull her away from the scene.

Charles' body lay sprawled on the ground, with his shirt unbuttoned. The prongs of his pitchfork were buried in the mud on either side of his neck and the handle wedged into the hedgerows, effectively pinning the body to the ground. The Slash hook was buried in his throat, leaving a wide gash across his neck that almost severed his head from his body. Searching nearby the men found Charles' walking stick, spattered with blood and matted hair, whoever the killer was, he had used Charles' own stick to beat him severely, before cutting his throat with his slash-hook, killing him outright. As they were coming to terms with the horrific scene before them, a man named Harry Peachey passed by and after calling him over, the group enlisted his help in alerting the police back in the village. Harry Beasley accompanied Edith home, who was clearly struggling to deal with the events and Alfred Potter agreed to stand guard over the scene until the police arrived.

The first policeman on the scene was PC Michael James Lomasney who arrived at 7.05pm after responding to Harry Peachy's news reaching the village station. Members of Stratford-upon-Avon CID were later to arrive, as well as members of the West-Midlands forensics team.

At 11 pm, Alfred Potter gave his first statement to the police, claiming that he had owned the farm for 5 years and had known Charles for the entire time he had been there, employing him on a casual basis for the previous 9 months to trim the hedgerows around the various fields. In the morning, he had been in the College Arms with Joseph Stanley, a farmer of White Cross Farm and after leaving at noon, he had seen Charles working about 500-600 yards away, from an adjoining field. He noted that there was around 6-10 yards of hedgerow left to cut and that the body had been about four yards further on from the spot he had seen him previously, which would be about half-an-hour's work. He described Walton as an "inoffensive type of man but one who would speak his mind if necessary" The body was finally removed at 1:30am in the morning. One of the first observations noted by police concerning Charles was a missing pocket watch that, despite being carried with Charles religiously, was nowhere to be found on his body or nearby in the field. Whilst not expected to be worth very much, it was at the time the only tentative lead for a motive that the police had.

The Autopsy

The official autopsy report stated that Charles Walton had bruising on ribs, chest and head, all of which matched his walking stick. His Trachea had been cut. He also had several defensive wounds, suggesting that he put up as best a defence as he could for a 74-year-old man. He had a cut on his left hand alongside bruises on his right arm and left hand.

Almost immediately the local police sent a message to Scotland Yard requesting help on the case. On the 15th February, the Deputy Chief Constable of Warwickshire sent a message requesting assistance, citing a nearby Prisoner of War camp as a primary concern. The message read:

"The Chief Constable has asked me to get the assistance of Scotland Yard to assist in a brutal case of murder that took place yesterday. The deceased is a man named CHARLES WALTON, age 75, and he was killed with an instrument known as a slash hook. The murder was either committed by a madman or one of the Italian prisoners who are in a camp nearby. The assistance of an Italian interpreter would be necessary, I think. Dr Webster states the deceased was killed between 1 and 2pm yesterday. A metal watch is missing from the body. It is being circulated."

The nearby camp was named Long Marston and was situated 2 miles from the village of Lower Quinton. It housed both Italian and German prisoners throughout world war 2, but by this stage of the war, as with many of the British camps, it had a rather relaxed view of security akin to modern open prisons. Many prisoners were encouraged to integrate into the local communities in a limited capacity, often working as labourers on the local farms. As is commonly the way, it is often an initial leap of logic to suspect an 'outsider' to a case and so it was here in the tight-knit community of Lower Quinton.

The Investigation

On the 16th February, assistance from Scotland Yard arrived in the form of Chief Inspector Robert Fabian and his partner, Detective Sergeant Albert Webb. Fabian was one of the foremost inspectors of the generation and highly respected. The pair were also joined by Detective Sergeant Saunders from the special branch, a fluent Italian speaker who would act as an interpreter when questioning the Italian PoWs.

With the arrival of Fabian, the investigation begun in earnest and despite Fabian writing in his later published biography that the people of Lower Quinton were cold and in some cases threatening towards the inspectors, even citing anonymous letters threatening Fabian directly along with his family, they managed to collect over 500 statements from residents of the village and surrounding areas.

Edith Walton was interviewed by the police and she told them that she had lived with Charles since she was three years old after the death of her mother. Charles paid all the rent on the cottage, as well as giving her a weekly allowance and supplying the households coal and meat. Along with his pension of 10 shillings a week and casual earnings from farm work, he had savings of £11, 11 shillings and 9 pence, money which had been left to him after the death of his wife. She also stated that Charles had left his purse at home on the day of the murder.

Harry Beasley was also interviewed and he stated that "Potter had a reputation as a decent man to work for". Concerning the night of the murder when the three walked up to Hillground and discovered the body, he stated that Alfred Potter had told him that he had seen Charles at work at 12:15 that day and that upon discovering the body, he was certain that Potter realised he was dead immediately.

The police took a second statement from Alfred Potter. He told the police that Charles Walton had usually worked on about four days each week when weather permitted. He said that he left it to Walton to say how many hours he had completed and implied that Walton was sometimes paid for hours he had not actually worked. When the police mentioned that they were hoping to take fingerprints from the murder weapons, he became angry, stating that he had in fact touched both the slash hook and pitchfork whilst discovering the body and that he had mentioned this to police previously.

Detective Sergeant Saunders undertook interviews with the Italians and despite finding that the security of the camp was lighter than anyone expected of a PoW camp, with the prisoners essentially being free to come and go as they pleased, no Italian connection with the murder was found and eventually the suspicions of the camp members subsided, as no solid leads materialised, nor any motives.

Becoming desperate, RAF planes were called in to photograph the entire village and the royal engineers swept the entire murder scene and surrounding area with mine detectors in an attempt to find any trace of the pocket watch, though nothing was found.

As leads faded away, paranoia and superstition crept in. Many theories were put forward which still linger today, blurring the facts of the case and taking it in an even darker direction.

Folklore and Witchcraft

Folklore and the pagan roots of the country are often heavily referenced in rural English communities and Lower Quinton was no exception. It was said that the devil attempted to throw a large clod of earth to smother a recently built Abbey. The Bishop of Worcester noticed the devil and with the power of prayer, altered the devil's aim, causing the earth to fall short of the Abbey which led to the formation of Meon Hill, the site of The Firs.
One year prior to the Charles Walton murder, there was a high profile trial of a woman named Helen Duncan that invoked the witchcraft act of 1735. We can assume then, that whilst uncommon, there was still some legitimate concern around pagan and folkloric beliefs at the time of the murder.

Rumors began to circulate among the village and there were a minority that held Charles Walton with some suspicion. The fact that he kept toads lead some to pass rumours that he had used them to sabotage the previous years harvest. Others noted that he had an unnatural affinity with animals . It was well known that he had trained horses, but it was claimed by some that he could also tame wild dogs and that birds would often flock around him and feed from his hand and would even "obey his requests" to not eat the seeds from his plot of land. Despite no mention in the official autopsy and police reports, there were also rumours that a cross had been carved into his chest at the time of his murder.

Upon his arrival, Fabian himself was presented with two strange tales of local history. Detective Superintendent Alex Spooner, head of Warwickshire CID presented Fabian with a book, published in 1929, entitled "folklore, old customs and traditions in Shakespeare land". The book contained a story of one Charles Walton, who in 1885 had seen a phantom black dog on the road whilst walking home from work for several consecutive nights. On the final night, he had seen the dog accompanied by a headless woman. Upon returning home, he found that his sister had passed away. Black dogs have long been a staple of British folklore, often signifying death and generally viewed as a dark omen, often with a satanic association.

The second piece of local history presented to Fabian was the murder case of eighty-year-old Ann Tennant, in Long Compton, just 15 miles from Lower Quinton. In 1875, she had been brutally murdered by a man named James Heywood with a pitchfork and slash-hook, then pinned to the ground in a way resembling Charles' murder. James Heywood later claimed that he killed the woman on the grounds that she was a witch.

We now know in fact, that the boyhood Charles Walton from the book was highly unlikely to have been the same person as the murder victim, no records have been found in any of the birth or death records pertaining to him having a sister who died in 1885.
We also know that the murder of Anne Tennant, in fact, did not hold many similarities at all to the murder of Charles Walton, except for the fact that a pitchfork had been involved in both cases. Ann had been attacked in front of several witnesses and died in her sister's house from injuries sustained by James Heywood, who stabbed her in the legs and head with a pitchfork. A slash hook was not involved at all.

Whether or not Fabian took any stock in either story or the rumours surrounding Charles at the time of the murder is debatable. He makes no mention of them in any of his police reports, however in his autobiography, published 25 years later, he refers to the case as "The Witchcraft Murder". He also wrote of an encounter with a black dog whilst walking on Meon Hill one evening and makes several references to Pagan lore and witchcraft concerning Charles Walton, going as far as to write:

"I advise anybody who is tempted at any time to venture into Black Magic, witchcraft, Shamanism - call it what you will - to remember Charles Walton and to think of his death, which was clearly the ghastly climax of a pagan rite."

Regardless of the veracity of any of the claims pertaining to witchcraft and folklore that surrounded the case, or the conviction of Fabians belief in them (he was a renowned self-publicist by the time he released his biography) they have persisted throughout the years, leaving a curious stain on the case which remains unsolved to this day.

One final twist to the case came In 1960. Whilst clearing the outhouses of Charles Waltons cottage, his pocket watch was finally uncovered. Whilst the obvious thought would be that he simply left it at home on the day of his murder, some have argued that being a man of such renowned habit, this is highly unlikely. It is also known that the police undertook an extensive search of his house and grounds which turned up nothing. This has led people to theorise that his murderer had in fact returned at a later time to place the watch there, before slinking back into the shadows of anonymity.

Lower Quinton remains as closed today on the subject of Charles Walton as it was to Fabian in 1945. When talking with the BBC, The landlord of the College Arms, Tony Smith, said:

"I can't talk to you about that. After 17 years of running this place I know there are some things we don't talk about. Talking about it would upset people and there's no sense in alienating people in a small village like this."

He added:

"In cases like this, there's always someone that knows something. Someone knows what happened, but for the sake of relatives and for not upsetting people, no one will say."

And thus, the murder of Charles Walton stays unsolved, a curious case which is deeply tangled in the local folklore of which it has itself become a part of.

Episode 8 - Hagley Wood: Who Put Bella in the Wych Elm

In 1943, four young boys out poaching in Hagley Wood came across a large Wych Elm, a broad, spider-like tree. One of the boys began climbing the tree to look for bird eggs and upon reaching the topmost branches, looked down to find the tree was curiously hollow. Inside the inky blackness of the broad trunk there was no trace of any bird nests, instead, he saw a human skull staring blankly back at him.

Hagley Wood, 18th April, 1943

On the 18th of April, 1943, four young boys from the local town of Stourbridge, Robert Hart, Thomas Willetts, Bob Farmer and Fred Payne were poaching in Hagley wood, part of the Hagley estate owned by Lord Cobham, deep in the west midlands county of Worcestershire. It was wartime Britain and as such, food was heavily rationed, it was not uncommon for people to stretch the boundaries of the law for a good meal. They approached a large Wych Elm and thinking it a good place to find birds nests for eggs, Bob Farmer scaled the branches and peered down inside the hollow trunk of the tree. Spotting bleached white bone and thinking it to be the skull of an animal, he reached in and pulled it out. Devoid of any flesh, aside from one small patch above the left temple, which also left a matted patch of hair draped across the skull, farmer was horrified as it became apparent that the skull was that of a human. He took a piece of material that was in the branches of the tree, wrapped it on a branch, wedged it into the skull's mouth and pushed the skull back down into the hollow. The four boys were now in a difficult position. They had discovered the remains of a human, a disturbing discovery that should be reported to the authorities, however, they were poaching and illegally trespassing on the land. In fear of reprisals, the boys decided to keep quiet about the skull and keep it amongst themselves. It was a plan that was doomed to fail and the thought of the remains quickly became too much for the youngest of the group, Thomas Willets, to keep to himself. He told his father of their grim secret shortly after returning home.

An Identity of Sorts

After hearing his son's story, the next morning, Willetts father contacted the police and the site of the Elm was visited by the Worcestershire County Police Force. The Police quickly found the skull but also found that any remains that were in the tree were so tightly wedged inside the hollow trunk, that they saw necessary to enlist the heavy-handed help of a lumberjack who cut down the macabre tomb so that the police could gain access. Once the job was done, they found they had unearthed not only the skull but an almost complete skeleton. They found some small scraps of rotten clothing in the nearby surrounding area and a single shoe along with the bones of a severed hand which was curiously missing from the rest of the remains inside the tree. The remains were transported to the West Midlands forensic science laboratory at the university of Birmingham, arriving on the 20th April. Professor James Webster, head of the Home Office forensic science laboratory in the West Midlands made a detailed inspection of the bones along with Doctor John Lund. Webster concluded that the remains were that of a woman, around 35 years of age, 5 feet tall with mousy brown hair. She had died 18 months prior to the discovery of her body, placing her death around October of 1941. Although the evidence was not conclusive, it was found probable that she had given birth at least once in her life, an eye-watering assumption that can be made by examining the pelvic bones for any changes resulting from childbirth. She also had an irregularity in the pattern of her teeth, which crossed over in the front on her lower jaw. There were no signs of any disease, nor was there any trauma to the bones, however, due to a wad of Taffeta material wedged into the skull's mouth, Webster concluded that she had died of asphyxiation. Furthermore, Webster was able to confidently conclude that the body had been placed inside the tree feet first, either whilst she was still alive, or very soon after death, as Rigor Mortis would not have allowed her to have been manoeuvred so tightly into the cramped space of the trunk. Once Dr Lund was supplied with the taffeta cloth from the skull's mouth, he was able to ascertain a complete image of her dress, the clothing being of poor quality and consisted of a brown skirt, peach petticoat, Brown knitted cardigan and cheap wedding ring. Her hair had not been artificially coloured or permed at all. All this gave us an image of a rather modest woman who would not have been uncommon in any street of Britain during wartime. This series of conclusions were remarkably detailed, however, they do present us with the case's first problem. Webster reported that the cause of death had been asphyxiation due to the wad of taffeta in her mouth, however, the young boys had stated earlier that they had wrapped material around a stick and wedged it into the skull mouth to lower it back into the Elm. If this is indeed the case and the cloth is assumed to be that which was used by the boys, how exactly did the woman die, if, in fact, she was even dead at the time she was placed inside the Wych Elm at all.

Bella

Despite the meticulous description that the forensic laboratory was able to provide of the woman, the police were no closer to ascertaining her identity. They drew up a sketch of the clothing and an artist's impression of the victim, which they used to issue publicly. The UK dental records were thoroughly searched and her description alongside the details of her lower jaw irregularities was published in dentists journals, all to no avail.

Hampered by the difficulties of undertaking such an investigation during wartime, the only thing the police felt they had any certainty of was that she was not a local woman, as there had been no reports of any missing persons in the area matching the description supplied by Webster. The case seemed to be in danger of grinding to a halt when a clue emerged almost six months later in the form of a somewhat cryptic message. Scrawled with chalk on a wall in large capital letters. It read:

"Who put Luebella down the wych-elm? - Hagley Wood"

The discovery of the message was followed by several more messages, all variations of the same theme and found throughout the Birmingham and West Midlands area. The messages morphed slightly each time before seemingly settling into the repeated phrase "Who put Bella in the Wych Elm?".

Whilst some presumed it was the work of a hoaxer, or someone with a twisted sense of humour, the woman's remains finally had a name and both the press and the police, starved of information, adopted it immediately. The Police promptly appealed for the graffiti writer to come forward for questioning, but unsurprisingly, no one materialised and the case once again fell cold.

Theories

At the time, there were many theories about Bellas identity, some were rather more typical in wartime Britain, that of her being a Nazi spy, for example, were openly put forward. Others were caught in whispers and were slightly more strange. One theory that continues to come up, again and again, revels in a world of black magic and folklore. The theory that Bella was a witch, or that she had fallen victim to a Witch Coven, shadows the case until this day.

The Occult

As controversial now as it ever was, the theory of black magic being involved in Bella's death was nevertheless a popular story back in 1942. Originally posited by Professor Margaret Murray and circulated by rumours, under the hanging horseshoes and tankards of gloomy pubs throughout the West Midlands, it quickly morphed into the many tales we have today. Murray was a renowned Egyptologist, anthropologist, archaeologist and historian. Formerly a lecturer at University College London, she was a respected figure of the time and had published several works in egyptology. The First World War, however, had hampered her further academic work in Egypt and so she turned her attention to witchcraft and would become a heavy influence on the founding of today's religious movement of Wicca. Murray was interested in one particular aspect of the case, that of the amputated hand. At the time and indeed, still today, it is an area of the case which has never been sufficiently explained. She theorised that the hand was a sign of occult murder and linked it with an artefact called "The hand of glory". Creation of the hand of Glory was a practice carried out by an occultist, whereby the hand of a malefactor, hanged for their crimes is severed from the body and the fat used to produce a candle. The candle would then be placed in the hand and would burn for the maker forever, though for no one else. It would also open locks and render people motionless or put them to sleep. The process of making the hand of glory is written in a publication from 1722, named petit Albert and it reads as such:

"Take the right or left hand of a felon who is hanging from a gibbet beside a highway; wrap it in part of a funeral pall and so wrapped squeeze it well. Then put it into an earthenware vessel with zimat, nitre, salt and long peppers, the whole well powdered. Leave it in this vessel for a fortnight, then take it out and expose it to full sunlight during the dog-days until it becomes quite dry. If the sun is not strong enough, put it in an oven with fern and vervain. Next make a kind of candle from the fat of a gibbeted felon, virgin wax, sesame, and ponie, and use the Hand of Glory as a candlestick to hold this candle when lighted, and then those in every place into which you go with this baneful instrument shall remain motionless"

Outside of magical candles, Murray also cited her research into witchcraft and Covens. One legend told that the spirit of a dead witch could be prevented from causing harm in the afterlife by having their body imprisoned inside a hollow tree. These theories brought the police no closer to finding the identity of Bella and whilst popular at the time, Murrays work in witchcraft has been academically discredited since her death. There was no evidence of the occult operating in the area, nor that the woman in the tree was any "malefactor" or witch. There were also no patterns, symbols or other iconography usually associated with ritual anywhere at the scene. Furthermore, the hand being left behind rather reduces the strength of any hand of glory theories, since it would have been needed if it were to be used in any such manner. The question remains however of why the hand was removed. Some have suggested that an animal could have scavenged it away from the other remains, dragging it into the undergrowth. This sounds plausible until it's considered that any animal doing so would have had to not only scale the tree, ignore several other bones and then remove just the hand from a space that was so tight that it needed the tree to be chopped down to remove the remains entirely. This would have been a very particular scavenger and one would assume, not the standard behaviour of such a creature that would normally take whatever it can get. Further stories of occult worship and witch covens during World War II have sprung up throughout the years, with varying degrees of evidence and it is on the back of this that the theory has remained, casting its dark shadow over the Hagley woods mystery.

Espionage

War time Britain was a time that saw ordinary life disturbed by a constant undercurrent of paranoia. The British government released leaflets, posters and news bulletins with slogans such as "title tattle lost the battle", "Loose lips might sink ships" and the ominous "talk less - You never know". Invariably, it wasn't long before rumours of espionage and Nazi spy rings were to be involved with the case and though followed up by police, none would harbour any solid leads at the time. Peter Douglas Osbourne, a Councillor for Birmingham city, tells a story originally told to him by his father when he was a boy one day when they were walking through Hagley wood. Upon seeing a large, blackened burnt down tree, his father told Peter that he was home on leave at the time the remains in Hagley wood were discovered and through his work as a special constable before the war, was the man that was given the grim task of standing watch over the scene on the night the police had uncovered the bones. After the war, Peter's father was travelling home from Italy when he met with a pair of RAF pilots. They shared stories to pass the journey and he told them of Bella and his night watching over her remains. Curiously, the men had seen a file during their duty which they believed was linked to the body. The pilot's story gleaned from this file was that of a woman who had been involved with espionage whilst working as part of

Goering's inner circle, though she was executed during the war. She had been educated at either Oxford or Cambridge and had very distinctive teeth, the front teeth, just like the remains of Bella, were crossed. He was told that dental records had been matched, but the police reports for the Hagley wood case had stated that although dental records were searched thoroughly, no matches were found and no dentists had come forward with information. It could be possible from this story that Bellas records were not held in Britain but her country of birth, or that any matches found were covered up by the intelligence agency. When Peter asked his father about the story years later, as an adult, his father had, for reasons unknown to him, taken a sharp turn. His father told him that he had nothing to do with it and that he didn't want to discuss it. Peter suggests that something had an effect on his father, leading him to clam up and not wish to discuss the case, though he is careful to not allude too heavily towards an intelligence service conspiracy. A further theory involving espionage that had a little more evidence in its support surfaced in 1953 when a local West Midlands newspaper named the Express and Star ran a serialised report on the case. The writer, Lieutenant Colonel Wilfred Byford-Jones had been writing a series of articles concerning Bella and the Hagley woods case, when he received a letter signed by a woman using the pseudonym of Anna, from Claverley, a town 15 miles from Hagley woods. The woman wrote:

"Finish your articles regarding the Wych Elm crime by all means, they are interesting to the readers, but you'll never solve the mystery. One person who could give the answers is now beyond the jurisdiction of earthly courts. Much as I hate having to use a nom-de plume, I think you would appreciate it if you knew me. The only clues that I can give you are that the person responsible for the crime, died insane in 1942, and the victim was dutch and alive illegally in England about 1941. I have no wish to recall anymore. Anna, from Claverly."

The police followed up the letter from "Anna" and found that her real name was Yuna Mossop. Yuna was married to a man named Jack Mossop, who in 1941 was working in an ammunition depot in Coventry. He was good looking and well dressed and appeared affluent despite living under the hardships of war. He apparently spent time walking around in an RAF uniform, despite never having been in the RAF and would visit Claverley often to visit his grandmother, always with a Dutchman, though his grandmother never knew who the mysterious foreigner was. Jack's family were nevertheless quite sure that something suspicious was going on between him and the Dutchman. According to Yunas story, it turned out that Jack had used his position in ammunitions to pass on information to this Dutchman, named La Rait and who was in fact a Nazi contact working as a go-between and selling Jacks information to a spy ring operating in the West Midlands, gathering information about ammunition locations for the Luftwaffe. As her original letter mentioned, Bella was a dutch woman, who arrived in England in 1941 and subsequently became involved (though to what capacity is unknown) with the spy ring. Yuna told of how all of these details were part of a confession from Jack to her and his grandmother, perhaps unwilling or simply unable to shoulder the guilt anymore, he then continued on and confessed to not only his activities with the German spy ring, but also to his role in the murder of a Dutch woman, her statement read:

"March or April 1941, said he had been to the Littleton arms with Van Rait and the Dutch piece and she had gotten awkward and passed out. They went to a wood and stuck her in a hollow tree. Van Rait said she would come to her senses the following morning."

According to Jack's story, the woman was still alive when he left her. He told Yuna that he had recurring nightmares where he saw the woman in the tree leering up at him. Less than a year later, he died, aged 29 in a mental hospital in Stafford. The police and MI5 both followed up and verified several of the details from Yunas account, but none of the men involved were found. During research for his 1969 book, "Murder by witchcraft", Donald McCormick purportedly contacted an ex-Nazi called Herr Franz Rathgeb, who had spent time in the English Midlands during the war. Rathgeb knew a German agent named Lehrer who had a girlfriend who also worked as a German spy. She was a Dutchwoman named Clarabella Dronkers, who had lived in Birmingham. In 1942. The details from Yunas testimony lend a strong if somewhat circumstantial narrative to the case. She told of how "Bella" arrived in England illegally in 1941, and at that time, there were, in fact, well-known rumours that two German parachutists had landed in the Hagley area and vanished. It's also known that a Dutchman named Johannes Marinus Dronkers was executed for spying by the British in December 1942. Finally, Rathgeb also stated that Clarabella was aged about 30, and sure as day, had irregular teeth. So was Clarabella really the "Bella" from the graffiti, whose remains were a mystery for so many years? No details of a Clarabella Dronkers existence have ever been proven and McCormick's book is littered with what we would call today "Alternative facts". Despite the compelling statement made by Yuna to the police and the testimony of Herr Franz Rathgeb, we are still left with scant evidence for any of the persons involved. After the police had taken Yunas statement and despite their follow up and confirmation of many aspects of it, the case fell cold again and eventually closed. Finally marked as officially unsolved.

A Final Theory

In a modern BBC documentary concerning the Hagley Woods murder case, a statement given to police dated 7th April 1944 was unearthed from the depths of the police files. The short message was from Detective Sergeant Renshaw and addressed to his inspector. It stated that "whilst speaking to a Birmingham prostitute, she had told him that a woman named Bella who used to frequent the Hagley road had been missing for about three years." This was presumably also followed up and led nowhere as there are no more details of the prostitute named Bella. We are as close today to finding out who Bella of the Wych Elm was, if indeed that was her real name at all and not just a creation of a dark sense of humour, as the police were in 1943. Stories of witches and German spy rings aside, the remains of the woman in Hagley wood could just as easily have been an unfortunate woman from any number of backgrounds. Who was the graffiti writer? and Van Rait? Where are they now? Was the hand removed as part of an occult ritual? Or simply scavenged by an awkward scavenger? We could perhaps find answers to many questions through analysing the remains with modern DNA techniques. A case so wrapped in mystery, however, could not possibly have such a simple ending. The remains of Bella have been missing from their last known location at the university laboratory for over 50 years, no one knows where or when they were removed, nor are there, in fact, any records left of the remains ever having been there in the first place. Predictably, all forensic evidence and records have also vanished. The Hagley Woods murder case is a mystery upon a mystery and we are no closer to answering the 60-year-old question - who put Bella in the Wych Elm?

Episode 9 - Eilean-Mor: The Missing Lighthouse Keepers

On the 26th December 1900, a small ship approached the remote island of Eilean Mor. It was a small eruption of land, uninhabited aside from a small battery of 3 men, whose job was to operate and maintain the isles lighthouse. The relief vessel Hesperus was to bring supplies and rotate a fourth member of the lighthouse team. As the ship closed in on the barren Isle, the sight of the lighthouse on the edge of a sheer cliff sprung out from a bleak landscape. Joseph Moore, the member of the lighthouse crew who would be rotating in, noted that curiously, there was no flag flying on the flagpole, nor were there any provision boxes placed out for restocking. The crew on the boat fired off several blasts of the horn, splitting the quiet air. As they waited for a sign or reply from the lighthouse, an ominous feeling hit Joseph, things, it appeared, were not quite right on Eilean Mor.

Eilean Mor

At barely a quarter of a mile in width and just 43 acres in total, the Isle of Eilean Mor is the largest of a chain of small crags of land that make up the Flannan Isles in the outer Hebrides. Around 60 miles from the coast of mainland Scotland, it is set in the remote and bitter wilderness of the North Atlantic Sea, which surrounds it on all sides. The nearest port is in Gallon Head at the northern tip of the Isle of Lewis and Harris, which makes up the largest Island in the Outer Hebrides. 40 miles to the south is the abandoned Isle of Kilda and in the west, there is 2000 miles of open water before the coastline of North America comes into view.

Rising sharply from the water, the Southern end of Eilean Mor is a steep series of cliffs that stand around 150 feet tall, with a large slope extending to the northern tip of the Isle, here the cliffs drop 200 feet straight down to the sea below. Completely uninhabited, there are only three buildings, the lighthouse, built in 1899, the keepers living quarters and a small, ramshackle ruin that was once a chapel named the "Blessing Chapel". It was dedicated to the Irish missionary St Flannen, who was among the last people to have been known to certainly occupy the Isle in the seventh century and from whom the Isles have taken their name.

In the near 1300 years since and preceding the building of the lighthouse, it is thought unlikely that anyone had occupied the Isle for any period of time. Falling under the authority of Lewis, there are historical reports that inhabitants of Lewis would undertake yearly pilgrimages during the summer months for the purpose of rearing sheep and collecting eggs, quills, fowl and down. These pilgrimages were known to take on something of a supernatural bent. If the wind were to change direction upon their setting sail to the islands, they would immediately turn around and return home. Upon arriving, the crews of the boats would remove their hats and make their way to the ruined chapel, strip their upper clothing off and pray three times, once on approach, once as they made their way around the stone ruin and a third as they were beside it. Until they had done this ritual every morning, no foraging could begin. They also followed a code of conduct on how animals on the island were killed, as well as being careful to utilise a traditional local dialect in place of their own. These customs and rules were so strongly observed that any members of crew new to the pilgrimage would be placed with a senior member who was to keep a close watch and act as an advisory at all times. In 1695, Martin Martin wrote that they observed these customs to "Prevent inconveniences that they think may ensue upon the transgression of the least nicety observed here". When making inquiries to the men and women of Lewis on the sanctity of the Isles, he was told:

"there was none ever yet landed in them but found himself more disposed to devotion there than anywhere else."

The Lighthouse

In 1895, the Northern Lighthouse Board saw fit to place a lighthouse on Eilean Mor and shortly after first constructing steep zig-zagging, stone stairways leading up to the island's summit on both the East and West sides of the island, the construction of the lighthouse started. Due to consistent bad weather, the construction took four years, rather than the projected two and when it was finished, consisted of both the Eastern and Western landings, a crane around halfway up the staircases and small steam-powered trolleys on rails to assist in carting supplies from the landing dock to the lighthouse. There was a small living quarters for the crew and the lighthouse itself, which stood 75 feet tall from the highest point on the North-Eastern tip of the Isle. The light itself stood 275 feet above sea level and could be seen for up to 24 miles out at sea when it was lit for the first time on December 1st, 1899. Whilst it was a modern lighthouse, it was not fitted with any wireless or telegraph equipment, but instead used a signalling device that the crew could use in an emergency to signal to a watch station in Lewis.

The Crew

The crew of the Lighthouse was 4 men strong, three of whom stayed at the lighthouse at any one time and a fourth member who would rotate out to Lewis for two weeks leave in order to rest and recuperate from the high levels of responsibility, unforgiving climate and oppressive isolation of the Island.

The most senior and principal keeper was James Ducat. he was 43 years old and married with four children. He had already spent 20 years in the lighthouse service. During construction of the light on Eilean Mor, he had spent 14 months acclimatizing himself with the Island so when the men made their move there full time, he was already familiar with every facet of the landscape. The second Assistant Keeper was Thomas Marshall. he was 28 years old and unmarried.

The third was a man named Donald McArthur, 40 years old and married. He was, in fact, an occasional keeper, standing in for the first assistant keeper who was away on extended sick leave.

Joseph Moore was the fourth and last member of the crew and was the man who, on the 26th of December 1900 stood on the Bow of the relief vessel Hesperus watching for the welcoming party as it approached Eilean Mor to restock food and fuel for the crew and rotate personnel.

And Then There Were None

As the small relief ship approached the Island, the first sign of anything unusual that Joseph Moore noticed was the lack of a flag flying on the flagpole. As they drew nearer, however, he also noticed that the usual store boxes, which should have been placed out on the landing ready for restocking were curiously absent too. Due to the previous day's bad weather, they were already overdue and Joseph expected the men to be keen to see them arrive. The crew signalled their imminent arrival by giving several blasts of the ship's horn and when still there seemed to be no sign of movement from the lighthouse, they sent up a signal flare, but the lighthouse stood ominously still against the steel grey sky. In his memorandum, written 2 days later, Joseph wrote:

"Captain Harvie deemed it prudent to lower a boat and land a man if it was possible. I was the first to land, leaving Mr McCormick, the Buoy-master, and the men in the boat till I could return."

"I went up to the lighthouse and on coming to the entrance gate I found it closed. I made for the entrance door leading to the kitchen and storeroom and found it also closed, and the door inside that. But the kitchen door itself was open. On entering I looked at the fireplace and saw that the fire was not lighted for some days. I entered the rooms in succession and found the beds empty, just as they left them in the early morning."

"I did not take time to search further, for I naturally well knew that something serious had occurred."

"I darted outside and made for the landing. I informed Mr McCormick that the place was deserted. He along with some men came up so as to make sure, but unfortunately the first impression was only too true. Mr McCormick and myself proceeded to the light room, where everything was in proper order. The lamp was clean, the foundation full, blinds on the windows etc."

In describing the living quarters, Moore noted that MacArthur's 'wearing coat' was left on its peg, an item of clothing that he would have surely needed in poor weather. Moore stated: "It shows that as far as I know, Macarthur went out in his shirtsleeves".

On the night of the 26th, Joseph and several other members of the Hesperus crew, Allan Macdonald the Bouymaster, and Seaman Campbell and Lamont stayed on at Eilean Mor. Meanwhile, Captain Harvie turned the Hesperus back to Lewis, docking at Breascleat, which housed the nearest telegraph station to Eilean Mor. He made an urgent telegram to the secretary of the Northern lighthouse Board in Edinburgh stating:

"A dreadful accident has happened at Flannans. The three keepers, Ducat, Marshall and the Occasional, have disappeared from the Island. Fired a rocket but, as no response was made, managed to land Moore, who went up to the station but found no keepers there.
The clocks were stopped and other signs indicated that the accident must have happened about a week ago. Poor fellows, they must have been blown over the cliffs or drowned trying to secure a crane or something like that. Night coming on, we could not wait to make further investigation but will go off again tomorrow morning to try and learn something as to their fate."

That night, Joseph manned the Lighthouse, ensuring it was lit at the correct time. The next morning, the men thoroughly searched the Island looking for some trace of the missing Lighthouse team but found nothing. It seemed as if the men had simply vanished.
An Investigation begins

Over the next two days, the men continued their search for any trace or clue as to what could have been behind the disappearance of the Lighthouse crew. On the East side of the Island, they found no sign of disturbance and everything was in order. Climbing down the sharp stone steps to the docking area, they found that all landing ropes and equipment were properly and safely stored away and in their correct place. As they made their way over to the Western Dock, however, small signs of trouble began to emerge.

Joseph found that at some point between his previous shift on the Island, ending on the 7th December and his return on the 26th December, some force, which he thought likely severe storm weather, had caused the iron tracks of the steam trolley to have broken in several places. Furthermore, a box which was used to store mooring ropes, usually wedged and anchored into a crevice high up on the stone steps had vanished. They also found that one of the cranes on the Western steps, used to carry stocks up to the steam tramway from the docking area, was destroyed.

On the 29th December, Robert Muirhead of the Northern Lighthouse Board arrived on the Island to conduct an internal Investigation on the missing lighthouse crew. He confirmed most of the details previously given to the Board of the discoveries the men had found concerning the damage to the Western landing. He also found a large block of stone weighing just over a ton had fallen down by the side of the pathway, along with a missing life buoy, usually secured to the railing by rope, had disappeared. In his report he documented his findings as such:

"Owing to the amount of sea, I could not get down to the west landing place, but I got down to the crane platform about 70 feet above the sea level... The Crane was found to be unharmed, the jib lowered and secured to the rock, and the canvas covering the wire rope on the barrel securely lashed around it, and there was no evidence that the men had been doing anything at the crane. The mooring ropes, landing ropes, derrick landing ropes and crane handles, and also a wooden box in which they were kept and which was secured in crevices in the rocks 70 feet up the tramway were displaced and twisted. A large block of stone weighing upwards of 20cwt had been dislodged from its position higher up and carried down and left on the concrete path leading from the terminus of the railway to the top of the steps. A life buoy fastened to the railing along this path, to be used in case of emergency, had disappeared, and I thought at first it had been removed for the purpose of being used but, on examining the ropes by which it was fastened, I found that they had not been touched, and as pieces of canvas were adhering to the ropes, it was evident that the force of the sea pouring through the railings had, even at this great height (110 feet above sea level), torn the life buoy from the ropes."

Muirhead then turned his attention to the station's logbooks. A diary type document that the crew used to record simple weather and sea conditions around the isle along with any details that the crew would have found to be of particular noteworthiness. The log was kept with impeccable punctuality up until the 13th of December and logs for the 14th and 15th were kept on a slate and written in chalk, which were to be transferred later to the logbook itself. The final entry was dated the 15th December at 9am. Joseph noted that the morning's work had been done and that they had eaten their lunchtime meal and cleaned up after themselves. Given that the sunset was as early as 4pm in the Winter and yet the light had not been lit, Muirhead felt quite sure to conclude that whatever grim fate accosted the men on the Island, it was almost certainly being carried out sometime in the early afternoon of 15th December. This was backed up further by a report from a Captain Holman, of the vessel Archtor, who had passed Eilean Mor on that evening and noted that the light was not lit.

So what did happen to the crew of the Eilean Mor lighthouse on that bitter Winter's afternoon? With no place to hide evidence and no way of deserting, the men appear to have disappeared off the face of the earth. However, despite Captain Harvey's dramatic telegram to the Northern Lighthouse Board, men do not simply vanish .

Theories

There are a myriad of theories that have been proposed over the years concerning the disappearance of the lighthouse keepers of Eilean Mor. They range from the plausible to the extreme in strangeness, but no matter the initial credibility of each, none offer anything more than circumstantial evidence.

Of the more bizarre, it has been put forward that the men were abducted by aliens, or became victim to a supernatural cult which had ties with the old traditions of the Isle linked with the spiritual history. There is, naturally, no evidence to support either, however, the theories are often put forward. Sea monsters and passing ships abducting the crew are also out there and equally unsubstantiated.

One more plausible theory carries that at least one of the men, suffering from a form of isolation sickness, became violent and killed the other two and then himself. This relies on the evidence of the effects isolation can have on a person and is backed up by the fact that the relief vessel was late to arrive at the Island. This exact scenario, in fact, did occur in 1960, when the relief keeper of another lighthouse in Scotland on the Isle of Little Ross, named Hugh Clark was shot by the assistant keeper Robert Dickson at close range with a .22 calibre rifle. Robert Dickson pleaded insanity and cited the stress and isolation of the job as a contributing factor to his mental decline. Concerning this theory, neither Moore nor Muirhead noted any conceivable murder weapons as missing and there was no evidence of violence found. It is a theory worthy of consideration, however.

Muirhead's initial supposition suggested that high winds were the cause, due to the damage of the western dock, however, upon later musings, he withdrew from this as his final conclusion. On the subject of high winds carrying the men over the cliff's edge, he stated in his report:

"As the wind was westerly, I am of the opinion, notwithstanding its great force, that the more probable explanation is that they have been washed away, as, had the wind caught them, it would, from it's direction, have blown them up the island and I feel certain that they would have managed to throw themselves down before they had reached the summit or brow of the island."

The Official Line

One of the theories deemed most plausible and indeed, was the final conclusion of the Northern Lighthouse Board at the time, posited that there was a storm of some kind, sufficient enough to cause damage to the Western pathway and landing port. The men were drawn outside, perhaps in an attempt to reduce further damage and subsequently washed away after being struck by a wave. The official report by Muirhead, dated 1901 stated:

"After a careful examination of the place, the railings, the ropes etc and weighing all the evidence I could secure, I am of the opinion that the most likely explanation of the disappearance of the men is that they had all gone down on the afternoon of Saturday the 15th December to the proximity of the West landing, to secure the box with the mooring ropes, etc and that an unexpectedly large roller had come up on the island and a large body of water going up higher than where they were and coming down upon them had swept them away with restless force."

This, however, would have had to be an incredible wave. In 2000 the British oceanographic vessel RRS Discovery recorded a 95ft wave off the coast of Scotland, however, it was in severe gale force winds. Modern satellite data has also proven that waves of up to 98 feet can be common in all oceans around the world.

The men of Eilean Mor, however, were thought to have been at least 110 feet above sea level. On the night of the 15th, the vessel Archtor, who reported the lack of light shining from the lighthouse, further reported the weather conditions around Eilean Mor as "Clear, but stormy". This is anything but specific, however, it does not sound like the weather was violent enough to have been notably bad.

In latter years, the principle keeper of the Eilean Mor Lighthouse, Walter Adelbert, who served the station between 1953 and 1957 carried out his own research on the waves around Eilean Mor, and found that waves could indeed reach the height of at least 200 metres, he himself being almost swept away by one when he attempted to take photos of the giant waves from the top of the cliff. He goes on to hypothesise that, in his opinion, the most likely scenario consists of two of the men going out to save the landing ropes as they were a necessary piece of equipment for a relief boat to land, and were subsequently struck by a large wave which took one of the men out to sea. The second man, fearing for his safety and requiring help in attempting to rescue the first, would have rushed back to the lighthouse to call MacArthur, who would then rush out, leaving his coat behind. The two men would have tried to help their colleague, however, a second wave could have then struck both men, taking all three out to sea.

However, this theory is not without holes. If MacArthur rushed out with the second man to help the first, why were all the doors found shut by Joseph Moore upon his initial arrival? Further, it has some contradictions at times. Walter states "Nobody goes out of a lighthouse in bad weather" But then posits that the men did just that. His justification is to save the landing ropes, however, were they really so significant as to be worth risking your life for? Could it not be possible to signal to land if they were lost, or in the worse case scenario, have the relief vessel turn back upon the revelation that they were lost and retrieve more? As there were two landings, is it far-fetched to believe that the ropes from the East landing could have been used temporarily for the West if needed?

And what of the coincidence of two giant waves, both over 100 feet tall could have struck all three men in rather quick succession? Two of whom whilst attempting rescue, would have surely been watching for this exact scenario?

Walter Adelbert also goes on to state in reference to the weather and sea conditions, that "Perhaps these poor fellows, being fairly new to the Flannans, did not realize the extreme danger". However, the men had already been on the Island over a year and James Ducat, the principle keeper had spent a further 14 months on the Island to acclimatize himself to the environment prior to the completion of the construction of the lighthouse. Although largely accepted as the most likely theory, it is far from tied up.

Now, in its 117th year, the disappearance of the Eilean Mor lighthouse keepers is just as cast in shadow as it ever was . We can point to the theory of a giant wave as certainly the most plausible, however, it is not without holes nor conjecture. Any new concrete evidence arising is unlikely and just as the bodies of the men were never found, concrete answers will most likely remain undiscovered too. The unfortunate fate of James Ducat, Thomas Marshall and Donald McArthur will persist as the mystery it was in 1900.

Episode 10 - The Devil's Footprints of 1885

In February of 1855, Britain was deep in the midst of one of the coldest winters recorded. Minus temperatures were reported from January to March, the nights were long and the conditions severe. In the early morning of the 9th February, people across the rural, South West counties of England were waking up after another night of heavy snowfall. As they went about their daily chores, a steady rumbling began to roll through the small villages and across the bleak farmlands. Rumors were spreading of a trail of prints in the snow. A trail which leapt walls, climbed haystacks, walked on rooftops and seemed to extend for miles upon miles, across rivers and through towns. Each step in the snow left a cloven hoof print, yet it appeared that whatever left it had walked upright on two legs.

The Winter of 1855

The winter of 1855 was the third coldest winter ever recorded in Britain, with average temperatures in February of -5 Celsius. Snow was reportedly falling until May and frosts were recorded right up until summer, freezing the ground up to a foot deep.

In the city of Exeter, county of Devon, the river Exe had frozen over for so long that people skated atop the thick icy surface in their hundreds. One of the more unusual newspaper reports from that February can be found in The Royal Cornwall Gazette, dated 23rd February 1855, and read:

"A singular occurrence in gastronomic science was tried on Tuesday week, on the ice in the centre of the River Exe, at St Thomas. The severity of the frost having coated the surface of the river with a thick crust of ice, capable of bearing several hundred persons, who skated and otherwise deported themselves thereon for hours, near the bridge. It occurred to Mr. Vickery, stove manufacturer, Fore Street, that a dinner might be cooked by gas in the centre of the ice-bound stream. The suggestion was seconded by Mr. Hox, of the Seven Stars, and in less than an hour several of the workmen from Mr. Vickery's establishment had laid down gas pipes from the street main to the middle of the Exe, where the gas supplied a number of little jets in one half of Mr. Vickery's improved cooking stoves. In this apparatus a large piece of beef and some poultry were roasted; and a leg of mutton and vegetables, a large Devonshire dumpling, and other etceteras were boiled. It was surely no wonder that so many skaters encircled the scientific cookery while the savoury steam issued forth with as much delicacy and richness as though the spirit of a Soyer "ruled the roast." The meat was admirably roasted, and the experiment altogether was as successful as it was novel."

This, however, was not the most unusual report from that February. Whilst the people of Exeter took part in a feast cooked on the frozen rivers of Devon, there were some for whom the frivolities would have been a welcome respite, for there had already been several weeks of reports of something much more mysterious that had been playing on the minds of many of the locals.

The Morning of February 9th, 1855

Around midnight on the night of 8th February, heavy snow clouds formed over the South West of England. The streets were quiet with a muted sound as the snow fell to a depth of 4 inches. As the morning began to break, there was a slight rise in temperature and it seemed that the snow might melt with the sunrise. As was the case throughout the cold, bitter winter of 1855 however, the temperatures soon dropped again, cementing the snow on the ground and creating thick ice sheets in the small patches where a thaw had begun. As the people of Dawlish in South Devon were rising to start their days, small rumours began circulating the village. At first, there were whispers of track marks left in the snow, but strange details were being mentioned. There was a case of the tracks leading up to a 12-foot high wall, stopping on one side and starting again on the other, leaving no trace of traversing the solid brick structure. Worryingly for the villagers, were the reports of tracks leading up to several doors and windows of houses before turning back on themselves or continuing across rooftops. Then were the tracks in the churchyard, which appeared to traipse freely among the graves. The physical appearance of the footprints was also causing a great uproar, there were later reports that described them as slicing through the snow "as if the snow had been branded by a hot Iron". Despite many of the locals being men and women of long rural lifestyles, no one could recognize them as anything that a known animal might leave and they seemed to appear to many, to resemble cloven hooves.

As word spread wider, a muted panic began to stir and in an attempt to put the matter to ease in the village, a group of tradesmen equipped with clubs and guns attempted to follow the tracks. Beginning in the churchyard, they walked East of the village for about a mile and a half to Luscombe Wood, North for half a mile to Dawlish Water, before doubling back 180 degrees to follow the path South for several miles to the village of Oaklands where the tracks continued and seemed to offer no clear material evidence of what or how they were created. After this 5 mile trek through the cold snow, they returned to Dawlish none the wiser than when they had begun. One of the men remarked that:

"The tracks had stopped and started suddenly, in the middle of fields - as though they had been left by a bird, or something more mysterious that had then taken wing".

Whilst people were initially perplexed by the prints, as the day wore on and reports from further afield began to filter across Devon, people began worrying and the muted panic was turning to outright fear for many. There were congregations of people huddled around the footprints exchanging rumours and hearsay that the trail had been seen as far West as Torquay, and even lead up to the bank of the river Exe, where they stopped abruptly and then continued again on the far bank, traversing the river, in however manner, with ease. The vast distance covered by the tracks in a single night was disconcerting to all but the most sceptical of the time.

The Press

The first newspaper report concerning the mysterious tracks appeared on the 13th of February and focused on the Dawlish prints. In describing the tracks, it read:

"Since the recent snow storms, some animal has left marks on the snow that have driven a great many inhabitants from their property, and caused an uproar of commotion among the inhabitants in general. The markings, to say the least about them, are very singular; the foot print, if foot print it be, is about 3 inches long by 2 inches wide exactly, in shape, like a donkey's hoof: the length of the stride is about a foot apart, very regular and is evidently done by some two-footed animal. What renders the matter more difficult of solution is, that gardens with walls 12 feet high have been trodden over without damage having been done to shrubs and walks. The animal must evidently have jumped over the walls."

As the first few days after the sightings of the tracks wore on, the true nature of the extent and scale of the event had now spread throughout the towns, villages and cities of Devon. There were reports of tracks stopping in front of a haystack, then again on the opposite side, appearing as if it travelled straight through. Some people had claimed to see them in guttering and through pipes of only a few inches in diameter and there were numerous sightings of the tracks appearing in enclosed gardens, fields and yards that appeared to have no entry or exit points.

On the 16th Of February, The Times picked up the story and printed an account of the prints which gave a good example of the feeling at the time:

"Considerable sensation has been evoked in the towns of Topsham, Lympstone, Exmouth, Teignmouth and Dawlish. In the South of Devon, in consequence of the discovery of a vast number of foot-tracks of a most strange and mysterious description. The superstitious go so far as to believe that they are the marks of Satan himself; and that great excitement has been produced among all classes may be judged from the fact that the subject has been descanted from the pulpit."

"There was hardly a garden in Lympstone where these footprints were not observable. The track appeared more like that of a biped than of a quadruped, and the steps were generally eight inches in advance of each other."

"At present it remains a mystery, and many superstitious people in the above towns are actually afraid to go outside their doors after night."

By the 17th of February, the press had taken the story and run with it. The Western Times actually running a piece that stated that there had been:

"a report that the town and neighborhood had been visited by no less a person than His Satanic Majesty. "

The Devil's Footprints

Whilst the newspapers ran sensationalist stories, capitalising on the mystery and fear of some of the locals, there were other voices making themselves heard through letters sent to several newspapers. Anything from flocks of birds, to otters and escaped monkeys, were being offered as explanations from some that considered themselves to be more rational. Spliced among them, however, were still some letters that offered personal accounts that continued the demonic narrative. One such letter was from a Mr R. H Busk, who wrote of an episode of men chasing a trail into the woods around Dawlish with a group of hunting dogs, the tail he spins was written:

"The track was followed up by hounds and huntsman, and crowds of country folk, till at last, in a wood (I think it was said over Dawlish), the hounds came back baying and terrified. This was the moment one would think real excitement would begin. Nevertheless, no one seems to have had the courage to rush in where the dogs feared to tread, and the matter ended in a battle of conjecture on paper."

As a lone voice, it could be easily dismissed, however, another source, written by a reverend J.J Rowe confirms the instance and wrote a passing reference in another letter, stating:

"The episode of the hounds and co. I well and distinctly remember."

Perhaps the most infamous of letters written during the time of the case, however, is that of a correspondence to The Illustrated London News, from a writer calling themselves simply "South Devon" and contained not only many details of the tracks that are still sighted 160 years on, but also included a page of sketches of the footprints. In this lengthy letter, South Devon wrote,

"It may probably be interesting to many to have a more particular account - which I think this unusual occurrence well deserves.

"The marks which appeared on the snow and which were seen on the Friday morning, to all appearance were the perfect impression of a donkeys hoof - the length four inches by two and three-quarter inches; but instead of progressing as the animal would have done (or indeed as any other would have done), feet right and left, it appeared that foot had followed foot in single line., the distance from each tread being eight inches or rather more - the foot marks in every parish being exactly the same size and the step the same length."

Concerning the distance travelled by the tracks, they went on to write:

"When we consider the distance that must have been gone over to have left these marks, one may say in almost every garden, or doorstep, the extensive woods of Luscombe, upon commons, in enclosures and farms - the actual progress must have exceeded a hundred miles. It is very easy for people to laugh at these appearances, and account for them in an idle way. At present, no satisfactory solution has been given. No known animal could have traversed this extent of country in one night, besides having to cross an estuary of the sea two miles broad. Neither does any known animal walk in a line of single footsteps, not even man."

It is also in this letter that the footprints were described "That this particular mark removed the snow, wherever it appeared, clear, as if cut with a diamond or branded with a hot iron."

The writer, Using the nom de plume of South Devon, cited their own experience of spending five months in the backwoods of Canada during winter and their extensive experience of tracking wild animals and birds to confidently state,

"I have never seen a more clearly defined track, or one that appeared to be less altered by the atmosphere than the one in question."

The contemporary press naturally had quite a field day with the letter and using the details from the letter, published many more stories, right up until March, whereby the appetite for news on "the devil's footprints" as they were now known, was clearly starting to thaw just as were the frosts in the ground. With no further leads, no fresh tracks and no evidence of what had caused the markings coming into frame, the history of the mysterious footprints left on the night of the 8th of February, 1855 gradually faded from the minds of the residents of Devon. Life returned to normal and the stories passed into local Legend. The question remained - What did leave the tracks in the snow during that cold and bitter winter?

Theories

Most contemporary theories of the time revolved around an animal of some kind as the culprit. Not a single theory, however, is backed with strong evidence and in many cases, can be thrown out with a cursory examination of the claims, such was their lack of credibility.

One thing of relative certainty that we can say upon looking back at the contemporary sources, is that the strength of the similarities between the descriptions of the prints from comparable reports covering the entire area, suggests that it's highly probable that the majority of "the Devil's Footprints" were created by either a singular or singular group of being.

Animals

When considering animals as a culprit, it should be noted that the circumstances of the overtly cold winter will have altered the habits of some animals into acting in ways that differ from their norm. Flocks of birds had, earlier that winter been driven ashore in Norfolk due to the harsh conditions at sea and with the nights being so cold, it might not have been uncommon for nocturnal and traditionally shy animals to venture into built-up areas in search of food that would have been scarce in their natural habitats outside of the villages and towns. Among the animals suspected of creating the prints at the time of the event were birds, hares, toads, otters, badgers, rats, donkeys, ponies and even monkeys and kangaroos.

Richard Owen, a renowned naturalist of the period was the man to put forward the idea that it was badgers creating the footprints. He based his theory on two key facts. Firstly, that badgers were known to travel great distances in search of food and secondly, that they were native to England. It is then, disturbingly easy to attack this theory and so it was by another naturalist named Rupert Gould, who stated simply

"A badger's paw-prints are staggered as it has rather a wide tread, and the result would be a double line imprint. In addition, a badger could hardly have made the tracks seen on the roof tops and probably could not have been responsible for those found in closed gardens"

This rather puts the theory of badgers to bed quite comfortably and so it is with most of the other animals suggested too. Whilst the tracks superficially resembled that of a horse or donkey's hoof, the size and once again the rooftop markings do the same for this theory and all the others, with the exception of birds.

Birds

The theory that Birds made the footprints was an attempt to explain the strange occurrence of tracks upon rooftops and seeming to jump clean over obstacles up to 14 feet in height. As stated, there was also evidence that large flocks of gulls had previously been driven ashore by the harsh winter in Norfolk. The lack of any noise associated with a large flock of birds arriving en masse is an obvious problem for this theory, however. The largest problem presented by the theory of flocks of birds, however, is the simple fact that no bird's feet are known to look in any way like the marks left in the snow.

Of all the animals then, we are left with perhaps one of the more bizarre contemporary theories of the time, that an animal such as a monkey or kangaroo had escaped a menagerie and roamed the countryside. The idea of an escaped monkey only appeared in one press report in an offhand remark and has little to no basis in fact whatsoever. An escaped kangaroo is at first glance, an utterly ridiculous suggestion. It was in fact, a fringe theory until it was repeated by the Revered G.M Musgrave during a sermon. Musgrave himself, however, later admitted that he had little stock in the theory and chose to repeat it in his sermon only to relieve fears in his parish that the devil was walking among them. Nevertheless, it is somewhat more likely than the monkey theory, given that there was actually a pair of kangaroos residing in a menagerie in Exmouth, however, neither were reported missing. Of course, we are also once again faced with the fact that the feet of a kangaroo are far distant from the marks left in the snow during the Devon mystery.

And so we can start to see that what should, at first consideration, be the most obvious answer to the mystery, is in fact faced with a myriad of problems. So what of the other, perhaps less obvious, theories?

Secret Balloon

Wandering dangerously close to the line of conspiracy theory, one theory put forward at a later date by author Geoffrey Household stated that an "experimental balloon" of some kind was responsible for the tracks. His source was a Major Carter, whose Grandfather had worked at Davonport Dockyard at the time and who stated that the balloon had somehow broken free and flown out across Devon on the night of February the 8th trailing two ropes with shackles tied to the ends. It was, Carter stated, these shackles which had caused the track-marks as the balloon flew across the towns and villages before landing in Honiton. Whilst this theory does explain how marks could have gotten onto rooftops, hopped large obstacles and travelled such great distances, it does not explain why no other evidence has ever been found. According to Household, the incident was quieted as the damage caused by the trailing ropes to property across Devon was too great and therefore a coverup was enforced. Whilst this theory may seem attractive to some, it leaves a lot to be desired in answering how trails were found that seemingly zig-zagged around gardens and stopped at peoples doors and windows, as a balloon should fly in a more or less straight, or, at best, slowly curving persistent line. It would also seem sheer fluke that a balloon would not have become snagged as it trailed ropes tied with shackles over such a vast area. Furthermore, if such great damage was caused by such a craft, where are all the reports of the carnage?

Meteorological Phenomena

J. Allen Rennie put forth yet another theory, this time pertaining to a rare weather phenomenon. Rennie claimed that he had witnessed marks like the devil's footprints on five other occasions. The first time he observed them was in Canada in 1924 and his companion was so scared upon finding them that he deserted the expedition. He described the phenomena as caused by "Some freakish current of warm air, coming into contact with the very low temperature which had set up the condensation" and left tracks that looked remarkably similar to those found in Devon in 1855. There are however two drawbacks to Rennie's theory. The first is that, critically, Rennies description of the markings left by his meteorological phenomena were much larger in size, being 19 inches in length by 14 inches in width and seven feet apart. Secondly and perhaps more damning, depending on how you take it, is that Rennie is the only person in history who has claimed to have seen such a phenomenon.

Human Hoaxers

So what of the idea of a complex hoax? There is some suggestion that at least some of the prints were left by human hoaxers. Five days after the original prints were left, there were fresh tracks left throughout a churchyard in Topsham that crossed right up to the door of the vestibule. The high church vicar of the Parish at the time was a controversial figure and some, including investigator of the case Theo Brown has concluded that at least these prints could be attributed to a human hoax. It is however highly unlikely that the entire case was a hoax, as the sheer scale would make leaving so many tracks in so many places, all in one night a conspiracy that would have been almost impossible to keep quiet.

The Devil

So we are finally left with the last theory, that it was the devil himself that had made the prints. Walking through the cold winter night. It is important to remember that in 1855 and especially in rural areas, people would have been far more susceptible to this idea than they might be now, hence how quick it was to gain traction once the press ran with the story. However unlikely you find this explanation, it is nevertheless a theory which at the time was believed by many. It was enough to keep people in their homes at night through fear of meeting the cloven-hoofed monster as he patrolled through the streets. An event worthy of note on the case happened almost 100 years after the fact, when, in 1952, a collection of papers and notes collected by the Reverend H.T Ellacombe, the vicar of the parish of Clyst St George during the time of the event were drawn to the attention of folklorist Theo Brown who published extracts from them. It is from these papers that we are now able to discern the identity of "South Devon", the person who wrote such an influential letter to The Illustrated London News. It is now clear that the author was "young D'Urban and he was 19 years old. It's unknown whether he had truly been a skilled tracker who had spent time in the Canadian wilderness, but it certainly makes the story less likely.

In the end, we are left with a bizarre event with little evidence and few sources with which we can draw information from. The mystery of the Devil's Footprints of 1855 will remain in folklore and likely never be solved. No one theory fits neatly or gives us any clarity on what may have caused the phenomena. Mike Dash, a writer for the Fortean Times and who studied the case in great detail believed that the best explanation is a combination of several theories, however still himself admits that if such mundane theories can explain away the Devil's hoof-prints so easily, how have we avoided any panic on such a scale since? In his paper on the subject, concerning the multiple theories angle, he wrote,

"There were simply too many prints, in too many locations, for any one entity - except perhaps, Milton's Satan - to have made them."

You need only an ounce of scepticism to disregard the theory that the prints were caused by Satan himself, however, the mystery will remain.

Episode 11 - Vampires: From Myth to Murder

Vampires are a staple in horror fiction the world over, the charismatic lady-killer or seductive succubi, biting necks and sucking the blood of their victims as they sleep. Equally popular in pop culture as they are to horror fans, poring over black and white B-movies, the character of the vampire holds universal appeal and to most, even those not usually prone to scepticism, remain completely fictional.

How can we explain then, the old folk stories, stated squarely and insistently as fact, that vampires, risen from the dead, stalked townsfolk and terrorised entire villages at night? Stranger still, that remains excavated in Bulgaria, Slovakia and right across Europe, staked into their coffins with Iron nails, teeth removed and bricks forced into their gaping mouths, have been found in their hundreds providing compelling evidence for said tales.

Creating a Monster

The image that jumps into your mind when someone mentions vampires will most likely differ wildly depending on your age and location. From the disturbing Count Orlock or the middle aged pale faced, seducers of Hammer films, to the high school catalogue models of twilight, literature and popular culture has shaped what we imagine of a vampire for centuries. Far from the rotting plague bringers of Medieval Bulgaria, or the demon goddesses in ancient mythology, in the west and increasingly throughout the world, we're faced instead with numerous affluent, well dressed vampires waiting to hunt prey at night, or pop to the nail salon for a quick manicure by day. Before we dig too deeply on the long and grim history of vampires in the real world, it's important to understand the distinction between what we expect of a vampire today, versus the blight infested monsters of folklore and more disturbingly, the reality of the middle ages and beyond.

It is often stated that the first work of pure fiction to include a vampire in its pages is that of an Anglo-Saxon poem entitled "The vampire of the Fens", dating from the 11th Century. There are however some who claim that the work doesn't actually exist at all. Proving to be incredibly elusive as it does, it's hard to argue. As to why or when this poem became a popular misconception is unknown, equally for what reason. It was not until 400 years later, in the 15th Century that a literary character would appear in a fictional tale with the tendencies that one can call "Vampiric". Brian J Frost, in his book "The monster with a thousand faces: Guises of the Vampire in myth and folklore" traces the next fictional work to be that of Sir Thomas Malory, with his tale of "Le Morte D'Arthur". Published in 1485, it is a Middle English retelling of the classic King Arthur tale, however Frost himself notes that it is a tenuous link, with only a single, side character, a queen, who drinks the blood of virgins to sustain her life. No other activities associated with the lore of vampires is mentioned.

After this, there was another long, 300 year hiatus in fiction of the stalking, blood sucking monster. It was in the 18th Century, after a "vampire boom" in popular folklore, that the popular work of Heinrich Ossenfelders "Der Vampir" was published in 1748. This poem is widely accepted as introducing the popular concept of the modern vampire into European Literature. The second verse introduces common themes as such,

"And as softly thou art sleeping To thee shall I come creeping And thy life's blood drain away."

In 1819, "The Vampyr", a short work of fiction written by John William Polidori was published. Described by British writer Christopher Frayling as "the first story successfully to fuse the disparate elements of vampirism into a coherent literary genre". It tells the tale of Lord Ruthven, a suave and sophisticated nobleman, and elevated the Vampire character out of the villages, where is once stalked, rotten and disease ridden, to the affluent and educated killer, enjoying the rank of high society that it has retained almost exclusively since. Lord Ruthven mysteriously enters London society, where he seduces a young woman, marries her and then promptly sucks her body dry of blood and disappears into the night.

In 1847, James Malcolm Rymer, writing in a serialised format and released in weekly pamphlets known as "penny dreadfuls", introduced Varney the Vampire to the literary world alongside many tropes now staples of our imaginations of the vampire. Sir Franics Varney was the first Vampire in fiction to sport sharp fangs, when he takes the life of a young woman and:

"With a plunge he seizes her neck in his fang like teeth."

Sir Francis Varney also boasted traits such as superhuman strength and of immortality, with his estimated age being placed around 200 years old. He also suffers death several times throughout the story, but is always able to reanimate. He stalks women at night, creeping through their windows to bite them, leaving behind puncture wounds and has the ability of "turning" others into vampires, which he demonstrates when he savages a female member of a family he is terrorising by biting her simply for revenge. Alongside all of these now instantly recognisable characteristics, Varney is also the first literary vampire who cannot stand his condition, but lives as a slave to what he has become, the "sympathetic Vampire" as it was later known.

It was in Joseph Sherian Le Fanus Gothic Novella, "Carmilla", again first published in serial format in 1871 that introduced a Vampire that possessed a dark, seductive and overt morbid sexuality. The main character was a female vampire using the false name of Carmilla, though she was in fact, as was now becoming the standard, from high society and known as the Countess Karnstein. Carmilla slept in a coffin and stalked around in the shadows with nocturnal habits, where she was able to transform into a black cat. She had unnatural beauty and preyed exclusively on young women. The story is narrated by her close friend and has, for the time, overt sexual overtones suggesting a lesbian romance between the two characters. "Carmilla" supplied vampires in fiction with another of its now core themes, elevating further, from affluent high society, to the seductive, sexualised undead that instil both fear and fascination among their victims and readers alike and a trait that would be exploited in both literature and film and made into a central point in numerous exploitation and B-movies right up until present day.

There are many that suggest outright that Le Fanus tale was a direct influence on the genres undoubtedly, most famous of tales, predating it by 26 years. That of one Abraham Stoker, or Bram Stoker for short, known the world over as "Dracula".

Dracula, first published in 1897 has been reimagined on stage and screen the world over, and has enjoyed bestseller status since its release. The lasting legacy of Stoker, was his incarnation of Dracula as the definitive Vampire in fiction and the cementing of an image in our minds when first we hear the word "vampire". From the Universal Studios films of the 1930s and 40s, through the output of the Hammer films in the 50s, 60s and 70s. When we see vampires on screen as monster of the week in the X-Files, in Buffy, Interview

With The Vampire, or even more recently with Twilight, all stem directly and take great influence from Stokers portrayal of the vampire.

There are, however, older stories of Vampires. Leaving the realm of fiction, we should also leave this perceived image of the vampire and enter into a darker world of folklore and mythology, where the lines between reality and fiction become increasingly difficult to distinguish.

Things that Stalk in the Night

In his book "From Demons to Dracula: The creation of the modern vampire myth", Mathew Beresford wrote:

"There are clear foundations for the vampire in the ancient world, and it is impossible to prove when the myth first arose. There are suggestions that the vampire was born out of sorcery in ancient Egypt, a demon summoned into this world from some other."

In folklore around the world and throughout cultures and history, we can see shadows of what we consider a vampire today, shaped by literature and cinema. Through legends and myths, there have long been tales of nocturnal beasts, bloodsucking undead and plague bringing revenants that rise up from their graves to terrorise the living in almost all corners of every society.

As far back as ancient Mesopotamian mythology we can find Lamashtu, the daughter of the sky god, Anu. Lamashtu was a demon and malevolent goddess who would kidnap children whilst they were breastfeeding, gnawing on their bones and sucking their blood.

She would eat men, drink their blood, terrorise people in their sleep and bring sickness and disease to crops and people alike.

In ancient Greece, Lamia would seduce men and drink their blood and later, the vrykolakas, undead beings risen from the dead. It was told they would roam the lands, ruddy and gorged with blood, bringing sickness and death. They would sit atop people in their sleep, suffocate them, drink their blood and at times grow wolf-like fangs.

In Mayan mythology, Camazotz were death bats, associated with the night, death and sacrifices. And in Aboriginal folklore, the Yara-ma-yha-who were little red men who would wait in trees for unsuspecting victims and then using suckers on its hand and feet, attach themselves to their prey and drain their blood.

In the Philippines, the Aswang are a shape-shifting demon dating as far back as the 16th Century that are shy and elusive, at night changing into animals such as bats and black dogs. They move silently, stalking prey throughout the night, eating unborn children and bring sickness to victims, leading to death. The Aswang then returns to steal the bodies of the dead for sustenance.

The Chiang-Shi of China are vicious reanimated corpses or undead demons, with red eyes and fangs that tear their victims to shreds before feeding on their blood. They can turn to vapour or mist and have the ability to gain the power of flight through the draining of their victims Qi. By daytime, they rest in caves or in their coffins, only leaving them at night to hunt for the souls of their victims.

The myths and legends are so numerous that it seems like we can find a regional example of an evil undead with vampiric associations anywhere we choose to look. Whilst they do have deviations and differences, the similarities are striking. All have nocturnal tendencies, supernatural abilities and feast on the blood of the living, whilst bringing plague, sickness or death to their communities. In the year 1047, the words 'Upir Lichy' were written in a document describing a Russian prince and directly translated, meaning 'Wicked Vampire' in Russian, Czech and Slovakian. This is possibly the earliest reference we have to vampires by name.

In eastern Europe, these vampires are ultimately as varied as the creatures before, but in general were not handsome seducers. They were ruddy skinned revenants that crept through villages at night, bringing sickness and plague and foul odours. They ate children and drank blood to gain life force in order to become a full human form again.

Of course, these creatures are all myths, legends and folklore, the embodiments of evil in a campfire story or twisted demigods of ancient mythology. The lines however, can often blur between fact and fiction when a myth takes hold and grips tight within a culture of fear.

The Bones in the Ground

In 1921, in the small coastal village of St Osyth, in Essex, England, Mr Charles Brooker, the owner of a house on Mill Street was carrying out some building work in his garden when his shovel, thrust into the ground, hit something hard. Upon investigation, he discovered what looked to be a pelvic bone, and after clearing the dirt around it, found two full skeletons lying in a row, head to foot. Unusually, the bones had been nailed down at every joint with heavy Iron nails.

With the village's history relating so strongly with the witch trials of 1582, people were quick to jump to the conclusion that it was the remains of Ursula Kempe, a woman who had been tried and hanged as a witch in 1582. Years later, in 2002, it was discovered that the remains were in fact those of a young man in his early twenties, somewhat damning the witch hypothesis, despite this however, it is still often written off as the remains of Ursula Kempe and the misconception seems unstoppable at this point.

Throughout history, evidence of such burials have been discovered showing similar practices. In some cases, rocks or heavy objects were placed on the bodies and in others, spikes, stakes and heavy nails were driven through the remains, pinning it to the burial site. An important aspect, as we shall see, lies in the folklore throughout Europe that tells of Iron having magical properties . Specifically in reference to vampire lore, the Eastern European vampire is thought unable to touch the metal without suffering great wounds or death.

These methods of burial are known as "deviant burials" and encompass a wide gamut of macabre ways in which to prevent the dead from rising. These deviant burials were carried out for a multitude of reasons, always however, as a method of securing the dead beneath the ground. In his book "Vampire Forensics", historian Mark Collins Jenkins states the purpose of such practices quite clearly:

"In graves thousands of years old, skeletons have been found staked, tied up, buried face down, decapitated ... all well-attested ways of pre-empting the [attacks] of wandering corpses,"

In 1959, in Southwell, Nottinghamshire, England, Archaeologist Charles Daniels unearthed another unusual skeleton whilst excavating a site which had previously been known for the discovery of Roman remains. Dated to be from 550-700AD, the skeleton had metal spikes driven through its shoulders, heart and ankles. Given that it dates from such an early period of history, many archaeologists are not quick to attribute the burial with Vampire traditions. Predating the earliest legends of vampirism in Europe by at least several hundred years, it's simply stated that the burial shows signs related to later vampiric burials and acts as both a curious anomaly and a warning to anyone who wishes to jump to a vampiric conclusion as an answer for deviant burials.

Moving away from England and into the heartlands of Gothic folklore, during a 1966 excavation of a 10th to 11th Century Churchyard around 30km North of Prague in Celakovice, in the Czech Republic, the remains of 14 individuals were found which had undergone the treatment of deviant burial. Each body was buried in separate graves, rather than mass burial, however given the brief history that the graveyard was known to be used, showed that they all died within a similar time period. They were all young adults, both male and female. They were found with heavy rocks covering their bodies, or spiked to the site with nails of varying length and metals.

In 1991, during archaeological research being undertaken at the ancient church of the holy trinity in Prostejov, Slovakia, a sixteenth century crypt was discovered that entombed the remains of a man whose legs had been cut off at the knees, his body weighted with heavy stones. Just to be sure, he was then placed in a wooden coffin that was reinforced with thick iron bars.

In 1994, archaeologist Hector Williams discovered the remains of an adult man on the Greek isle of Lesbos. His tomb had been hollowed out of a solid stone wall and unlike the other bodies buried nearby who had been wrapped in cloth, he had been buried in a thick wooden coffin and then nailed into it with 8 inch long iron spikes through his neck, pelvis, and ankles. Interestingly, in this case was also the discovery that the man was almost certainly a Muslim, making it the only non-Christian corpse found to date that was buried in such a manner.

In 2005, in county Roscommon, Ireland, Archaeologist Chris Reed discovered the bodies of two men buried side by side. One was of a man in his later years, probably between 50 and 60 years old and the other was a young adult, thought to be in his twenties. During their excavation of the site, 137 bodies were unearthed in total, however setting the two apart were large black stones jammed in their mouths and in one case, with such force and the stone of such size, that it almost dislocated the jaw entirely. The bodies dated from the 8th century, which again placed them firmly before the times of popular vampire lore, however Ireland has its own tales of revenants, remarkably similar to the vampires of the Balkans, which could be attributed to the deviant burial.

Similarly, in 2006, in Lazzaretto Nuovo, Italy, two km North East of Venice, Italian Archaeologist Matteo Borini, whilst excavating a plague pit used in the 16th and 17th century, found the skull of a mature female. The skull was dated to the 1576 Venetian plague suggesting the victim had died of the disease, however unlike the numerous other victims unceremoniously buried in the pit, she was found with a brick shoved into her mouth with such force that her teeth had all been broken.

The same can be seen in the remains found in Kamien Pomorski, Poland, when in 2008, archaeologist Slawomir Gorka excavated a cemetery used periodically between the 13th and 18th centuries. Of the 275 sets of human remains that were excavated, six were found to be deviant burials dated to the 16th or 17th century. Five of the six had been buried with Iron sickles placed across their abdomens and in one case, a male that had been buried with it's legs nailed to the ground, its teeth removed and a stone forced into its mouth.

Such burials were attributed to vampires due to the legend that a vampire will feed from its burial shroud to awaken and reanimate after death. It was thought that by placing a brick, stone or wad of earth into the mouth, this could halt the process of returning as a vampire in its earliest stages.

Taking this one step further, In 2013 on a building site next to a roadside in Gliwice, Poland, four sets of remains were found dated to the 16th century, all of which had had their heads removed prior to burial and placed between their legs.

In Bulgaria, in 2013, during an excavation nearby the ancient Thracian city of Perperikon, Nikolai Ovcharov unearthed the remains of a 40-50 year old man, dated to the 13th

Century that had a piece of Iron plough hammered through his chest with enough force to have broken his scapula bone.

The following year 2014, 200 miles to the East of Perperikon in the black sea town of Sozopol, two sets of male remains were uncovered thought to be from the 14th Century. Both had heavy iron pieces of plough rammed through their chests in the same way as the remains in Perperikon, however, these men also had had their left leg removed below the knee.

The list of burials attributed to vampirism continues on and on. According to the head of the Bulgarian National Museum, Bozh idar Dimitrov, there are one hundred such burials just like the examples above that have been discovered in Bulgaria alone.

These are of course, all archaeological finds of long dead persons, but there are stories too of living vampires who stalked through the night that date right up to modern times.

The Bones No Longer in the Ground

There are, throughout history many stories of famous vampires and folklore legends, the rumours surrounding Vlad the Impaler being one particularly well trodden path. In this episode however, we'll look at two of the more obscure, but historically well documented and highly influential cases.

In the 18th century, Eastern Europe and the Balkans was swept by several waves of vampire epidemics. One of the more famous and well documented cases dates back to 1725 and revolves around a Serbian Peasant from the town of Kisilova named Peter Blagojevich. Whilst there are some slight variations to the tale, the generally accepted version is as such:

Peter Blagojevich lived and died as a peasant during a turbulent period of Serbian history and the Ottoman occupation. He was married, had a son and scraped out a meagre existence in a bleak period. A short time after his death, in 1725, as night fell, Peter's widow laid her son in his bed when a sharp rapping knocked on the front door. Collecting the lamp from the kitchen, she cautiously opened the door, only to see to her shock, Peter standing in the doorway, looking very much alive. He apparently wanted his shoes. This evidently, was the sanitised version of the tale, as in another, he demanded food from his son and then brutally murdered him, drinking his blood and fleeing into the shadows. In both cases, the incident was enough to see his widow take her leave of the village, fearing for her safety. Over the next two weeks, people in the village began to fall ill and pass away with no prior history of illness. There were nine deaths in total and several victims, whilst lying on their deathbeds, told of how Peter had visited them at night and crushed them in their sleep.

The military representative of the village, a man named Frombald, was swamped with requests from the other villagers to exhume Peter's body and stop him from rising again. Despite initial scepticism, his attitude quickly changed when the villagers threatened to desert and leave the village to ruin if nothing was done. Frombald, along with a member of the local church, marched through the graveyard and tore open Peter's grave. What they saw astonished Frombald, who noted that the body had not decomposed at all, in fact, he had "new skin and nails" and his hair and beard had actually grown. In his report, he wrote:

"There was not the slightest smell of death.... The face, hands and also feet, and the whole body, were so recreated that they, in his lifetime, could not have been more complete. In his mouth did I see fresh blood, which, after the general opinion, he had sucked from those killed by him."

The villagers in their haste to end the fear staked Peter's body through the heart, which upon being struck, forced a large amount of fresh blood to pour from Peter's mouth. His body was then cremated to ensure the job was done. In his report, Frombald wrote that he wanted no responsibility for allowing the villagers to do as they had, as "they were beside themselves with fear". Upon receiving his report, the authorities took the whole thing completely in stride and nothing more was uttered about the case.

One other case, equally well documented from the time of the vampire epidemics, was that of Arnold Paole, a peasant militiaman who lived in Meduegna, Serbia. Common at the time, these militiamen were recruited from the poorest villages and paid off with small plots of land.

Whilst serving the militia in Greece, Paole later recalled to his wife that he had been visited by an undead revenant in his sleep and took it upon himself, as was the local tradition, to enact revenge by visiting the undead's grave, exhuming the body and burning it. He then ate dirt from the grave and smeared himself in the blood of the undead creature, which he was assured would remove any ties the being had with him.

Upon his return to Serbia, he worked his land as a farmer until he one day slipped from a hay wagon, breaking his neck. As the days passed after his death, things were, in general, normal for the villagers of Meduegna. There were whispers though, that several inhabitants had been visited by Paole at night and it seemed as if one by one, they were beginning to die suddenly from an unknown disease. Forty days after Paoles death, and after four people who had all complained of receiving visits from the dead man during the night had all died, his grave was ordered to be exhumed by the local military administration. Two military officers, a local priest, and two army surgeons made up the group that would carry out the grim task and in their report, signed by all five men, stated their findings as follows:

"fresh blood had flowed from his eyes, nose, mouth, and ears; that the shirt, the covering, and the coffin were completely bloody; that the old nails on his hands and feet, along with the skin, had fallen off, and that new ones had grown".
"his body was red, his hair, nails and beard had all grown again."

They proceeded to stake his heart whereby Paole reportedly shrieked in pain, before lying still again. They then burnt the body and scattered garlic around the remains.

And there are still more, in the United states there was the vampire epidemic of 1892 which culminated with the well documented tale of Mercy Brown, who upon exhumation, was found to have suffered no decomposition and whose heart was burned in an attempt to cure disease. In the UK, the beast of Croglin grange has fascinated people for centuries and remains an unsolved mystery, despite being investigated both in contemporary times and extensively throughout the past 80 years.

Far from existing only in films, literature and myth, we can see that through burials spanning hundreds of years and in well documented and reported cases that it appears as if there is a more sinister truth to the myths than we might have expected.

Cultural Origins

As we saw earlier, there are descriptions of mythological creatures throughout history that cover a vast geographical distance. It is, however, the folklore of the Balkans and Eastern Europe that refers to the Vampire directly by name and it is from here that we see the most crossover from folklore into popular literature and film. Superhuman strength, the Vampiridzhija, or vampire slayers, living nocturnally, drinking the blood of victims to sustain their life-force and bringing plague and disease are all features of Balkan and Eastern European folklore concerning Vampirism. It is from these accounts that the western view of the contemporary vampire stems and it is from here, with so much physical evidence found buried in the ground, that the question begs, can vampires really exist?

The earliest writings on vampires were frequently authored by clerics, monks and high ranking church members. These historical texts refer to vampires as unclean spirits, wreaking havoc on the living. The Russian Upir, a word meaning revenant and often associated as the root of the term Vampire, was originally someone who was considered a heretic or sinner. Banished from their churches and communities, it was believed that they were susceptible to demon possession after death and would be used by the devil as a reanimated corpse to terrorise the living. It is from these early supernatural and spiritual origins that the Vampire rose to prominence in folklore. In the Slavic countries, where the perpetuation of vampire mythology was strongest, there was not a widespread belief of witches. This leads one to hypothesise that the vampire could well be a substitute scapegoat, cast out by church and society, for many of a region's ills, just as witches were in England. Giuseppe Maiello, a professor at Prague's Charles University, once wrote that:

"If in a small community there was a typical epidemic and people began to die... they were sure it was the action of one or more vampires."

Early accounts of Vampires follow a consistent pattern, whereby a family or village would suffer a grave misfortune, either in a loss of crops, or a spout of deaths from infectious disease or plague and in a society that perpetuated fear through spirituality, doubled up with the absence of any scientific or medical knowledge, vampires became an answer that people were able to grasp as to why bad things were happening.

As was the case on many occasions and as we saw earlier with both Arnold Paole and Peter Blagojevich, graves were exhumed and with a lack of medical knowledge, people's worst nightmares were confirmed when the site of a body which looked to be in a healthy state or, at the very least was not decomposing as was expected, was found in place of a rotting corpse.

If, as was the case with Mercy Brown, in the US, the body was buried in winter, putrefaction could have been delayed by weeks. Intestinal decomposition and the rotting of the gastrointestinal tract could form a substance known as "purge fluid", a dark substance that would flow from the nose and mouth. A similar result could be caused by bloating forcing blood from the mouth. In both cases, if a shroud was used, these fluids could break down the material, giving the impression that the corpse had recently sucked blood and as in the case of Lazza ret to Nuovo, reinforced or even created the theory that a vampire must consume its shroud as part of the first step to reanimation. On top of all this, it's a well known medical fact now that hair and nails continue to grow for a period after death and that blood moving to the surface of a cadavers skin can make a body appear flushed, rather than pale as might be expected. It's unlikely that these observations would have been known among laypeople of medieval Europe.

This would have been compounded in times of plague and great sickness, where it became common practice to reopen crypts, vaults and grave sites to bury the newly dead by the common folk in great numbers. It is important to note that in all regions where vampire burials have been discovered, there have been severe and extremely damaging cases of plague and sickness. The correlation then, between sickness, death, limited medical knowledge and the perpetuation of spiritual beliefs, is a convincing argument as to how the belief and fear of the vampire was so strong for so many centuries and why we now find so many deviant burials, undertaken as preventative measures for things which were seemingly based in fact and stooped in evidence.

Final Conclusions

Far from characters existing only in literature, we are confronted with a long and complicated history that spans centuries and crosses numerous cultural and physical borders.

It is clear from the evidence of burials that people took the myths of the vampire very seriously and why not? When confronted with what was tantamount to solid evidence to a medically ignorant population of the 16th and 17th centuries, there is little reason to doubt and every reason to fear. Although the tales of vampires stem entirely from myth, the absolute belief in their existence created something which was tactile and real.

As for the existence of vampires in modern times and the many cases reported of blood drinkers, living a shadowy existence, is another story. One thing we know for certain however is that for as long as humans have maintained a practice of burying their dead beneath the ground, we have held a fear of those same bodies re-emerging from the tomb and preying on the living under the darkness of night.

Episode 12 - The Fire From Within: Spontaneous Human Combustion

In 1951, Mary Reeser sat down in a chair, feeling a deep sleep weighing heavy on her eyes from the sleeping tablets she had taken, she began to nod off, cosy and warm. She was found the next morning, her body a pile of ashes. Her left foot was all that remained. She had been consumed by fire, though the room she was in showed little sign of fire damage, a stack of newspapers remained untouched by flame just feet away from the ashes on the ground.

Milan, Italy, 15th Century

During the reign of the monarch Queen Bona Sforza in the 15th Century, a Polish knight was enjoying an evening of frivolity. He poured himself a glass of fine brandy, promptly drained his glass, and took a seat, pouring himself a second. The brandy was strong, it burned as the alcohol slipped down his throat, Gosh did it burn. As smoothly as it had gone down, he felt the burn in his throat spread back up. A burst of fire erupted from his mouth and his body burst into flames.

The tale of the polish Knight is often retold and often misinterpreted. Despite these inaccuracies, however, it stands as one of the earliest known documents that speak of the phenomena known as Spontaneous Human Combustion. The original Latin text, written by Thomas Bartholin and published in 1654, is poorly written and is undoubtedly the source of the problems. The Knight, often said to have been Italian, was, in fact, Polish and was unnamed in the original text, the often cited name of Aldolphus Vorstius refers to the man who told Bartholin of the events and was a well known Botanist and Scholar of the time. He himself heard the story from his father, Aelius Everardus

Vorstius. So, this third-hand account, poorly written and poorly translated, has throughout the years stood as the shaky foundation of a phenomenon that has held much controversy for over 400 years and claimed the lives of over 200 people.

Spontaneous Human Combustion

Spontaneous Human Combustion is still a murky and controversial subject, feared by some, casually explained away by others. The phenomena itself refers to a seemingly rare event whereby a human, without any apparent source of ignition, spontaneously ignites from within, in most cases killing the victim and often leaving behind nothing but a smouldering pile of ash. In early cases, there was a great deal of mystery upon the subject. Not least because the thought of a human body suddenly bursting into flames is a perplexing event in itself even by today's standards, but because the average layperson in the earliest days of reported incidents had little idea of how combustion worked in the first place. Early theories put forward to explain the phenomena ranged from undiscovered elements, as was the theory of Johann Becher and his student, George Stahl in 1677 when they attempted to unshroud the mystery using a hypothetical element that would later be named Phlogiston. Needless to say, they were way off the mark, but the basic theory was that all combustible matter would build up this "phlogiston" and release it upon ignition, whereby plant matter would absorb it from the air, hence why wood, grass and hay etc. all burn so well. The logical step for them was that this spontaneous human combustion was simply a build-up of excess phlogiston causing an ignition. This concept of everyone walking around as ticking time-bombs is plainly viewed as incorrect now, but such were the times.

Another theory that gained traction in the 18th Century was the puritanical concept which can be likened, literally, with the modern proverbial phrase "you are what you eat". This theory gained some ground and proposed that heavy drinkers were prone to bursting into flames due to the amount of highly flammable alcohol they were consuming. Worthy of note is that during the Victorian era, many were devoutly Christian and still held to the belief that alcohol represented a grave evil and therefore the theory was much easier to accept by the majority than it might be assumed.

When all else failed, the last common theory floated during the earliest cases of spontaneous human combustion were just people being simply unlucky, suffering at the hands of freak accidents, as was initially concluded in the case of Countess de Bandi Cesenate.

Verona, Italy, 1731

The case of the Countess de Bandi Cesenate is another historical case of Spontaneous Human Combustion which occurred in 1731. This time in Verona, Italy and this time documented to a far greater degree than that of the Polish Knight.

On the evening of April 3rd, the Countess was observed by her maid as being of "normal good health", however after suppertime, she had retired to her bed, complaining of feeling 'dull and heavy'. After talking with the maid for several hours until she fell asleep, she was left alone in her room and nothing unremarkable happened for the rest of the night.

In the morning, however, her mistress had not risen at her usual hour and so she took it upon herself to rouse her, fearing that perhaps she might be ill. Instead of any sickness, however, she found upon opening the curtains of the bedchamber, that the Countess had suffered a much worse fate. The scene she found was described in reports as such:

"Four feet distance from the bed there was a heap of ashes, two legs untouched, from the foot to the knee with their stockings on: between them was the lady's head: whose brains, half of the back part of the skull, and the whole chin, were burnt to ashes; among which was found three fingers, blackened. All the rest was ashes, which had this peculiar quality that they left in the hand when taken up, a stinking moisture."

"The air in the room was also observed cumbered with soot floating in it. A small oil lamp on the floor was covered with ashes, but no oil in it. Two candlesticks on the table stood upright, the cotton was left in both, but the tallow was gone and vanished. Somewhat of moisture was about the feet of the candlesticks. The bed received no damage, the blankets and sheets were only raised on one side, as when a person rises up from it, or goes in"

Not known as a drinker, it was concluded that she had got up from the bed during the night and been struck by "silent lightening" that had crept through a crack in the window or down the fireplace, though this was later amended and her copious amounts of perfume was finally fingered as the culprit.

Perhaps more interestingly, was not the conclusion of what caused the fire, but what had not caused the fire. In "Philosophical Transactions of the Royal Society of London," published in 1745, Mr Paul Rolli wrote of the case,

"Such an effect was not produced by the light of the oil-lamp, or of any candles, because common fire, even in a pile, does not consume a body to such a degree and would have besides spread itself to the goods of the chamber, more combustible than a human body."

Rolli then goes on to theorise that flammable gases within the human body, along with alcohol could combine to become a potent fuel that could either, with the aid of an outside source, as in the case of the silent lightning, or even without, could spontaneously combust and quickly incinerate the body in a flash. This theory tidily answered many of the questions, such as why the limbs of such cases were often left unburnt and also why nearby flammable objects were left untouched; The fuel had simply burnt out with an intense and sharp burst of flame.

In 1800, Pierre Aimi Lair published what would become the definitive criteria for Spontaneous human combustion to take place. The study was titled "On the combustion of the Human Body, produced by the long and immoderate use of Spirituous Liquors". His eight Criteria were that:

All victims had made "immoderate use of spirituous liquors." All were elderly or advanced in age. All were ignited by an outside source of fire. The extremities were left behind un-burned. Strangely, that water sometimes had the effect of fanning the fire rather than extinguishing it. The fires confined their damage to their victims. The fires reduced bodies to ashes and a stinking, penetrating soot. and finally, that all victims were women.

Needless to say, there were many inconsistencies with Lairs study and he admitted as much himself. Nevertheless, alcohol again remained forefront and confirmed what most people already believed, and so it remained as an accepted truth.

Public interest in Spontaneous human combustion was greatly expanded in 1853, when, needing to kill off a character in his book "Bleak House", Charles Dickens modelled the victim's death on none other than the earlier case of Countess di Bandi Cesante.

As scientific theory advanced and the discussion of spontaneous human combustion fell out of the spotlight of medical discussion, public interest waned. It wouldn't be until 1951 when a now infamous case burst into the headlines, baffling officials and the public alike. That of the case of Mary Reeser.

Mary Reeser

In 1951, Mary Reeser was a plump, 67-year-old widow who lived alone in her apartment in the sleepy city of St. Petersburg, Florida. On the night of July 1st, 1951, her son, Dr Richard Reeser was paying her a visit. She apparently suffered from mild depression and had difficulty sleeping and as was becoming usual, she told him of how she had taken two sleeping pills and would later take two more if she still couldn't sleep. At 9:00pm, Dr Reeser said goodbye to his mother, along with the landlady, Mrs Pansy Carpenter. They later confirmed that Mary had been wearing slippers, a nightgown and robe and had left her sitting in the chair, quite well.

At 5:00am, Mrs Carpenter awoke to the smell of smoke and thought it to be coming from an overheating water pump, went out to the garage and turned it off, before heading back to bed.

She awoke again at 8:00am when there was knocking at her door. A courier from the Western Union was delivering a telegram addressed to Mrs Reeser that needed signing for, so after doing so and straightening herself up, Mrs Carpenter went to Mary's room to deliver the correspondence . When there was no answer, she began to feel as if something might be wrong and tried to open the door, upon grabbing the door handle, however, she found the metal to be hot. Slightly panicking at this point, she rushed back to her own apartment and called the police. Upon their arrival, Mrs Carpenter took the police to Mary's door, where they promptly forced it open, only to be met with a gust of heat, as if opening an oven. Inside they found a pile of ashes in the corner, thought at the time to be the burnt remains of Mary's chair and a lamp. The table clock had stopped at 4:20am and the plastic power socket it was plugged into had melted, as had all other sockets that were placed higher up the walls. The mirror had cracked and there were candles on the fireplace that had melted, leaving only their unburnt wicks in a lump of wax. There was a thin ring of soot around the upper parts of the walls, but the rest of the apartment was left relatively untouched by the apparent fire, including a stack of newspapers piled up just feet from the ashes. It wasn't until the fire service showed up that the horrible fate of Mary Reeser was discovered. Among the pile of ashes, they found Mary's left leg, still wearing the slipper, part of her skull and some vertebrae nestled amongst the metal springs of the chair. Bill Bennet, one of the firefighters said of the scene:

"I'll never forget it, the sheets on the studio bed were still white."

Mary Reeser had weighed 170 pounds at the time of her death, her remains had been reduced to just 10 pounds of ash.

The Investigation

On July 7th, the police chief for St. Petersburg enlisted the help of the FBI on the case. He sent a box of evidence which included glass fragments found in the ashes, six small objects "thought to be teeth", a section of the carpet and the slipper from Mary's left foot. He also included a note which read:

"We request any information or theories that could explain how a human body could be so destroyed and the fire confined to such a small area and so little damage done to the structure of the building and the furniture in the room not even scorched or damaged by smoke. This fire is too puzzling for the small-town force to handle."

At first, the FBI were puzzled by the case, upon consulting with local funeral homes, they were told that a body would take upwards of 4-5 hours to burn to ash in temperatures upward of 2500-3500 degrees Fahrenheit. After several months, the FBI concluded their report on the case, stating that it was their belief that Mary Reeser had fallen asleep in her chair whilst smoking a cigarette, which had dropped onto her clothing, catching her alight and burning her to death. It read:

"Once the body became ignited almost complete destruction occurred from its own fatty tissues," the FBI reported, adding that the absence of any scorching or adjacent damage was due to the fact that "heat liberated by the burning body has a tendency to rise and form a layer of hot air which never came in contact with the furnishings on the lower level."

"Once the body starts to burn, there is enough fat and other inflammable substances to permit varying amounts of destruction to take place. Sometimes this destruction by burning will proceed to a degree which results in almost complete combustion of the body."

Professor of Physical Anthropology at the University of Pennsylvania, Dr Wilton Krogman happened to be visiting the area of St' Petersburg at the time of the case. Krogman had investigated over 30 cases of fire death as a consultant to the FBI and so it was he who became involved with the case of Mary Reeser. Although he never stated his opinions publicly at the time, he wrote in 1961:

"Never have I seen a body so completely consumed by heat. This is contrary to normal experience, and I regard it as the most amazing thing I have ever seen. As I review it, the short hairs on my neck bristle with vague fear. Were I living in the Middle Ages, I'd mutter something about black magic."

Michael Faherty

Another modern case of Spontaneous human combustion can be found in the reports on the death of Michael Faherty, a 76-year-old man living in Clearview Park, Ballybane, Galway in Ireland.

On the night of December 22nd, 2010, at 3:00am, Tom Mannion was awoken abruptly by his neighbour's fire alarm screaming into the night. He looked out of his window and noticed thick acrid smoke billowing out from the house of Michael Faherty next door. He rushed over and began to bang on the door, shouting out to Tom, but received no response. He called the fire service who sped to the scene and extinguished the flames.

With the fire out, Gerard O'Callaghan of the divisional crime scene investigation unit inspected the scene inside. He found that there had been a fire in a small sitting room which had centred on Michael Faherty, whose body was almost entirely destroyed by the fire. His remains were lying on his back, with his head close to an open fireplace. There were black soot patches both underneath the remains and on the ceiling above. Aside from this, however, there were no other signs of damage and a mobile phone, razor and a box of matches on the mantelpiece were completely untouched.

The police found no evidence of forced entry, robbery or violence at the scene and promptly ruled out a murder investigation. Speaking at the inquest, Gerard O'Callaghan stated,

"I took samples of the fire debris and forwarded them to the forensic science laboratory at Garda headquarters in Dublin to establish the presence of accelerants (eg. petrol, diesel, paraffin oil) - there were none found - and I found no evidence to suggest any foul play had occurred."

The state pathologist, Professor Grace Callagy, noted in her post-mortem findings that Faherty had Type 2 diabetes and hypertension, but concluded he had not died from heart failure. She also stated that many of his internal organs and some bones were missing, apparently burnt away in the fire, meaning that the fire had to be at least 1000 degrees, and that cause of death was therefore incredibly difficult to determine.

Although a strange case, the news of Michael Faherty's death became a national talking point when, at the inquest, Keiran Mcloughlin, the west

Galway coroner stated:

"This fire was thoroughly investigated by the most experienced fire experts in the country, and I'm left with the conclusion that this fits into the category of spontaneous human combustion, for which there is no adequate explanation."

Theories:

Time has moved on and with it so has our understanding of biology, combustion and chemistry. The earlier theories put forward by Paul Rolli et al. are now largely baulked at. In their place, however, sit no shortage of strange and bizarre suppositions. One early theory which is still often repeated is that of static electricity building up within the body. As is ball lightning, whilst moved on slightly from the crafty "silent lightening" considered in the case of The Countess, it is still a fringe theory concerning its involvement in spontaneous human combustion. There are many other theories ranging from paranormal phenomena such as connections with poltergeist activity to UFOs, as well as many that feel it's simply unexplained. On the sceptical side, it is often noted that victims are old, infirm or suffer from a difficulty with mobility and are often found near a source of ignition, suggesting common accidental death. There is one theory, however, which remains as the commonly offered explanation for many, namely, the Wick Effect.

The Wick Effect

In 1999, a paper titled "Combustion of animal fat and its implications for the consumption of human bodies in fires." was published in the forensic science journal "Science and Justice". It detailed the experiments carried out by John DeHaa n and SJ Campell. The experiments burnt pigs wrapped in cotton and polyester shirts to simulate that of a human body. It laid the groundwork for what would become known widely as The Wick Effect and a theory which has been used to officially explain all of the previous cases of spontaneous human combustion in this episode.

The wick Effect states that a human body, when met with a low flame is kept alight by the melting of its own fats melting into the surrounding clothes, essentially turning a body into an "inside-out" candle. The fat acts as a source of fuel and this prolonged burning state is what both destroys the body and contains the damage to either the body alone or its nearby surrounding area. In their experiments, DeHaan and Campell were able to witness pigs bodies burning up to a period of four hours before they extinguished them. There are discrepancies in the experiments however to the results seen in cases of purported Spontaneous human combustion. The pig in the experiments had

had their internal organs removed, making it far easier to burn through than a body which would have the organs intact. The pig's body was also burnt with the aid of gasoline, a far more potent source of ignition than a candle, ember, oil lamp or cigarette, all of which are the usual culprits in cases of spontaneous human combustion. Furthermore, after such prolonged burning, the pig's carcass burnt through the floor entirely, a significantly more pronounced amount of damage than that witnessed at the scenes previously stated.

Dr Wilton Krogman himself stated in his 1961 piece on Mary Reeser:

"I find it hard to believe that a human body, once ignited, will literally consume itself - burn itself out, as does a candle wick."

Conclusions

Spontaneous human combustion remains a controversial topic. On one end of the spectrum, we have people adamant that all mysteries are solved and there is nothing unexplained about such deaths. On the other end, we see just the opposite, but equally as adamant, that there are too many questions left unanswered and too much speculation passed off as evidence. In the middle, we can say that of true certainty that these deaths have happened and at very best can only be placed aside as unusual. Despite their grim details, fascination and speculation remain. Brian Dunning, author of many books related to scientific scepticism suggests a new title for spontaneous human combustion, that of simply "Unsolved deaths by fire".

Episode 13 - The Clapham Woods Mystery: Satanism & The Occult

Nestled on the southern edge of the rolling hills, woods and grassland of the south downs in the south-east of England lies the leafy rural village of Clapham, in Sussex. Settled for thousands of years, evidence of the pagans, druids, Saxons and Romans is rich and seeps throughout the local area. In the 1970s, it was an idyllic rural British village, but on the outskirts of the village, obscured by the woods, evidence of a much darker group began seeping out, strange disappearances of animals were reported. Then came the bodies...

Clapham, Sussex

The South Downs is a long range of rolling chalk hills that borders Winchester in the West and stretches for over 70 miles eastwards, across counties to the chalk cliff faces of Beachy Head, in Eastbourne. Holding national park status, its farmland, dry valleys and steep hills are interspersed with thick wooded areas dotted throughout, small villages and towns nestled amongst the green landscape.

Inhabited and settled for thousands of years, there is archaeological evidence of Neolithic mines, and Iron age forts scattered throughout the green hillsides. Two of these forts are atop large hills on the outskirts of Clapham. The first is named Chanctonbury and sits at a height of 782 ft, and there is Cissbury that stands at 600 ft. The visible remains of the fortified walls form large circular indentations on the vast hilltops are known simply as Cissbury ring and Chanctonbury ring. Along with Rackham Hill, they form "the devil's triangle", a triplet of large earthen hills said to have been created by the devil, when he scraped up mounds of earth and threw them aside in an effort to create a valley and flood the area to destroy the Christian churches. Upon hearing the crowing of a rooster, the devil was cut short in his work and fled, leaving a large valley, now known as Devils Dyke.

The village of Clapham sits quietly alongside these hills. The church in the village was built in the 12th Century and dedicated to St Mary in 1406. The local farmland of Lee Farm acted as a leper colony in the 13th century and the surrounding area, with its high vantage points played important roles in invasions from the Saxons and Romans and was used in armoured vehicle training during World War II. In modern times, Clapham is a quiet, rural village with a population of 275, a footprint of 2 square miles and consists of only a handful of streets and dusty, tree-lined footpaths. Six miles to the South West lies the town of Littlehampton and 5 miles to the South East, Worthing, with the City of Brighton and Hove just 12 miles along the busy dual carriageway, built in the 20th century as a modern alternative to what was once the main trading route connecting Chichester and Brighton.

With such a long, rich and often violent history that encompasses eras of invasion, plague, witch trials and religious persecution, it should come as little surprise that the folklore and legend of the area run equally as deep. There are tales of Saxon coin mints, lost to time under the hills of Cissbury that hold vast sums of ancient wealth, however, the stories are not only of romantic fortune but speak also of strange happenings amongst the woods and atop the hills that belie the leafy and idyllic facade.

High Strangeness

The devil has a long and varied history in folklore throughout Sussex and lends his name to many places. Many of the churches have at some point in the distant past had their northern entrances bricked up as a form of preventing evil from entering the sacred houses. There are reports of Alistair Crowley using the Chanctonbury Ring to practice his particular form of paganism and it is suggested by those that subscribe to such theories that ancient ley lines cross and weave all along the ancient ruins, standing stones, mines, and forts of the South Downs.

In a woodland area outside of Clapham village, there are numerous reports of strange happenings that draw from the folk history of the area. In 1967, when a group of University students attempted to spend the night within Chanctonbury ring, they left in a sudden panic, leaving all their equipment behind though none of the group ever told details of their story.

In 1968, a UFO research group who used the hill for its high vantage point and seclusion from light pollution, were shocked to the core when, as they were walking up to the Ring, were swept by waves of cold, bitter air. Many of the members complained of feeling nauseous, whilst others had trouble breathing. Upon leaving the ring, all of their conditions returned to normal.

This is a common story for the Chanctonbury ring and Clapham wood, which have winding, leafy pathways, spidering throughout the overgrowth that prove popular with local dog walkers and hikers. The stories are numerous of sudden, sweeping sickness, dizziness, weakness, problems with taking breath and perhaps most disturbingly, feelings of being pulled by an unseen force that has affected both human and animal alike. Talking with local press, a Mrs Goodman reported that whilst out walking her dog and beginning to feel uneasy, she experienced a great struggle trying to get away from the wood, claiming that:

"It was as though I was being pulled back and my legs grew weak. It was quite frightening. There is something strange about that wood."

Among the walkers, it's often discussed and remarked upon by the lack of wildlife in the Clapham wood and Chanctonbury area, in particular, the stillness of the air and peculiar lack of birdsong. David Bennet, the Clapham Churchwarden was a keen ornithologist and enjoyed recording the song of the nightingale, however, he noted that since the mid-1970s, the presence of any song at all had completely disappeared. The woods are left with an uncanny silence, rarely found anywhere else on the South Downs.

In 1975, the Worthing Herald, a local newspaper carried a story which detailed mysterious accounts on the behaviour of dogs in the area, "Wallace" a three-year-old chow belonging to Mr Peter Love was being taken for a walk by his son in an area of the wood locally known as "The Chestnuts" when it simply disappeared. Despite a thorough search, no trace of the dog was ever found. Following the publication of the story, numerous other local residents contacted the paper to report on their own experiences and a week later, a two-year-old collie belonging to Mr John Cornford also disappeared in almost the same spot of Clapham woods. This dog, too, was never found. Aside from disappearances, there were also two reports of dogs becoming agitated and in the case of Mr Rawlins, whilst out walking his golden retriever, the animal became partially paralysed and later had to be euthanized. Mrs Wells told of how her collie became so agitated as they neared the Chestnuts she immediately turned around and took the dog home, whereby it calmed down as soon as they left the vicinity. This story was emulated by the owner of a pug who noticed her dog shaking violently and began foaming at the mouth upon their approach to the area. Thinking the dog was having a type of fit, she rushed it to a local vet who found no physical problems and pronounced it perfectly healthy.

Dogs are one story, but horses are quite another. There was one report of a rider who tethered his horse to a tree whilst he went into the overgrowth to relieve himself and upon returning, the horse had completely disappeared and was never found.

On the rocky and overgrown hillside, there is also the existence of a mysterious pit, where nothing appears to grow and no one seems to know how and when it was created. There are theories of an ancient Lime Pit as well as some who claim it was a second world war bomb that dropped and created it as a crater. The truth is completely unknown and completely unrecorded however and it's simply referred to as "the pit".

Alongside vague stories of "dense mist" which seemed to take the shape of animals, a fox and a bear, there are three well known haunting legends surrounding Clapham woods and Chanctonbury ring.

The ghost of an ancient Saxon man was said to have stalked around the ring, scrabbling on the ground and always seemed to be looking for something. In 1866, a local ploughman uncovered a hoard of Anglo-Saxon silver coins in a small pit on the hillside and ever since reports of the Saxon ghost ceased.

There are many folk tales concerning running around the ring at midnight, sometimes circling clockwise, sometimes anti-clockwise, six times or twelve times, the means are varied, however the end result is the same and that is of upon completion of the rite, the ghost of a druid is said to appear inside the ring.

Finally, the visage of a medieval astrologer who took up residence in the ring to study the stars. His shining ghost is said to glide in and out of the trees following a sudden lowering of the temperature and has been seen and reported on numerous occasions by people from all walks of life. In 1935, Dr Philip Gosse who lived within viewing distance of Chanctonbury ring and held a special fondness for the area said of the ancient mound:

"Naturally the Ring is haunted. Even on bright summer days there is an uncanny sense of some unseen presence which seems to follow you about. If you enter the dark wood alone you are conscious of something behind you. When you stop, it stops. When you go on, it follows. Even on the most tranquil days when no breath of air stirs the leaves, you can hear a whispering somewhere above you, and if you should be so bold as to enter the Ring on a dark night, as my wife and I did ... We never shall repeat that visit; some things are best forgotten if they can be."

The folk-tales surrounding the area are widespread and most everyone knows at least one tale of strangeness that has taken place there. Beyond stories, however, lies real evidence of something much darker, much more physical, lurking in the shadows of the wood. A threat which could in part at least, explain the disappearances of the animals and possibly much much more.

Enter the Occult

Aside from the various other reported phenomena, Chanctonbury has also been the focal point for several reported UFO sightings. Offering fairly easy access, as well as a high vantage point and a level of seclusion able to remove a night sky watcher from the light pollution of the nearby city of Brighton and Hove and large towns of Worthing and Littlehampton, it has been the sight of choice for many nightwatchers over the years. In 1968, local UFOlogist Charles Walker was attending one such nightwatch taking place on Chanctonbury ring. The group took a break from their extended vigils when a sudden bout of sickness and temporary blindness struck many members of the group. Being of curious mind, it was this event, which he found difficult to explain that prompted Charles to begin investigating the area of Clapham wood and Chanctonbury. What he was to discover, was beyond anything which had been uttered of the area so far.

In the late 1970's, Charles was investigating the numerous reports of missing dogs in Clapham woods in relation to his own research. He had placed an advert in the local paper appealing for information that included his personal telephone number. Unsurprisingly, he had received a number of prank calls and so he was somewhat suspicious of a wild goose chase when, one evening in 1978, he received an anonymous call from a well-spoken man suggesting they should meet. Arrangements were made for the pair to meet at 9:00pm that night in the now renowned area of the woods named the Chestnuts, close to the disappearances and strange happenings that had been taking place. The problem for Charles was that the call had come in at 8:30pm. With little time to decide, he jumped on his bike and rode to the meeting spot without giving too much thought as to the motives behind the caller.

As he walked up the overgrown footpath to the meeting point, he felt a moment of fear as he suddenly realised, now he was out in the isolated woodland surrounded by nothing but darkness in all directions that perhaps he was not entirely safe. Alone he waited.

After several minutes of pacing back and forth, however, he began to suspect that perhaps the caller had led him on a path to nowhere. Just another prank. There was no sign of the caller and he turned to leave and make his way back down the path to the warmth of the humming traffic below and the lights of the busy main road. As he began to move away, however, a voice echoed out from the darkness of the bushes. It offered Charles details of information he had coveted for several years prior. Writing in "The Demonic Connection", the man was said to have spoken thusly:

"Don't attempt to look for me. For your safety and mine, it is imperative you do not see who I am."

"I am an initiate of the Friends of Hecate, a group formed in Sussex. The nearest I can describe our activities to you is that we are followers of Satanism. At every meeting we hold we sacrifice some animal or other. My fellow initiate who is with me tonight will confirm that if you doubt what I say. We hold meetings in Clapham Woods every month, and dogs or other domestic or farm animals are sacrificed. It all depends on what is easy to obtain at the time."

Charles then apparently asked if the group were connected with the missing dogs in the area, to which he got the reply,

"I have already told you that our cult demands a sacrifice at every meeting."

And then went on to add a last ominous warning to Charles:

"There are people in high places holding positions of power and authority who are directly involved and will tolerate no interference. We will stop at nothing to ensure the safety of our cult."

Friends of Hecate

Hecate refers to the ancient Greek goddess born of Perses and Asteria who takes three forms. Pictured with three human forms as well as the head of a dog, snake and horse, she was the goddess of the moon, Selene the moon in heaven, Artemis the huntress on earth and Persephone the destroyer in the underworld. It is suggested that her initial form was that of a friendly and benevolent birth deity, however, since the medieval period has become most commonly associated with her darker aspects, that of the crossroads, long referenced in folklore as gateways to the underworld, of witchcraft, herbs and poisonous plants, ghosts, necromancy and sorcery and she is commonly referred to as the goddess of night terrors. Closely associated with dogs, she is the keeper of Cerberus and although it's proposed that originally the dogs were symbols of childbirth and fertility, this interpretation later gave way to the concept of dogs as manifestations of souls and demons which accompany her. As her sacrificial animal, it is said that dogs were often eaten in solemn sacrament to her.

Francis Kings book, published in 1972 "sexuality, magic and perversion" details how to invoke the goddess Hecate with a recitation as follows:

"Come infernal.. Bonbo, Goddess of the broad roadways, of the crossroad, thou who goest to and fro at night, torch in hand, enemy of the day, friend and lover of darkness, thou who dost rejoice when the bitches are howling and warm blood is spilled, thou who art walking amid the phantom and in the place of tombs, thou whose thirst is blood, thou who dost strike chill fear into mortal heart, Gorgo, Mormo, Moon of a thousand forms, cast a propitious eye upon our sacrifice."

One could perhaps write off the group as a small bunch of cranks, or perhaps just people with unique interests who mean little harm. The animal disappearances could have little to do with the group and they could be simply using the disappearances as a convenience, a form of legitimacy where none existed. To do so, however, would be much too simple, for it was not only dogs and animals that went missing in Clapham Woods.

Mysterious Deaths

Police-constable Peter Goldsmith was 46 years old, a well-known police officer in the area and a former Royal Commando. He lived in the local village of Steyning, around eight miles to the North East of the village of Clapham, on the far side of Chanctonbury, with his wife Edith and two daughters. On Friday, 2nd June 1972, He failed to return home and his wife promptly reported him missing. The next morning when he failed to show up for work at the station, the police launched a full-scale search party consisting of local police, tracker dogs and helicopter. By the 20th June with no evidence found, the search operation was ramped up to include over thirty officers, eventually increasing to over 95 officers, ten dogs, light aircraft, helicopters and a diving unit and yet still no trace of Peter was found. On the 22nd September a police spokesman admitted to the local press that despite following up several leads, they had drawn a blank.

At 3:00pm on the 13th December 1972, whilst beating for a pheasant shoot on a nearby private farmland, Mr Edward Llewellyn Harris discovered the body of Peter Goldsmith laying underneath a thick patch of brambles. He was lying as if asleep and covered by leaves, in his left hand was a small disc attached to a metal ring and lying next to the body, a small brown bottle which was tested for poison but gave negative results. Due to extensive decomposition, the exact cause of death was impossible to ascertain, however it was heard at the inquest that his passing had occurred at least three months prior to the discovery of his body and that there were no signs that foul play had occurred.

Giving further evidence at the hearing was PC John Grigson, a long-term colleague and friend of Peter, who told of how leading up to his disappearance, Peter had seemed worried recently and was "rather quiet and slightly nervous about something." It was also revealed at the inquest that he was last seen at 3:30pm with a brown holdall, heading towards the South Downs and that 6 months prior to his disappearance, Peter had been working as the Coroners Officer investigating the death of an unidentified woman's body which was found just half a mile from where his own body was found, the details of the case however, do not seem to exist. The final judgement on his death was an open verdict and thought to most likely be suicide.

Mr Leon Foster was 66 years old and had been missing for three weeks when his body was found in Clapham Woods on 4th August 1975. Mr Hugo Healy and his wife had been looking for their missing horse when they came across a pair of legs sticking out from a thicket. Thinking it to be a homeless man, they reported it to the landowner's wife, who contacted police. PC Owen Strathmore found the body as reported laying on the ground next to what he thought was hay as if laid out on the ground like a bed. The pathologist on the case was unable to find a cause of death owing to the decomposition of the body, however, stated that it appeared he had not eaten or drunk anything for several days prior to his death. The coroner Dr Mark Calvert-Lee, unable to ascertain any obvious cause of death once more ruled an open verdict.

Reverend Harry Neil Snelling was 65 years old and lived with his wife in Steyning. He had been the rector of Clapham and Patching from 1960 until 1974 and was well known in the local area. On the 31st October 1978, he had visited the dentist and called his wife to tell her that all had gone well with the appointment and he would be walking home. When he did not arrive home later that evening, however, his wife reported him missing and the following day, as with the case of Peter Goldsmith, a full search party was organised comprising 25 police officers, tracking dogs and light aircraft. As the days passed and no evidence was returned, local civilians joined in with the search operation and yet nothing was ever found.

Three years later, in August of 1981, a package arrived at Worthing police station containing a letter, a wallet with Harry Neil Snellings credit card inside and a rough map with directions to his body. The letter was written by a Canadian hiker named Michael Raine, who apparently had stumbled across the remains of the Reverend whilst out walking, however did not have time to report to the police, as he was due to fly to Africa the following day and presumably did not want to be held up by an impending investigation. Upon following the map and description, police found the remains of the reverend 150 yards from the edge of Clapham Wood in a spot that they knew to have thoroughly searched during the investigation.

At the inquest, his wife positively identified several items found on the remains. The pathologist Dr John Shore stated that there was no sign of injury to the bones. Due to the lack of evidence, the verdict was recorded as open once again.

Jillian Matthews was a 37-year-old divorcee, living in Steyning. She had had a history of Schizophrenia but was generally thought to be coping well in recent times, however on 28th September 1981, she went out to the shops and never returned.

Six weeks later on Saturday 14th November, Alan Budd and Andrew Martin from Clapham were beating on a pheasant shoot when they stumbled across the body of Jillian, lying uncovered on the ground and quite in the open. Investigations found that Jillian Matthews had been raped and strangled, but no further evidence could be found despite combing the surrounding area. On the 25th November, a police spokesman told local press that:

"It is thought that there are a number of people in the Steyning area who are reluctant to speak directly to the police"

A confidential phone line was set up, but no information was ever gleaned and the perpetrator has never been found.

Anthony Flowers, the head keeper of the pheasant shoot for that particular piece of land commented to police,

"Strangely enough, we had been over the exact spot a fortnight before but had not seen anything."

Hecate Revisited

There are some, including Charles Walker and Toyne Newton the authors and researchers of "The demonic connection" that believe the friends of Hecate may well have had a hand in at least some of the mysterious murders of Clapham Wood. It is not without basis either.

After his meeting with the initiate in the darkness of the Chestnuts, Charles Walker refused to stop his investigations into the occult practices and rather, armed with a name for the group, intensified his research. In November of 1978, not long after his rendezvous, Charles was riding his pushbike home when he heard a car pull up behind him and begin to follow him at low speed, the car then proceeded to accelerate into the back of him, knocking him off his bike and sped off quickly. Not being deterred easily, when back on his feet, Charles resumed his investigations and later found a mural on the wall of a barn situated near Clapham Wood of a satanic figure, he described it as:

"A huge horned head with a scaly Luciferian body and forked tail, set against a backdrop of vivid flames"

Later in the same year, Charles found evidence of a satanic altar in the centre of Chanctonbury Ring.

Meanwhile, Toyne Newton had published several articles detailing his own and Charles' research into the area of Clapham wood and Chanctonbury for the paranormal magazine "The unexplained". The magazine received quite a large amount of correspondence from readers to Newton and they duly forwarded them on to the author. Most were from readers who wanted to discuss the subject or had questions, however one was unsigned, typed up on an old typewriter and opened with the harrowing line:

"In your article on Clapham Wood, you ask if the mysterious events are linked to a black coven? I can tell you they are but it is much more than that."

The letter could be easily dismissed as a hoax by a reader who is spinning a tale for Newton, however, the very next line dispels the idea almost without question:

"A few years back, a friend of mine joined them, they are called the friends of Hecate."

Given that Newton had not mentioned the group's name in any of his articles, there could only be one way for the writer to have had the information and that is through direct contact either as they say "a friend" or they were a member themselves. The letter goes on,

"They meet in the woods and barn up by the church and make ritual sacrifices at the time of Orion and The Archer."

"Lots of Patching and Clapham people are in it but the top ones come from London, two women and a man, the man is a doctor, about 45, the women about 30 and 60."

"They always go back to London after the meetings so no one knows who they are or that they are connected with what goes on, I think this is when there is a human sacrifice."

"My friend said there are other groups the same in Winchester and Avebury, a big group in London, I can't remember them all but lots of people are involved as there are different grades and thousands of members in the outer one, but only about 200 at the inner circle. It is all very secret, the inner core members are protected by the others who they use as spies and guards to make sure everything is kept secret."

"At Clapham there is about 30 members, who they are I don't know, it is only because my friend has gone to live abroad that I can tell you about it. He was sick of it all, especially the sacrifices. He was very frightened when the police were looking for the vicar you mentioned and when I said I was going to join the search party on the downs he said no need they'd got him. I thought he meant the police had found him but they hadn't and when I asked him later on, he told me to shut up."

The letter goes on to mention their reasons for using Clapham Wood, and about dark forces and finally signs off:

"I can't sign my name but be warned, they are much more powerful than a black coven." In his research, newton had previously come across a source who had told him about a group of Londoners, who had secured exclusive shooting rights on some of the land around Clapham Wood, saying:

"People who have purchased exclusive shooting rights from the privately owned estates come down from London. Big money changes hands and they don't bag many birds. I know, because I've seen them."

It was Newton's belief that the Friends of Hecate were purchasing the exclusive rights as cover and sights the fact that three of the four bodies in the mysterious cases were all found on privately owned land, and two by beaters during a private shoot. He also suggests that by owning said rights, they would have a very private and well-guarded venue for holding their ritualistic meetings.

Since publishing "The demonic connection", Charles Walker has continued to investigate the area and has both video and photographic evidence of ritualistic trinkets and incense found around a large beech tree, which is often found with obscure satanic symbols scribed onto the bark in chalk.

Conclusions

The wood is, apparently now clean of the occult according to posts made online by Charles Walker. Or maybe not. Reports have once again started to filter through of missing animals in the local paper and despite the hurricane of 1987 which destroyed the ring of trees that sat on top of Chanctonbury and which much of the reports of high strangeness entered around, the myths surrounding the area persist and questions on the mystery of Clapham wood end up simply requiring more questions.

Why did the initiate of the Friends of Hecate contact Charles Walker in the first place? If it was to offer veiled threats concerning his investigations, why did he offer up information so freely in regards to their name and practices? Furthermore, if they made sacrifices at their meetings and as suggested the animal was "what is easy to obtain at the time", why did they have to steal them from dog walkers? Surely there are much easier ways of obtaining domestic animals from breeders and animal shelters that would cause much less suspicion and fuss. Why not just breed them themselves?

Still though, the group can't be immediately dismissed. There is little doubt that many of the references made not only in the name but in the practices are far and away too obscure for a common prankster, especially in a time before the internet, where information was not so easily gleaned on such matters. The letter, as bizarre as it is, can also not be easily explained as it contains much too much information that could only have been gleaned from first-hand experience.

The writer of the book "The demonic Connection", Toyne Newton, has it seems written further publications that detail a supposed occult plot involving the European Union and British Sovereignty which is unfortunate and leads one to roll eyes a little too easily, however, even if we are to disregard the wider conspiracy, there is certainly historical evidence that the occult have and seemingly, will always, be drawn to Clapham and Chanctonbury due to its long and winding history. Posting online, Charles Walker said of Friends of Hecate:

"There is a tremendous amount of material that has not been made public as yet, and may not be for some time. Investigations in the area are ongoing and we have in fact made contact with at least two people who were, for some years, involved at a low level with The Friends of Hecate."

As far as the deaths are concerned, there remain many questions, In the case of Peter Goldsmith, if no foul play had been detected, why on earth would he have gone to the trouble of concealing himself underneath a bramble bush to commit suicide? And how did he do it? Who was the girl whose body had been found six months prior and why is there so little information in regards to any case?

There is little to be gleaned from the case of Leon Foster, but the questions surrounding the Reverend Harry Neil Snelling are numerous. If the remains were indeed found where his body originally lay, how had the police and search party, consisting of both a large group of trained officers and civilians not discovered it during the search? Who was the Canadian hiker and how was he allowed to simply vanish after supplying the police with such sensitive information? And exactly how had he died?

There seems little doubt that Jillian Matthews body was dumped at a much later date due to it being in such an open and obvious spot, but who was the killer and how was there so little evidence?

If the two mysteries are indeed connected remains to be seen but will most likely remain unanswered.

The disappearances of the animals and the deaths of the four victims during the 70s and 80s will likely never be fully resolved, remaining a mystery shrouded by the overgrowth in the still, uneasy air of Clapham Wood.

Episode 14 - The Hinterkaifeck Murders

Post war Germany was a difficult and at times bleak period. In the rural heartland, amongst the farms of Bavaria lay Gröben, a small hamlet populated by farm hands and peasants. The isolated and suspicious community toiled with the rigors of daily life to earn money that became increasingly worthless as the days passed. On the outskirts of a small patch of wood, half a kilometre outside of Gröben lay Hinterkaifeck farm, an old stone building home to the Gruber family. In the winter of 1922, strange events were to befall the residents, scaring away the maid and seeding unease. These events however, merely foreshadowed a much darker future for the Grubers, one that would end in brutal fashion and that has held no answers for almost a hundred years.

Hinterkaifeck, Germany, 1922

Built between 1862 and 1864, Hinterkaifeck farm, owned by the Gruber-Gabriel family, was situated in Bavaria, Southern Germany, surrounded by vast, flat farmland and isolated by forest trees. To the South lay the border of witchwood, a small and dense patch of woodland that continued to stretch along the Western boundary of the farm. The closest neighbour was half a kilometre to the East, at the end of a long dirt road, in Gröben, a small village hamlet made up of 25 buildings with a population of around 75 people, the vast majority of which were peasants and farmers. The larger village of Waidhofen was situated 2.5km to the south and the city of Munich sat 70km away to the North of the vast farmland. The town of Kaifeck, which the farm took its name, sat around 1 km away.

The farm building was a large stone structure, resembling an "L" shape, with the living quarters atop the long end of the "L", and attached a stable, a barn which took the corner and a machine house which made up the shorter, bottom of the "L". Outside in the large, open yard was a small tool shed and bakery which doubled as a laundry room as well as a well which supplied the farm with water.

The history of the Gruber-Gabriel family is mired with rumour and hearsay. In general, they were well known and thought to be a relatively well off family. You could go so far as to say that they were widely disliked within the local area. Their negative image is a sentiment that is repeated time and time again within the numerous contemporary testimonials of the family which painted them as hard working, helpful in matters of business, but reclusive in their private life, never hosting visitors or travellers and extremely guarded with their money, which, if we are to believe all the local talk, was a healthy sum. A statement given to police in 1922 by Kressenz Bichler, a local farmer who occasionally helped out on Hinterkaifeck, summed the family up as such:

"The Grubers were very diligent and frugal. They lived very withdrawn lives and if possible avoided any interactions with other people."

Still, rural Germany of the early 1900s was not an easy time to live and the family had worked hard amid war, famine, hyperinflation and political turbulence. Andreas Gruber was the patriarch and father, who lived with his wife Cazilia, his daughter Viktoria and two grandchildren. The grand-daughter was also named Cazilia and the grandson Josef. The deeds to the land had passed to Cazilia senior in 1885 and after their marriage in 1886, Andreas took co-ownership until 1914, whereby sole-ownership was passed down to their daughter, Viktoria.

Andreas was 62 years old and led the farm work on Hinterkaifeck. He is spoken of as a helpful, but at times vicious man who was rumoured to beat his wife and children. His second child was born in 1919 but had died aged two years old and in a statement to the police, it was clear that rumours once again twisted through the village concerning the Grubers. Lorenz Schlittenbauer, who had known the family since birth and lived on a neighbouring farm said of Andreas concerning his children:

"The children probably died due to lack of care and not being fed enough. I myself and also my father had often experienced hearing the children locked in the cellar for days as we passed by the farm. I'll tell you frankly, the people were not good."

Andreas had forbidden his daughter Viktoria to remarry after the loss of her first husband and had twice been convicted of crimes against morality for an incestuous relationship with her between 1907 and 1910 and again in 1919.

Andreas' wife Cazilia was 72 years old and was widowed from her first husband in 1885, after which she inherited the deed and took full ownership of Hinterkaifeck until her marriage one year later to Andreas in 1886 where she signed over co-ownership. She had lived a difficult life and had reportedly been beaten by her father and later her husband Andreas. Nevertheless, she was tough and spoken of merely as "A busy woman" by those from the village.

Viktoria was born one year after the marriage of Andreas and Cazilia and was 25 years old. She was the first child of Andreas and Cazilia, her sister Sofia was born two years later, but died aged two years old. She had previously married Karl Gabriel in April of 1914, however after a short and unstable marriage, compounded by Andreas' hostile actions towards the husband, Karl had been drafted to fight in the first world war 8 months later and died serving Germany on the front lines, leaving behind Viktoria, who was pregnant with their daughter Cazilia junior. Tall and slim, she was relatively well spoken of and was said to be the only one of the Grubers who often left the farmstead and spent time in Waidhofen, where she sang in the church choir. In May of 1915 she had been sentenced to one month prison service for an incestous relationship with her father Andreas and in 1919, she gave birth to her second child, Josef whose father was a hotly disputed fact in the area.

The two grandchildren, Cazilia and Josef were 7 and 3 years old. Cazilia was attending school in the nearby village of Waidhofen.

The paternity of Josef is a complicated knot and was the subject of much talk in Gröben. Viktoria claimed a local man from a neighbouring farm, Lorenz Schlittenbauer, was the father of Josef, who she had previously had a short relationship with in 1918. She had supposedly been forbidden from marrying him by her father Andreas, who locked her in the wardrobe when he came to ask her for marriage. Lorenz denied the child as his and promptly reported Andreas and Viktoria to the police, stating the child was born from a further incestuous relationship. Andreas was convicted for a second time but one month later, Lorenz rescinded his claim, accepting Josef as his son and Andreas was released from prison. He was ordered to pay a one off sum of 1800 marks (about 600 dollars in today's money and adjusted for inflation), although he later claimed that with her father in jail, Viktoria had come crying to him, begging for his help and that he had received the money to pay the child support from Viktoria herself, which suggests that the Gruber family were hoping to buy Lorenz' statement of paternity as a means to exonerate her father and free him from jail, which seemingly worked.

It's hard to extract fact from rumour and many of the statements pertaining to the Gruber family are derived from hearsay and gossip, either from the local village folk or from the maids that worked at the farm over the years. It's clear however, that they were not a well understood family, whose reclusive tendencies likely had a role to play in the suspicions and feelings of the local people. Despite all this bad feeling in the area however, they worked hard and survived the harsh environment for many years, but things were about to get very strange on Hinterkaifeck.

Stranger Things on Hinterkaifeck

As winter drew in around Hinterkaifeck in 1921, a sinister series of events fell upon the homestead. The bitter, dark nights brought more than just a cold chilled air and several strange occurrences foreshadowed a grim future for the Grubers.

At first there were footsteps in the attic. The maid who worked on the farm at the time had had such trouble sleeping through the continuous soft thudding above their heads that by the time she finally decided enough was enough and quit her position on the farm, she was pale and gaunt and utterly exhausted from lack of sleep. Viktoria had reportedly told people whilst out shopping of the noises in the attic also and Cazilia junior had also had trouble sleeping due to the nightly commotion and had at one point fallen asleep in class. When asked if she was having trouble at home, she told the teacher that she had been chasing her grandmother through the woods the night before, though the reasons for her night time flight were never established.

Andreas himself had heard the steps and finally, with the loss of the maid, took it upon himself to investigate, telling neighbours that he was not afraid, as he had his rifle ready. His searches amounted to nothing however and no-one was ever found on or around the farm, yet still the footsteps thudded across the wooden beams. Suspecting burglars, Andreas searched around the outhouses and found that the door to the machine house had been tampered with, the metal of the lock seemed to have been torn and ripped from a crushing tool and the wood around the door showed scratches, though nothing was removed or stolen from the property. Andreas asked around with his neighbours, though all claimed to have seen nothing suspicious.

As the winter drew on into the early months of 1922, Andreas found a series of footsteps from the nearby treeline of the witchwood that led to the farmhouse, however no tracks led away. This incident was confirmed by several people who had spoken to Andreas about the possibility of burglars in the area and the postman who had seen the tracks himself. The postman also mentioned a curious event, whereby members of the family had asked him if he had mistakenly delivered or dropped a newspaper, as they had found a Munich Newspaper on the edge of the wood, nearby their property, though no one living there had bought nor in fact, ever read a paper from Munich, nor did they ever travel so far away. The postman merely confirmed that he had not mislaid any post and found it quite strange that the Grubers were so concerned. The postman however, could probably sleep at night, without the thudding of footsteps above his head or tracks being left to his house in the snow.

Lorenz Schlittenbauer later told police in a statement of how Andreas had approached to ask if he had seen his house key recently, as the only key to the house had been lost and Andreas was completely at a loss as to where it may have gone, suggesting that someone had stolen it rather than it being misplaced, he had searched high and low across the entire farm but turned up nothing.

At least the new maid was ready to start work and on the afternoon of March 31st, 1922, Marie Baumgartner arrived on the farm to work as a live-in housemaid. As the night drew in around the farm and the animals fell silent in the barn, Andreas and his family were eating their first and last meal prepared by the new maid. By the time the sun would rise over the tops of the trees and thaw the ground of the farm yard, the entire family would be dead.

One by One

On Saturday 1st of April, whilst speaking with a coffee merchant, Lorenz Schlittenbauer was asked if he had seen any of the Grubers, as he had stopped in on his rounds, but found no one at home, a situation most unusual for the reclusive family and most merchants were accustomed to finding them at home whenever they needed to conduct business at the farm. Lorenz mentioned he had not, but thought little of the situation. However as the days passed and whispers reached out across the village, suspicions began to arise. Several other traders and merchants stated they had not seen anyone at the farm and a mechanic who visited the farm to fix one of the machines found the door to the machine house locked and no one at home when he knocked. In fact, he dismantled the door to the machine house, undertook his work and once finished, put the door back together and yet throughout the whole time, saw no one. Two of Viktoria's friends had stopped by the farm on Sunday morning to meet Viktoria for their regular journey to church in Waidhofen, however met no one there, and the entire Gruber family did not attend church that Sunday. On Monday, the schoolteacher took notice of Cazilias absence from school, she often missed days, so her missing class on Saturday was not thought of as unusual, however missing Saturday and the following Monday was less common. Many people noted an unusual quiet coming from the farm as well as a lack of smoke from the chimney. In the Solitude of Groben, the sound of machinery and farm work would easily have carried across the flat fieldland and the sounds of daily work was a familiar drone, ringing through the air. The farm had been noticeable for its lack of activity for four days. For a family that was not well liked in the village, word soon spread of their absence and there were many who noticed the fact that Hinterkaifeck stood silent.

On the afternoon of 4th April, Lorenz Schlittenbauer asked two of his sons to go and check on Hinterkaifeck farm. In a statement to the police, he said:

"I asked my two sons, Johann and Josef, to go to Hinterkaifeck farm and knock on the windows and have a look if they could see anyone inside. I also told them to let the Grubers know that the mechanic had fixed their engine. Shortly thereafter, my sons came back and said they had not seen anyone, though they had heard something whining in the barn along with the cattle."

Now showing real concern for the lack of activity on Hinterkaifeck, Lorenz went to two of his neighbours, Jakob Sigl and Michael Poll, and the three men went down to the farm to investigate. Arriving at 5pm on Tuesday the 4th April, the rusted gates of Hinterkaifeck creaked at the hinges as the group stepped into the barren yard. All the doors to the various sections of the building were closed except the machine house, which was left unlocked by the mechanic. The three men entered and once inside found a door leading to the barn, which they rammed open. As Lorenz entered the barn, followed by Jakob and Michael, there were several young cattle standing in the doorway connecting the barn to the stable at the far room of the large room, but otherwise the building stood empty and still. The barn was dimly lit as the light outside began to fade. As Lorenz approached the animals he stumbled across a pile of hay on the floor, causing Michael to gasp from behind him. Michael let out a short sharp sentence that bounced off the walls of the stone barn: "There's a foot!".

Lorenz stopped and looked down at the bundle of hay on the floor covered by a large wooden board, he had not noticed himself stumble, but now, looking down and moving the board and hay aside and pulling the foot out to the corner of the barn, Lorenz could clearly see the body of Andreas Gruber. Under the hay, the three men also found the bodies of Cazilia junior, Viktoria and Cazilia senior stacked on top of each other, crudely covered with hay in an attempt to conceal the gruesome scene. Andreas was dressed in his trousers and undershirt, Cazilia junior in her nightshirt, Viktoria was fully dressed, but had no shoes on and Cazillia senior was also fully dressed. All of the victims had severe and gruesome facial and head injuries.

Jakob and Michael left the barn to stand in the yard, whilst Lorenz continued further into the building. The Grubers dog, a pomeranian, was tied in the stable, but otherwise the building was in good order and the cattle had feed in their trough. As he entered the house, he found the body of Josef, still in the remains of his cot which had been demolished. Opening the door to the yard and reconvening with the two men, all three entered the sleeping quarters and found the feet of the maid poking out from under the foot of the bed. Lorenz shifted the large wooden frame aside and uncovered the body of the maid, fully dressed, her backpack still packed next to her body from her arrival to Hinterkaifeck on Friday. She too had large head wounds and lay lifeless.

A Complicated Investigation

In the days after the discovery of the bodies, initial investigations were underway immediately. The locals were reportedly very fearful and it took much of the police resources communicating with them about the goings on, taking statements and keeping them away from Hinterkaifeck farm. Although no official autopsy report exists, a telegram in the police files details the injuries to the victims as such:

Cazilia senior: 7 large head wounds, a cracked skull, the right side of her face had severe wounds, exposing bone.

Andreas: The right side of his face and head had been torn open and skull smashed.

Viktoria: Injuries to the right side of the face, cracked cranium, 9 star shaped head wounds and the right side of her face and skull had been smashed.

Cazilia junior: A shattered skull, she reportedly had been found with tufts of her own hair in her hands, thought to have been torn out from pain of death. Doctors surmised that she had probably died 2-3 hours after the incident and was the only one of the victims that had had any chance of being saved after the attack.

Josef: Shattered skull. His cot had been smashed by a severe blow, breaking it where it stood.

Marie: Right side of her face and skull had been smashed.

All of the victims suffered severe head injuries from a blunt object which was considered as the cause of death outright. Police quickly pieced together a mode of killing that entailed the perpetrator luring each member of the family into the barn one by one, possibly by untying cattle, whereby he made short work of dispatching them before moving on to the next. They then entered the house and killed Josef in his cot and finally the maid.

On the 5th April, Criminal Inspector Georg Reingruber arrived at the crime scene from Munich, though only stayed a few hours before departing. These few hours were all the head of investigations and his team ever spent physically at the scene and instead chose to communicate remotely via telephone and telegraph for the remainder of the case's life. The majority of the manpower on the ground came from the local town of Schrobenhausen, though an incomplete list showed that upwards of 50 investigators worked on the crime scene from numerous divisions and local municipalities. Over 100 statements were taken from the villagers and surrounding farms and a 100,000 Mark reward was advertised for information regarding the murderer, which rose quickly to 500,000 Marks.

Due to the victim's state of dress, Maries backpack still being packed, Cazilias absence from school on Saturday and as many smaller details arose, it was generally accepted amongst the police that the murders had taken place on the night of 31st March. However, the possibility also began to arise that the perpetrator had stayed on the farm for some considerable time after the act, possibly even days. Although somewhat conflicting of the idea that the farm was seen as quiet, motionless and devoid of life over the weekend, there were several statements too, that people had seen smoke coming from the Bakery ovens chimney in the days after the accepted time of murder. One statement made by Michael Plockl, unfortunately now lost in full was recorded in part during the prosecution and stated that:

"One witness noticed that on the morning of Saturday April the 31st, the oven door was closed, but half open in the evening. The chimney had given out smoke in the evening and he saw a fire in the oven and an electric torch in the forest nearby the farm."

The dog, tied in the barn was reported on as though he looked to have not been fed, although several statements claimed that the cattle had all seemed to have been fed, as the commotion and noise they would likely to have made from missing meals would have been heard among the people of the village, however the farm had sat silent and Lorenz Schlittenbauer commented in his statement concerning the discovery of the bodies that the barn was clean and in good order.

The police were quick to begin naming suspects and publicly made efforts to be seen as proactive. In the months that followed, the list of suspects grew, fortunately for all involved, gaining in credibility and most were less questionable than the first.

Josef Bartl

Josef Bartl had escaped a mental asylum and was the original suspect of the case. Criminal Investigator Reingruber alerted police to the possibilities of Bartl almost immediately and searches were ordered to find the man, however all were deemed unsuccessful. Reingruber has faced criticism over the years for his premature judgement on Bartl and it appears that the brutality of the crime and the known escape of the madman were the only connecting factors to the initial suspicions of police. There is one story of Bartl begging a stranger for something to eat and a place to hide and when they offered him a suggestion, Bartl gave them a 100 Mark, stained with blood. This further piqued the police interest, however upon forensic investigation, no traces of blood linked the coin with Hinterkaifeck and bartl was never found. The obvious case against Bartl as the murderer is the lack of any proof whatsoever that he had ever been to the farm, nor knew of its existence. There is also the fact that the hospital he had escaped from lay over 70 Km away. Despite the initial link with the murder investigations, he is seen as a fringe suspect in modern times.

Initially, finding that some marks were missing from victims wallets and after finding very little in the way of paper money in the house that was well suspected of being there, the police concluded that the brutal scene was that of a robbery that had gone wrong.

Anton and Charles Bichler

Following the suspected burglary lead, two brothers from Groben were also initial suspects. Anton Bichler was known to have had an intimate relationship with one of the previous maids on Hinterkaifeck and had worked on the farm during harvests. The Bichlers were known in the area after having been convicted of several petty thefts and they had spoken openly about coveting the wealth that the Grubers were apparently stashing on Hinterkaifeck. They were arrested in April for the murders, but were later released as both could provide watertight alibis that kept them away from the area, working in the town of Schrobenhausen before and after the night of 31st march.

After taking a detailed inventory of the house and finding large sums of gold marks and valuables, investigations moved away from robbery as motive, however, in doing so the investigations opened up to a slew of suspects and motives based around local gossip and hearsay.

Karl Gabriel

One of the more out there suspects of the time was Karl Gabriel, Viktorias dead husband. In a letter dated 29th April, 1922, the police in Schrobenhausen contacted Munich and asked the following:

"After the comprehensive investigations into the murder case have hitherto produced no result, I would urge the police authorities to make enquiries at the care centres in Munich, as well as other offices in Bavaria, whether the husband of the murdered owner, named Karl Gabriel, while according to a death announcement dated 12/12/1914 and published in the Schrobenhausen weekly, should have fallen at Neuville and not returned with a prison transport just before the murder."

This was seemingly a desperate move by the police, but the relevant questioning was nevertheless carried out. Their thinking behind the suspicion of Karl Gabriel was based around their initial suspicions that the perpetrator was seemingly well acquainted with the layout and goings on of the farm and that nobody had ever been returned from the war after his reported death. The police surmised that if Karl had in fact survived, he may have returned to the farm to find that Viktoria had had a child, rumoured to be from an incestuous relationship with her father, offering a powerful motive and as such, he may have flipped and taken his vengeance out on the family.

When we look at the suspect clearly however, the suspicions quickly begin to fall apart. Firstly, if he were to return, where had he been in the seven years prior? There are also strong rumours deduced from numerous statements that Karl and Viktoria had had an unhappy marriage, he had left the farm at one point in their short married life and returned to stay with his parents. He reportedly had had a tough time living with Andreas, who beat him and there are even suspicions that he volunteered to fight in the war as a means to escape rather than be drafted. Perhaps the most damning testimony of their marriage however, came from Jakob Sigl, who over thirty years later, in 1952 wrote of their marriage:

"I am of the opinion that the couple did not have a good relationship with each other and that Karl Gabriel had married Viktoria Gruber in the main for the money and property of Hinterkaifeck and that Viktoria was the only daughter".

If this was truly the case, what motivation would he have had to come back at all? The final nail in the coffin of this line of enquiry however was struck when several testimonies of Karls regiment were collected, all of which stated they had seen his body on the battlefield and personally attested that he was very much dead. With the suspect of Karl, we are left with a disappeared body Vs hearsay. In the first place though, one can certainly suggest that the initial suspicion was tenuous at best. Adding spice to this suspect is the story of a German speaking Russian soldier who met with German soldiers on the russian front during the second world war who claimed to have been the Hinterkaifeck killer. Some have speculated that the man was, in fact, Karl, but the story remains unsubstantiated.

Lorenz Schlittenbauer

Heavily implicated with the crime in much of the English information on the Hinterkaifeck murders is Lorenz Schlittenbauer. Whilst it is true that he was a suspect of the case, it has to be said that much of the suspicions that lie with Lorenz are based around facts which are simply untrue but often repeated. One such case is the damning suggestion that on the night of the murder, Lorenz slept in the barn of his own farm and therefore had no alibi. In the german records of statements however, this is shown to have been a contemporary rumour and as Schlittenbauer states very clearly:

"People like to talk. It is not true, I was with my wife."

However, even if we disregard this, there still stacks a heavy case against Lorenz. In the first, Schlittenbauer was well acquainted with the farm. His own farm lay on the other side of the witchwood, less than half a Km away and he had known the Grubers and worked with them for a long time. He had intimate knowledge of the house and was reported to have had a short lived sexual relationship with Viktoria and was even planning to marry her after the death of his first wife, however after Viktoria fell pregnant with Josef, the complicated situation of the paternity arose and as we heard, Andreas forbade the communion. The issue of paternity and Lorenz turning Andreas into the police led to a feud which according to Lorenz was not a drawn out affair and he held no bad blood towards the Grubers after all was done, however, it is still a black mark against him in regards to the case.

There were also further rumours that Viktoria was demanding further child support money from Lorenz, however, given the family's circumstances, it is deemed unlikely that this would have been very successful and considering the original support money was paid from their own money in the first place, seems out of sorts with the facts of the whole affair. In his statement to the police, Lorenz was quite clear that all financial matters pertaining to the child had been settled and there was no enmity between the families. It seems that It is more likely that this was mere village gossip.

More damaging to the cause of Lorenz Schlittenbauers innocence was his behaviour upon discovering the bodies of the Grubers. Rather than to take care to not disturb the crime scene, he immediately moved almost everything in close vicinity to the bodies, furthermore, he made sure to have witnesses watch him do it. At the time, Jakob Sigl, one of the men who went with Schlittenbauer to Hinterkaifeck thought his behaviour suspicious and said later in a statement to police that:

"Poll and I immediately told Schlittenbauer when we found the bodies that he should be careful to leave things as they are, but he replied he had to see things for himself. He then told me to feed the cattle, but I told him that we were going home and reporting to the police."

"He was very busy, he went straight to the cellar to fetch milk and feed the pigs. On the way home, Poll and I said nothing. It was very striking that Schlittenbauer changed everything that could have been changed and knew exactly where everything in the house was. In my opinion Schlittenbauer did not often go to Hinterkaifeck as Andreas wouldn't have allowed it."

Lorenz Schlittenbauers destruction of the crime scene went further when, as people began arriving at the crime scene to see for themselves the reality and before the police had arrived, Schlittenbauer made no effort to stop people from disturbing the scene and told Johann Freundl, a local man that "people were already there and he could do nothing more now."

There is also the matter of his behaviour concerning the possibility of the murderer still residing at the farmhouse. When questioned by police why he wasn't scared after discovering the bodies to enter the house alone, he replied:

"I was so worked up that I didn't think of anything, I assumed my boy had to be starving. Even if I wasn't completely sure that he was my child or not, I still felt compassion for the boy and I wanted to look after him at once."

Lorenz also spent a lot of time cleaning the crime scene, feeding the animals and even took care of two of the pigs at his own house. Was this merely a coping mechanism on Lorenz's part? He had just discovered a brutal scene involving people he had known his entire life, one of which could possibly have been his son. Were his actions at the time then, that of a murderer covering his tracks? Or of a grieving man, stricken with shock?

There were many in the village that suspected him, and Lorenz actually received damages from one man for slander after repeatedly being accused. There are still many small things that go against and for his innocence, he appeared to know the house very well and even knew how much money was on the farm and many speculated that living so close, he could have come back and forth through the woods relatively unnoticed, however, if this was the case, how had he managed to explain such absences to his family? Furthermore, if he had really spent so much time on the farm, many other statements concerning the farm after the days of the murder would have been incorrect. He also suffered asthma, and some doubt his physical ability to carry out the attacks, however, he appears to have run his own farm quite well despite this condition.

Finally, and importantly, was that despite extensive questioning, the police never arrested him, nor found any particular reason to suspect him above others. In the final report on Lorenz Schlittenbauer the police wrote:

"Subsequent to interrogations, there were some inconsistencies in Schlittenbauers statements that were revealed. He, however, presented his answers in such a way that legitimate doubts about his guilt have to arise. He repeatedly declared his innocence in tears and declared that he was well aware that he was a suspect in the area, emphasising that this was chiefly due to his energetic involvement as a local guide and his willingness to help."

"There are no indications for further action"

Lorenz Schlittenbauer remains a suspect high on the list even today, and it is not unfounded, but often it's simply because his motive fits a narrative surrounding the child Josef so neatly rather than consideration of other factors. If it really was Lorenz Schlittenbauer who murdered the Gruber family, this also calls into question the importance of the footprints in the snow, the newspaper and the break in attempts in relation to the murders. Ultimately, the suspicion of guilt has to be decided by considering whether or not one believes him to have been so calculated as to plan the discovery and all of his subsequent actions or he was simply doing what he could in a time of great stress.

Two final pieces of information pertaining to the case lies curiously, with the discovery that Viktoria donated 700 gold marks, a vast sum of money and that which would have amounted to all of her savings, to the church in Waidhofen around two weeks prior to the murders. The pastor of the church surmised it to be from Viktoria, as no one else would have had the means to have donated such a sum from the local area.

And last but not least, the uncovering of the murder weapon one year later. Initially, the weapon was presumed to be a pickaxe found in the barn and pointed out by Schlittenbauer, however in February of 1923, after all inheritance disputes were settled, the new owners of Hinterkaifeck demolished the farmhouse and found a Mattock, stashed in a hidden nook of one of the outer sheds. Upon inspection by forensics it was found that it had human blood on the body and was unquestionably the murder weapon, however the police claimed that they had searched the area thoroughly. It has been suggested that the murderer had placed it on the farm some time after the initial investigations had finished, where it could be hidden and hoped to never be found.

Conclusions

There are endless lists of suspects for the Hinterkaifeck case and the podcast would go on forever to list them all. With so much gossip and hearsay in the small, isolated community it is often difficult to differentiate fact from rumour and the more you dig, the darker it gets. Speculation of motives range from extortion, blackmail, inheritance squabbles, local revenge and even the political turmoil of the time has found space to squeeze into the picture.

Despite over 30 years of official investigations and incredible efforts of the public to document and preserve the details, the true perpetrator will likely never be discovered and if they do, will almost certainly be long dead. The events that unfolded on the 31st March, 1922 on the isolated farm are therefore a sad, deeply dark and savage tale of murder and suspicion that haunts long after the final words in the report were written.

Episode 15 - Terri Hoffman & The Black Lords

"First degree lesson 1:

This is your very first lesson, it is yours in a special way since the knowledge contained within it is sacred, secret and mysterious. This information has been treasured and carefully guarded since ancient times, for knowledge gives its possessor power. By being exposed to the teachings of the masters, you will not only become aware of the truths which others rarely possess, you will also learn how to use and control energies few have mastered."

Cults. They're all fun and games until someone dies. Or a dozen people die, as was the case with "Conscious Development of Body, Mind and Soul", a peculiar cult mired in mysterious deaths and suspicious suicides.

Terri Hoffman

Terri Hoffman was born March 21st, 1938 in Fort Stockton, Texas. Set to a bleak backdrop of an alcoholic father and poverty, Terri began to see things, people, which no one else could see. Sitting under a tree one warm summer day aged just four years old, she was visited by three men wearing "splendid robes" who told her to think about God and that she was special. Inconvenient as such visions are, there existed a brief hiatus in Terris visions, as she thought about God, her mother gave birth to her stillborn sister and then shortly after passed away from Tuberculosis.

It wasn't until she was 9 years old, when her father, unable or unwilling to raise her alone, sent her to a Lutheran Orphanage in Round Rock that the visions came back to her more fluently. Whilst she sat alone, bullied and outcast, she was consoled by these visions of great masters who would tell her that she could be anything she wanted, she was special. The visions taught her how to pray and she even saw Christ himself.

During her time at the Orphanage, she learnt from one of the Nuns about Karma, reincarnation and the Akashic records - A compendium, encoded in a spiritual plane that told of all human events, thoughts, words, emotions and intent ever to have occurred in the past present and future. It was also during her time at the orphanage that she became convinced, aged 9 or 10, that she was the reincarnation of St Teresa of Avila, a 16th Century Roman Catholic Saint and mystical theologian who wrote profusely on subjects concerning meditative prayer and had visions of Jesus and Mary, visited heaven and dabbled in levitation now and then.

Two years later, aged 11, Terri was adopted by a Dallas couple who renamed her Terri Lee Benson. She began a life of normality and entered school, but made few friends and shortly after her 15th Birthday, met 18 year old John Wilder, a truck driver with a penchant for school girls. On May 2nd, 1953, the couple ran away together and got married in Durant, Oklahoma, both inflating their ages on the wedding certificate by three years.

The newly married couple moved to a farm near RedBird Airport, 6 miles outside of Downtown Dallas. 18 Months later, Terri gave birth to her first child, Cathy. In 1954, she began to seek something more during her quiet days as a housewife and visited meditation sessions as well as taking hypnosis classes and became increasingly interested in metaphysics and spirituality.

In 1958, she gave birth to a son named Kenneth. In 1963, she gave birth to her second daughter, Virginia. Financially the family struggled, but it was a peaceful life. The family moved to Farmers Branch, a small suburb of Dallas, Texas, a setting in which Terri's spirituality could flourish in the long days, mixing with well to do housewives, bored of the everyday and all looking for something more from life. In the mid to late 60s, she began holding classes herself that consisted mainly of high schoolers. She didn't charge for the classes and taught meditation and prayer. She handed out pamphlets of her teachings, heavily influenced by a wide range of Eastern thought and spiritualism. The first lesson from the pamphlets opens with the paragraph from the start of this podcast.

She also taught about Karma, death and rebirth. On Karma, she wrote,

"We can be sure that the people who have been killed in volcanic eruptions and dire catastrophes have deserved these violent deaths and that they have been reborn in these places to fulfill their destiny. They reaped as they sowed in past lives."

And on Death, she wrote that there was nothing to fear:

"You will also become conscious of the continuity of life. Death then, will not exist in reality; for you will realise that your existence is not dependent upon the mere maintenance of your physical body. The result of noble death is rebirth."

Peter Muth, a former member stated that:

"Another thing Terri taught us was that Death was just another state of consciousness and it wasn't a bad thing, it wasn't anything to fear."

A creed that would later drown in its ominous undertones.

Conscious Development of Mind Body & Soul

Terri's classes began to cause quite a stir and Terri herself was becoming a local guru to her small tribe of hopeful devotees. She told them of how she could read the Akashic records, let them know if their partner was their soul mate and of how she could levitate in her bed and heal people from miles away. She hinted on her ability to cure cancer and during meditation sessions, would turn off the lights, shine a torch on students and theatrically talk to the dead people of their past lives. Naturally her students ate it all up, many of whom were drug users, dropouts and the disenfranchised looking for acceptance. She signed one photograph for a female student, writing a note to her which read:

"To a sweet and dear friend, may the love, wisdom and power of God be with you, lead you and guide you all your life, bringing to yourself and others true blessings. Always be an example. Keep God in your heart, bring him to your mind and then live good all day. I send you peace, joy, love, light and harmony. Love always, Terri."

As Terri's claims became more and more out there, her students became more and more devoted to her. They would visit her in her home for private sessions, obtaining counselling and hypnosis sessions from Terri and told family members in excited tones of Terris great spiritual deeds. Seeking her opportunity, in the late 1960's, Terri officially founded an organization and named it "Conscious Development of Mind Body and Soul". All of this spiritual elevation was taking it's toll on Terri's home life however and her marriage to John Wilder begun falling apart. On the 28th December, 1970,

Terri filed for divorce. Wilder and Terri's mother responded by getting Terri sectioned.

Terri's hospitalisation didn't last for long however and soon she was back at her day job, talking with gurus, philosophers and Gods long since dead. Her divorce with Wilder was settled on March 23rd, 1971. Terri took custody of her daughter Cathy and her share of the divorce settlement included a 1968 Mustang, some stocks, a shotgun, rifle and pistol. John took custody of the two youngest children, Kenneth and Virginia, took the house and all the family's bank accounts.

A few months later, now aged 33, Terri was remarried to Glenn Cooley, a young 20 year old student of her classes in New Mexico. Now that John was out of the picture, Terri's spirituality could surely flourish.

Black Lords & The White Brotherhood

By the mid 1970s, Conscious Development of Body Mind and Soul was hitting big strides in Dallas. Terri was teaching her mantra to hundreds of the local residents and the organisation's fame had begun to spread nationally, attracting thousands of interested followers. All proceeds were flowing directly into Terri's personal Bank account.

At its core, Terri had a devout band of long term students, which she now deemed ready to become teachers in their own right. She was to be the master of masters. The group needed a higher purpose though, something to bind them together and in 1977, Terri found just the answer for them.

During her teachings, Terri began to enlighten the inner circle to the spiritual planes' darkest secrets, told to her by Plato and Babaji, a hindu god during her meditations. There was, according to Terri, a band of evil spirits named the "Black Lords" who disrupted the physical plane with their negative vibrations. Naturally nobody except Terri could see them, since they existed only in the spiritual realm that Terri could walk freely around in, but with her help and guidance, the group could go to war and fight these wicked hellspawn and save humanity from itself. This Holy War was to be kept secret, no one outside of the inner circle should know of their practices, for danger of them falling prey to the Black Lords negative vibes. The band of brave women and men of the inner circle were named the White Brotherhood and Terri became the Anatamaji, or Divine Revelator. Instructions on how to rid the spiritual plane of the existence of Black Lords were a simple affair:

"To kill them, one must take them to the pits of hell where their soul and lower bodies will be dissolved."

It was all so simple, but there were also Black Overlords, who could not be dissolved. These were dealt with by taking them into "electromagnetic caves" instead.

Soon the war began and weekly meetings were held in secret from all outsiders in a sports hall in Dallas. A protective circle was first drawn out on the floor and each member was to bring a cup and bag of earth, representing Gabriel, a Fan as a shield representing Ariel and a rod and staff, representing Archangel Michael. Terri assured the members that full size swords needn't be carried around and that it was merely a gesture, therefore members would use cocktail sticks, biros and letter openers in place as their holy weapon of choice. A former member Joyce Tepley described the battles:

"We were taught to use these weapons to kill Black Lords. Members would make a series of gestures with their swords and then touch the rod to their shoulders which they believed to be a power centre for the body and then you'd project it outward, with your thought along with it and know you were eliminating the Black Lords. That you really were in battle."

At the end of each session, some of which lasted several hours, Terri would give a body count of how many Black lords had been defeated, the group always had to do better. There were emergency battles held and the members would be called together to rush into battle. Each member was told to wear a robe that when properly made could lend them up to 15 times more power.

The members of the White Brotherhood felt no pain from their battle wounds, Terri, naturally, absorbed their pain and told them all how she suffered for them in their place. Black Overlords, holding such great power as they did and needing to be dissolved in electromagnetic caves, were often attaching themselves to members of the organisation who had fallen out of favour or family members of the White Brotherhood. Terri warned the group:

"Stay alert, curtail most of your social contact with those outside the group. It's for their protection. The Black forces may use them to get to you. Keep your sword near you, especially when you go to bed. Protect your animals, car, place of work and your home with protection rituals."

Terri began to sow the seeds of Paranoia and fear deep into her flock.

Glenn Cooley

When Glenn Cooley first met Terri, he was a twenty year old student at North Texas State University with an occasional penchant for drug use which he had fought with the aid of the Conscious Development meditation group. After their expedited marriage in New Mexico, the couple returned to Dallas and moved into a comfortable house. With the success of Conscious Development of Body, Mind and Soul, Terri had begun to expand on her literature and Glenn partnered with Terri running the Jewellry side business, CD Gems, which sold handmade jewelry that offered protection for its members. After 6 years however, Glenn was growing tired of Terri's organisation. His mother later commented that he had come to her and confessed that he wanted out of it all.

His wish soon became a reality and on 24th November, 1976, Terri filed for divorce and five days later, Glenn filed a waiver to speed up the process and on January 27th 1977, the divorce was granted. Everything had been so smooth sailing that the pair remained working together throughout the proceedings, during the divorce Glenn was awarded all proceeds that the pair would derive from CD Gems. Five days later however, Glenn was found dead in a Cabin on Lake Grapevine, owned by his parents. He was fully dressed, lying propped up in the bed. There was a half empty can of beer on the dresser and a foam substance around his mouth. When they moved his body, police discovered two pills under his body and at the autopsy, traces of Valium and Librium, a hypnotic and sedative of the benzodiazepine family of drugs, were found in his blood. Cause of death was attributed to suicide by Drug Overdose.

His body was discovered by Terri and two other members of Conscious Development of Body, Mind and Soul, who claimed she had found a note in her safe on February 2nd, one day after his death, that had been left by Glenn. The note read:

"I, Glenn Cooley, give to Terri Cooley all of my property, both personal and real. This includes 2 boats, a 1972 Buick Limited, all jewelry and equipment for its making, all furnishings for the house on Dunhaven Road and all cash."

"I ask that this last will of mine not be contested by anyone in any way for any reason."

"Last but not least, I give all my love to all my family and friends."

Glenn had also signed over full ownership of the house to Terri 2 weeks prior.

His final estate was valued at $2565, a figure that deeply puzzled Glenn's parents, who estimated there to be around $85000 worth of jewelry making equipment, metals and gems in their house. Glenn's mother had also found Terri's behaviour during the funeral highly suspicious. She said of Terri:

"She was crying and talking and then she would stop and look up at me to see my reaction. I didn't understand it."

Terri of course, denied this fact and spoke of the situation:

"For them to blame me for Glenn's death is just totally awful. I did nothing but love that man. I tried to help him as long as we were married; I tried to help him after we divorced."

She also claimed that she had not felt things were right with Glenn for some time and had tried to talk him out of going to the cabin alone. However, there is also another side to the story. Years later, in 1989, a former member of the group claimed that she and Terri had visited the cabin on the night of Glenn's death and although Glenn was lucid at the time, he had already taken the fatal cocktail that ended his life. The purpose of this trip remains unknown. Furthermore, when Terri learned of Glenn's parents intentions to testify against her at the inquest, Terri called Glenn's sister to warn her that there was every possibility that Glenn's history of drug abuse might come up in public.

When word spread around Conscious Development of Body, Mind and Soul of Glenn's death, many members blamed the Black Lords.

Shortly after Glenn's death, Terri remarried with Ben Johnson, another member of the group and one of the three who had previously discovered the body of Glenn. Terri also began taking blood from members of Conscious Development, telling them that it had become poisoned by the Black Lords. This bloodletting advancement was a new way to expel negative energies and though Terri expounded on it's many benefits, it proved to be too much, a step too far for some and by 1978 membership started to dissipate. Joyce Tepley, a defector, later spoke of her decision to leave.

"I was relying on someone else's judgment of me instead of my own judgment of what's right and wrong, and using Terri as the ultimate authority of my life, rather than me as the ultimate authority. Once you give up your own decision-making process to someone else, however wonderful they may be, you've lost your integrity."

However at the same time as members were slipping away from Terri's grip, war weary from their prolonged battles with Black Lords and not overly keen on donating blood to the cause, one member, Sandra Cleaver, was doubling down on her commitment.

Sandy, Devereaux & The Black Overlords

Sandy Cleaver was tall, attractive and popular at school. At DePauw University, she met Chuck Cleaver, the Basketball team captain and four years after their graduation, the pair were married. Chuck took a well paid job and they moved to Dallas. Four years later, Sandy and Chuck had a daughter, Susan Devereaux Cleaver, known as Devereux and for a long time, lived a happy family life. Despite outward appearances however, Sandy had had a troubled life. Her parents divorced when she was a young child, her mother consequently spent years in and out of various mental health institutions and after school her sister had died in a car crash, whilst her father had also died in a light airplane accident in 1966.

She lived a comfortable life with a large trust fund, however, she suffered from past traumas and began seeking spiritual answers to her misfortunes. She became obsessed with walking a path of meditation and homeopathic medicine. At one point, Chuck found her packing to leave for a trip to a homeopathic practitioner who had promised to place Devereaux into his special invention that would "tune out the world's bad vibrations". Chuck was definitely not keen. This path eventually led Sandy to Conscious Development of Body, Mind and soul and to Terri. Sandy excitedly told Chuck of how Terri was the reincarnation of St Teresa, and of how she could use crystals to cure cancer. She also took to calling herself and openly telling people that she was a high priestess of Atlantis in a former life. Chuck, fairly understandably, felt this behaviour was unsettling and when he told Sandy as such, she replied that:

"I really have to help Devereaux overcome all the problems that are caused by your bad vibrations!"

Sandy became more involved with Conscious Development of Mind Body and Soul and this caused real strain on her relationship with Chuck who continued to vehemently oppose Sandy's new spiritual leanings, which compounded the issue. Sandy took counselling classes with Terri, who offered to protect Devereaux with one of her protective shields that would:

"Protect her from anything, except the negative vibrations from your husband, which are very powerful."

Sandy begun to actually believe that her husband's negative thoughts concerning her spirituality and relationship with Terri was creating bacteria that would infect Devereaux and during an argument with Chuck one evening, took out a knife from the kitchen and screamed that at times, she thought Devereux would be better off in heaven.

In 1971, one month after Terri divorced her first husband John Wilder, Sandy filed for divorce, citing that she and Terri had decided that Chuck was blocking her spiritual development. The custody battle for Devereaux was long and drawn out, although his attorney felt Chuck had an excellent chance of securing rights, and privately, so did Sandy's attorney. Eventually however, with fear of what Sandy might do to Devereux if she lost custody, Chuck agreed to settling for visitation rights, however wrote a provision into the settlement that Sandy must only take Devereaux to recognised physicians permitted to practice in texas.

With her spiritual development now unblocked, Sandy bought and installed a printing press in her house to produce the literature for Conscious Development of Body, Mind and Soul and begun working full time for CD Gems and in 1976, around the time that the war with the Black Lords was beginning, Sandy helped Conscious Development of Body, Mind and Soul legally become Incorporated, with Terri sitting as the sole member on the Board of Directors. Sandy was named Secretary-Treasurer. All income flowed directly into Terri's personal bank accounts.

Devereaux meanwhile became isolated and alienated from her mother and found the members who came to the house regularly "weird", unlike her mother, she was not a participant in Conscious Development of Body, Mind and Soul and even appeared to be embarrassed of her mother when her school friends visited. This strained their relationship, Devereux felt her mother was uninterested in her and alienated, whilst Sandy thought Devereaux was infected with bad vibrations. Terri tended to agree, suggesting that a Black Overlord was the cause of all the family's problems.

In August 1978, just as membership of Conscious Development of Body, Mind and Soul began dwindling, Sandy wrote a will that would leave everything to Terri and four days later, Devereaux, now aged 13, also wrote her own will also leaving everything to Terri, this included her $125,000 trust fund.

In February 1979, Sandy sat down on the bed with Devereaux and asked her if she would like to join her on a trip to Hawaii with one of her Conscious Development friends. Devereaux was thrilled that her mother had included her and jumped at the opportunity to holiday and socialise with her mother.

On the 25th February, she took a raft out to sea with her mother when a wave struck the pair, knocking them overboard. Sandy was rescued but Devereux could not be found for over three hours, eventually rescuers found her body. She had drowned.

Autopsy reports showed no sign of foul play and no traces of drugs and alcohol. Terri informed Chuck of his daughter's tragic and untimely death and he rushed off to Hawaii immediately. When he reached the hospital that Sandy was staying in, he found Terri already there. Curiously, whilst he was gone, one of Terri's followers called in on Chuck's house and left Devereaux's will with a family friend. The will read,

"I give, devise and bequeath all of my property, including all rights, titles and interests of whatever character I may own in and to any property, real, personal, or mixed, whatever situated to Terri Johnson, who has been to me like a second mother."

She also included that it was not to be contested in any way. Terri claimed to know nothing of the will's existence, however it was signed and witnessed by three Conscious Development of Body, Mind and Soul teachers. As it turned out, the document was not legal as Devereux was only 14.

In 1979, Terri's own son Kenneth, whilst working construction, fell through a hole in a roof 30 feet to his death. Two months later, Sandy took out a life insurance policy for $300,000 and at the end of 1979, legally signed over all of her property to Terri, including her $180,000 house, which she now paid Terri rent to live in. After the death of Devereux, Sandy became depressed and drew even closer to Terri, as well as her 78 year old housekeeper. Meanwhile, Terri was busy divorcing her third husband, and remarrying Don Hoffman, an engineer and member who had been married for 22 years, before separating from his wife Alice, who had signed a waiver, allowing Terri and Don to marry immediately following the divorce, rather than waiting for the usual one day's grace period. Don promptly quit his job and devoted himself fulltime to Conscious Development of Body, mind and Soul.

In August of 1981, Sandy wrote a 13 page letter to her Brother Croom, that was something of an autobiography and expounded the virtues of Terri. In September of the same year, she left for Colorado to visit a patch of land that Conscious Development had bought with a vision to build a retreat for the members. After a little cajoling on Sandy's part, she talked Louise Watson into accompanying her, despite Louise not wanting to take the trip, as she had been feeling unwell. The neighbours thought it was slightly strange that she had not asked them to look after the cats as she usually did. They left for their road trip in Sandy's car on September 8th and two days later, on September 10th an Air Force Academy Paramedic helicopter whilst on a routine flight spotted Sandies car lying at the bottom of a 450 ft cliff. The road was perilous so police found little to be suspicious of, however, it was noted that there were no skid marks on the road, suggesting that Sandy had not tried to break or veer away from the edge of the sheer cliff, instead it seemed like she had driven straight off by her own accord.

Terri arrived on the scene two days later, ever present in such situations that were now becoming commonplace, to collect the bodies and cash in on the wills of both parties. Louise had earlier written a will, leaving everything to Sandy, which now transferred straight to Terri.

Trial

Sandy's brother, Croom found the whole affair entirely unwholesome. On November 10th 1981, His attorney James Barklow filed papers on his behalf contesting the will, stating that:

The will was executed as a result of undue influence exerted over the deceased." It went on further too, " Sandy was controlled by Terri's use of hypnosis, pavlovian conditioning and psychotherapy. Sandra Beatty Cleavers' will was but one of several persons whose wills were changed pursuant to the direct influence, suggestion and psychological control of Terri Hoffman."

Terri's Attorney opposed this last line of investigation and won a motion to prevent anyone talking of any of the other deaths during the trial, however Terri clearly felt her chances were perhaps not looking so good, especially after the publication of an article in a local Dallas magazine that detailed Terri's involvement with Conscious Development of Body Mind and Soul. Fearing that the new found local fame would not sit well with the Jury, she settled with Croom Beatty. Terri agreed to pay $50,000 to Croom immediately, followed by a second cash payment of $62,500. Sandys house would be sold with the split 40% to Beatty, 60% to Terri and the remainder of Sandy's estate, valued at $332,000 would be split equally.

After the trial, Terri claimed to be taking Sandy's death particularly hard. Along with the spotlight from the Dallas magazine, she stopped all her meditation classes, instead taking small, private massage and spiritual classes in her home. Along with her husband Don, they embarked on revising much of their literary material, which had not been updated since the group's inception and had little talk of Terri's new abilities of being able to read people's auras, which she now offered as a service directly from her home. She also entered into a short lived real estate investment and by the mid 80s was running a perfumery named Perfume Oils International Inc. Despite this apparent enforced downsizing of Conscious Development of Body, Mind and Soul, Terri still had much work to do in both the spiritual and physical realm.

As she said previously, her masters do not visit her always, and not always when she wants them.

Robin Otstott

Robin Otstott was a former writer of the Dallas school curriculum and worked as a school counsellor, working with difficult children. When she met Terri in 1974, she was 41 years old and had been divorced for two years, in secret, she was struggling behind closed doors. She quickly became deeply involved with Conscious Development of Mind Body and Soul and was terrified of the Black Lords, though she participated in the weekly battles, playing her part for the spiritual war effort. She filled her home with protective crystals which she bought from CD Gems and twisted copper piping into "protective shields" which she placed under her bed.

Robin was the benefactor of one of Terri's lesser known abilities. By the 1980s, Terri claimed to her followers that she trained "dematerialised" CIA agents and used her powers to protect them. By the middle of the eighties, Robin was in a close personal relationship with an invisible CIA agent named George Geoffries, a man she had never met and no one had ever seen, but Terri assured her truly existed. Terri explained to her that they would never be able to meet or marry in the physical realm for reasons of national security. Robin kept detailed journals of their relationship, describing dates, romantic walks and even a camping trip to Colorado, where she had bought tracts of land along with several other core members of the group.

From 1980 until 1986, she had frequent therapy sessions with Terri and Don, however her mental health never improved. She became more and more introverted and began cutting ties with her family and social group and was writing of her depression openly in her journal entries. One of Robins friends said of her:

"Her whole life revolved around her son until she met Terri Hoffman, then her whole life revolved around Terri Hoffman."

Her journal entries spoke of how her physical and spiritual bodies were actively fighting one another and in one entry wrote:

"I don't want to work with my soul in the physical."

At one meeting, she physically attacked one of her closest friends, Tamara Taylor, though later blamed the Black Lords and maintained that she had no control over her actions. The other teachers pushed Robin away and in March 1987, Tamara herself wrote Robin a letter stating that:

"I have made the decision to stop talking with you. In looking back at the numerous things which have befallen me, I was able to determine that on many occasions I had talked to you and given you information which was then used against me by your other bodies following her phone call."

On April 2nd, Robin sent out a cry for help to Terri, the contents of the letter showed how far her mental state had deteriorated and the level of paranoia she was living among. She claimed in the letter that "Martin", Tamara's very own invisible CIA boyfriend, had threatened to kill her if she harmed Tamara. At the top of the letter, she had pencilled in a small amendment:

"Please tell me if this situation happened. It felt very real and it's very serious to me."

In April, she contacted her ex-husband and explained that she had caught Hepatitis from a banana skin. Concerned for her welfare, he set up a doctor's appointment for Robin on the 21st of April, which she attended. Following the appointment, she visited Terri, stopped into a store on the way home and bought a revolver, then promptly drove home and shot herself in the head. Her suicide note was a letter to Terri and it read:

"I am apologizing to Terri 3000x a week on all levels of my being for the highly offensive, rude and vulgar comments made to her last week. I love her dearly and beg her forgiveness someday."

Her will, written 2 months prior to her suicide, left her Colorado land, all her jewellery, personal files, clothing and furnishings went to Terri, her son had right of refusal on anything left over and anything he didn't want was also to go to Terri. Later, the results of her blood tests would come in, she showed no sign of any illness or disease whatsoever.

Mary Levinson

Mary Levinson was born in Indiana in 1957, the second of 4 children. Her parents were the owners of a locally famous chain of 13 clothing stores, however Mary never showed any interest in the family business like her brothers, instead she loved animals and art.

She suffered chronic pain in her knee from a problem which she avoided treating until she was into her twenties, her brother Carl suggests this had to do with their mothers Christian Science faith. She also had difficulties with Anxiety and depression and whilst at university, made an attempt at taking her own life. After hospitalization, she spent much of her life visiting counselors and therapists, but continued to struggle with coping with her troubles.

In 1984 she married Dr Robert Schrock and the couple moved to Chicago, where Mary became involved with a local Chicago based arm of Conscious Development of Body Mind and Soul whilst also continuing to see her psychiatrist up to three times a week. Due to the problems with her knee and stress, most of these sessions were carried out by phone. She also began taking weekly phone sessions with Terri Hoffman and they quickly became central to her life. She separated from Schrock in 1986 and found a new boyfriend, a Dr Robert Keyes who she met at a Colorado retreat with Conscious Development of Body Mind and Soul. Her divorce lawyer later stated that

"I would say that Mrs Hoffman's teachings were probably the most important thing in her life during the time that I knew her."

When her mother visited her in Chicago, she made her wait in the lobby for an hour whilst she finished a phone call with Terri and later even asked her parents for a loan so that she could move to Dallas. Her parents, wary of the group, denied her the loan.

In the summer of 1987, she removed her brother as beneficiary of her life insurance policy and replaced it instead with Dr Robert Keyes. She also visited her parents during a vacation where she would introduce Robert to her family, however after her mother scolded her for pushing Hoffman's teachings on to one of her brothers, the pair left early. Her mother claimed that since then, her relationship with her daughter became strained and they rarely heard from her.

Mary then began selling off her possessions including antique furniture, heirlooms and jewelry. Her mother sent her a cheque for a thousand dollars, thinking that she was having financial difficulty whilst she was waiting for her divorce settlement to finalize. When it finally came through, Mary withdrew the entire sum of $125,000 in cash.

On November 30th, 1987, a maintenance worker at the Hillside Holiday Inn in Chicago found the door to room 114 double bolted and alerted police, who responded around 7 pm and broke into the room, finding Mary lying dead on the floor, fully clothed between two beds. On the bedside cabinet was a pen, pad, motel room key and over 100 various pills, most of which were benadryl. They also found a briefcase on one of the beds which contained a manilla envelope holding $118 in cash, drivers license, a cut up VISA card and a tape recording left for family. Her autopsy report noted that she had a small puncture wound from a needle on her wrist and had overdosed on sleeping pills.

On the tape, she claimed to have used all of her money, including the $125,000 from her divorce settlement to pay of small debts, donate to animal shelters and

"I also donated money to institutions - charitable institutions - which I shall not name."

Her parents later found that Mary had used her mother's credit card to buy over $3000 worth of jewelry in the weeks leading up to her death, though none of it was found in her possessions. She had paid her attorney $1000 to settle her estate and to make sure that no one else was to be involved. In a letter written by Mary and read to her parents by Mary's attorney, she again reiterated that she had given all of her money to non-profit organisations which "would remain nameless".

Mary's ex-husband said that after her suicide, Mary's psychiatrist had told him that he had not seen Mary for four months leading up to her death and that he had been concerned over Terri Hoffman's influence:

"He said the type of group that doesn't define between life and death isn't good for Mary, they make it so that it was no big deal to step into that other room."

On the tape recorded for her parents, Mary stated,

"I want you to understand that I am fully rational and I have come to this decision after a long time of thinking," she said. "I am actually looking forward to it."

Charles Southern Jr

Charles Southern Junior was a respected English professor and assistant chairman of a local Community College in Chicago, illinois. He was fascinated with spirituality and religions. His mother told of how he studied all sorts of African and Eastern religions. He joined a local sect of Conscious Development of Body Mind and Spirit and rose to take part in Terris core group of teachers, battling the evil forces of the Black Lords and routinely visited Terri in Dallas. In 1987, his family found him walking the streets of Chicago mumbling in an incoherent language to himself and took him to the Michael Reese Hospital to be sectioned, fearing that he was a danger to himself. He stayed in hospital for five days and his mother visited him every day, as did two members of Conscious Development of Body Mind and Spirit, when they came, Charles would ask his mother to leave the room. After his release from hospital, he claimed that he had become disenchanted from Terri's teachings, though remained active in the group. He had booked a trip to India during his two week holiday in December 1987, and though his family was concerned with his mental state still, he reassured them that he was now fine and so they carried on as usual, stating that Charles had travelled a lot in his life and with his repeated assurances, there was nothing to do except trust in his judgement.

When they failed to hear from him for two weeks after the date he was scheduled to return from India, his parents drove from Cincinnati to Chicago to visit him and after breaking into his house, their worst fears were confirmed. Charles was nowhere to be seen, however, folded inside out atop a African ceremonial stool were his dress hat and coat, a Nigerian tribal symbol for death. They also found his passport, with no stamps from Indian customs and a small vial of a drug, Curare, a drug used in anaesthesia causing total paralysis. There were also poorly written documents scribbled on note paper and barely legible. At the top of one was the line:

"I came under a bad influence and tried to battle it myself."

Almost no other words on the page are legible, except the name Terri Hoffman. In another scribbled document, they found that Charles had named Terri as executor of his estate. He remains missing until this day.

Don Hoffman

Don Hoffman, Terri's fourth husband was found dead in a Marriott Hotel room by a maid at 8:30am on 17th September, 1988. Don had two children from his previous marriage with Alice, whom he had divorced in a flash and married Terri within a day of the papers being filed. After their marriage, he had quit his job as an engineer to work alongside Terri and the couple had worked hard to keep Conscious Development of Body Mind and Spirit afloat throughout the difficult period of the early eighties. Their eight years of marriage, not a bad run on Don's part considering Terri's track record, was ended abruptly when Don took a lethal concoction of drugs including Benadryl and Ecstasy. On the bedside table was a tape recorder, legal pad, pen and a neat stack of benadryl capsules. Written on the first page of the legal pad, he had written:

"My car is in parking place No.136. - R. D. Hoffman".

He had also left a three page suicide note that claimed he had an inoperable Cancer and that he would rather end his life than suffer Chemotherapy. The autopsy report discovered the drugs in his system that had killed him along with a curious revelation. Don had no sign of Cancer.

Prior to leaving home for the Hotel, Don had recorded three video messages for his family, in them he told them about his fatal cancer, about how his doctors names were to remain a secret and that he had burnt all of his medical records, though for what reason was not explained. He assured them not to grieve long for him and that "Death is just a transition from one life to another life." He also told them:

"Y'all help Terri as much as you can. Her heart is kind of weak and any undue stress or pressure on her right now would be really bad."

Don's children weren't buying it and were deeply suspicious. They called Terri and secretly taped the conversation. Terri informed them that at the time of his death, she had no idea about Don's cancer nor who the doctors were that apparently diagnosed him. Though she had spoken to him in his next life and that he was now "free from pain". She went on:

"The whole thing is really crazy, I don't understand it yet. I need to talk to him some more."

When asked about why there was no disease found during the autopsy, Terri explained that she had recently spoken to Kaltu, another one of her spiritual masters, Kaltu had told her that:

"What Don had was definitely cancer. He said the Black Lords were trying to create an illusion so that the medical examiner wouldn't find any cancer - so they would hurt us all more."

She then offered them some land in Colorado and told them that Don had told her from beyond the grave that he didn't want any conflict within the family. On April 19th 1989, Terri filed Don's will, which of course, left everything to Terri.

David & Glenda Goodman

David Goodman was the eldest of three sons, born in Chicago, he moved with his family to Santa Maria, California. He married Peggy, his high school sweetheart in 1961 and when they had a son, he dropped out of college to support his family. After raising enough money and his son grew, he went back to college and earned a Math degree and MBA from Berkeley. He had a second son in 1965 and in 1967, began studying a PhD in Management Science at Yale. Things were going well, but suddenly, in 1961 on the 10th anniversary of their wedding, Peggy left David and took their son. He started working at a community college as a professor, however, struggling with the whirlwind events surrounding the breakup of his marriage, David started seeking answers. He joined transcendental meditation classes and attended Hare Krishna meetings and eventually, in 1973 wound up meeting Terri and the Conscious Development of Body Mind and Soul. He was quickly drawn in by Terri's abilities and excitedly told his brothers of how Terri could read minds and was "training him". By 1978, he was spending $150 per month on Terri's counselling services.

In 1978, Terri introduced David to his soulmate, a Conscious Development member and presided over their marriage. It was also around the mid-to-late 70's that David's co-workers noticed David becoming distant at work. In truth, he was tired of academics and on the side, had entered into a partnership with John Peavey to develop a stock market trading system. The pair wrote a book titles "Hyperprofits" which was published in 1985 and became a bestseller. Despite working in a partnership, David largely kept himself to himself and rarely spoke of his private life. Peavey said of him,

"I spent more time professionally with him than anyone. I just never really knew the guy personally. He didn't seem to want to get involved with anybody. It was weird."

Peavey had not even been aware that during their time working together, David had filed for divorce from his soulmate and remarried a different soul mate, Glenda in 1984. Once again, they were introduced by Terri and she performed the ceremony.

In 1987 he resigned from his professorship, citing no reason. He left all of his books and possessions in his office and never spoke to another member of staff. He just disappeared from the college. Glenda had also cast off her children during the same period, pulling them out of high school and sending them to live with their father and only permitting them to visit for two weeks every summer. By 1988, the couple had cut their family off completely, telling them that they had no choice due to the family's "negative energies".

On October 20th, 1989, the couple shot themselves in the head in their home.

When police found the bodies one month later, they also found a collection of journals that had documented the years leading up to the couple's suicide and they made disturbing reading. They were full of daily entries, written in their own hand, but with detailed instructions from "Masters". They showed how over the space of three years, David and Glenda had turned to the masters to control every aspect of their lives, even as far as getting advice on shopping for soft furnishings from "Markus".

They were seeking the highest truth and the highest level of spiritual advancement, the masters suggested to them they needed to give Terri money in order to do this and after building an extension on their old house, they gifted it to Terri, along with over $110,000 and a new car "In appreciation for all she has done". They also spoke of "white pills" that they received from Terri.

Through this gifting however, they had earnt a certain level of spiritual advancement. Glenda had received a revelation at 5am one morning that she and David were, in fact, Adam and Eve reincarnated and they had lived 800,000 previous lives together. They took on new identities and began calling themselves Jupiter and Venus. In one entry, Glenda wrote,

"Terri and Markus took Jupiter and Venus by the hand and led us to a beautiful glittering house in the purple realm. It was to be our house."

However, being mere reincarnations of Adam and Eve was still not enough for Glenda and David. The journals explained how they needed to have a 50-50 relationship with God, apparently meaning that 50% of all their earnings should go to Terri. When they still failed to achieve all that they wanted spiritually, and had cut off their families, the couple found them on a bleak path. David wrote one day:

"Can't you see that we can't take this anymore? Give us your true energies."

Eventually the journal entries turned to suicide. Glenda wrote how suicide would be a path to success and away from sufferings of the physical world. She wrote to David of how they should look forward to being able to come and go from the physical world at will, "Just like Terri can".

Trial (Again)

On March 3rd 1989, Don Hoffman's children, filed a case against Terri Hoffman claiming that she had induced Don to kill himself and seven weeks later contested the will. Their attorney was James Barklow, the same man who contested Sandys will and during his investigations into Terri, he found a note in her trash. The note read:

"Here is your bulk order plus the samples. #1 is a new formula that is a bit more complicated to make and will cost 35 cents more per capsule. It should have more amphetamines and a balancer to neutralize bad effects. #2 is the basic E formula, without the last step performed in purification to remove all amphetamines."

Barklow Believed that these drugs had been the tablets that several followers were taking, suggested by Terri as "Vitamins" and were the capsules found at many of the scenes after the suicides.

On October 22nd 1991, Terri Hoffman filed for bankruptcy protection, claiming that the publicity had derailed her businesses, however failed to mention several bank accounts that she operated, along with artwork and property, but for the Hoffmans, things were not going well.

"We had a number of offenses we tried to assemble, but bankruptcy fraud is all that's happened so far, and that's not even connected to anything except the property she got."

The prosecutors shared their files with the FBI involved with her Bankruptcy claims, however they were told in no uncertain terms that they didn't want to get involved with aspects outside of the direct case of Hoffman's financial problems.

"We did not want to go into the hocus-pocus."

In the end, nothing came of the Hoffmans case against Terri, the prosecutor stated:

"It just doesn't translate into a grand jury proceeding. It's been an interesting endeavor, but I just never could quite get there."

On November 23rd 1994 Terri Hoffman was convicted on 10 counts of

Bankruptcy Fraud and sentenced to 16 months imprisonment, of which she served less than one year, released in May 1995.

A New Millennium Dawns

After prison, Terri appeared to go dark and there is scant record of her activity for the next 6 years, until she remarried for the fifth and final time in 2002 to Roger Keanely and changed her name to Terri Lilya Keanely. She remained married to Roger Keaneley until her death on October 31st, 2015.

Her website, still available for viewing at HeavenandEarthPhotography.com explains how she developed a new form of photographic art, her photos are of clouds, which she sold on her website until her death. In Terri's words however, they are not merely clouds, but "Various spiritual beings that have revealed themselves" to her. Never one to shy away from how special she was, she lists no less than five areas of expertise, from Floral Design to Seminar Leader.

Among her long lists of Honours, Awards and Publications, she listed all of her Conscious Development of Body Mind and Spirit literature as a "Multi-volume study course.", Whilst her biography was apparently included in the dedication sections of "Great Minds of the 21st Century" and "Hall of Fame of Great Women of the 21st Century", two publications for which there are no references.

The site talks openly about Terri's fantastic spiritual powers that she has had throughout her life, however, unsurprisingly, there is not one single mention by name of Conscious Development of Body Mind and Soul, though she appears to have offered low-key classes along the same lines up until her death. The final line of a Dallas obituary read:

"She gave us the opportunity to experience many different vibratory frequencies so that the next time we are exposed to a being, situation, or an energy, we can now attune to it and recognize it/them because she presented those new vibratory frequencies to us. That has truly been a gift from God."

"So our leader has left us on the physio-astral but nevertheless still exists on all the other levels. Thank you, for all your love, tutelage, and care. Until we meet again."

Conclusions

It's safe to say that Terri had a knack of attracting people with short life spans, especially those with insurance policies or large estates. Those who side with Terri believe that it was simply a hazard of Terri's line of work, becoming involved with people in difficult stages of their lives. Somewhat more credible however, is the idea that these vulnerabilities are exactly what Terri needed to successfully prey on.

Terri's lawyer, Fred Time said during the legal suit following the deaths of the Goodmans:

"What's wrong with giving a large gift in return for spiritual guidance? Call up some of the big churches and see if anybody died and left them money."

However, Leonard Goodman's words probably speak it best when he diplomatically said:

"Maybe it was double suicide, but one word from Terri would have stopped it. If my son hadn't been involved with Terri Hoffman, he'd be alive today. So would a lot of other people."

Mary Levinson's parents grieved alone until they heard of the legal suit against Terri, they now believe she was involved. Likewise Charles Southern Junior's family have also come to believe that Hoffman was embroiled in their son's disappearance.

Moreover, there are still more suspicious incidents, Jill Bounds from Dallas, a somewhat unorthodox therapist, heavily involved in all things metaphysical, was a former member of Conscious Development of Body Mind and Soul and had fringe connections with Terri at the time of her brutal, and unsolved, murder that is a riddle in it's own right. In the end, we are left with so many mysterious cases that are all tied up with Terri and her organisation that it's difficult to know where to start. With her death in 2015, the only certainty is that all we have are questions.

Episode 16 - Peter Stumpp, The Werewolf of Bedburg

Peter Stumpp snuck out to the forest on the edge of the village, he slipped on his belt and felt the familiar rage burning inside of him. As the woman he had spotted by the village square left the packed street and waved goodbye to her friends, he sensed his opportunity. Bounding across the field toward her, she barely had time to let out a scream before he tasted the familiar metallic zing of the blood. The deed done, he left the remains on the ground and skulked off back to the woods, removed the belt and now, in the shape of a man, walked casually back to the village, as he turned into the busy street, he greeted passers by with a spring in his step. Peter Stumpp held a very dark secret close to his chest.

Background

Today, we know of Peter Stumpp primarily due to the work of Augustus Montague Summers. A literary scholar and clergyman with an interest in the occult, who rediscovered a 16 page pamphlet that detailed Stumpp's crimes and execution in his 1933 publication of "Werewolves in Lore and Legend". The pamphlet's original title is practically a book in itself, but is generally shortened to "The most damnable life and death of Stubbe Peeter". Originally written in High Dutch in 1590, somewhat as news, but perhaps more so as entertainment. It was brought to English shores and translated by a man named George Bores to be sold on Fleet Street. who claimed to have witnessed the entire ordeal. There are no surviving copies in its original language thanks to the destruction on the German landscape during the 30 years war, a conflict which also destroyed the birth records of Bedburg and which makes it impossible to know Peter's exact date of Birth. Two copies of the English translation survived and now reside in the British Museum and the Lambeth Library.

The document is written in beautiful middle English and as such deserves it's space forefront to our story. The opening paragraph lays out the events we will delve into as such:

"A true Discourse. Declaring the damnable life and death of one Stubbe Peeter, a most wicked Sorcerer, who in the likeness of a Wolf committed many murders, continuing this devilish practice 25 Years, killing and devouring Men, Women, and Children. Who for the same fact was taken and executed the 31st of October last past in the town of Bedbur [Bedburg] near the City of Collin [Cologne, Köln] in Germany."

Peter Stumpp

Peter Stumpp was born in the village of Epprath, near to Bedburg, thirty miles West of Cologne, Germany in the mid-16th Century, Extrapolating from the text, all we can do is guess at a year, but it was probably around 1545-1550. Though his name has some variations on the spelling, a running theme often found in old English documents, they are all a variation of Stumpf, the german word for stump and is generally thought to refer to his missing left hand, a disability that whilst seemingly severe, had not stopped him earning a decent living from the land as he had worked as a farmer. A widower, He was well known and relatively wealthy within Bedburg, he took a mistress and had two children, his first child a son whose name is not mentioned and his second, Sybil or Bil a younger daughter.

At the age of 12, Peter became interested in the dark arts and practiced black magic, necromancy and sorcery. This occult path led Peter to making a pact with and selling his soul to the Devil around the age of 20 and in trade, the Devil gave him a belt in return for his eternal servitude. Once again, the original text really needs to speak its piece on the deal:

"The Devil, who hath a ready ear to listen to the lewd motions of cursed men, promised to give him whatsoever his heart desired during his mortal life: whereupon this vile wretch neither desired riches nor promotion, nor was his fancy satisfied with any external or outward pleasure, but having a tyrannous heart and a most cruel bloody mind, requested that at his pleasure he might work his malice on men, women, and children, in the shape of some beast, whereby he might live without dread or danger of life, and unknown to be the executor of any bloody enterprise which he meant to commit."

"The Devil, who saw him a fit instrument to perform mischief as a wicked fiend pleased with the desire of wrong and destruction, gave unto him a girdle which, being put around him, he was straight transformed into the likeness of a greedy, devouring wolf, strong and mighty, with eyes great and large, which in the night sparkled like unto brands of fire, a mouth great and wide, with most sharp and cruel teeth, a huge body and mighty paws. And no sooner should he put off the same girdle, but presently he should appear in his former shape, according to the proportion of a man, as if he had never been changed."

And with that swiftly made deal, Peter began his life as "the Werewolf of Bedburg."

The Werewolf of Bedburg

During the next 25 years, Peter maintained his reign of fear over the village of Bedburg, by day mingling with the village folk, apparently living quite amiably among them. It was however, his dark streak that he is famed for rather than his social skills and he used this guise of sociability to lure women out into the fields alone, or await them to leave the village by themselves and sensing his opportunity would rape and murder them "plucking out their throats and tearing their joints asunder". When he was unable to coax or follow a young lady by herself, he would tear into groups of young girls in his wolf-like shape, separate off the one he had taken a liking to and kill her promptly. When the deed was done, he would then remove the belt, resume his shape of a man and slip back into society, with no one any the wiser and even greeted his recent victims' families with a smile. Within a few years, he had murdered 13 young girls and two pregnant women, apparently eating their unborn children.

When times were less fruitful and Peter was unable to find women or children to kill, he turned instead to the local cattle, reportedly killing lambs and various farm life, eating them raw in the fields.

During his murderous activities, he maintained a work and home life, taking care of his family. He took care of his family so well in fact that his daughter, who was apparently very beautiful, gave birth to a child born out of an incestuous relationship that Peter committed her to. Incest being simply not really enough unless you're going to go all in, he also carried on an incestuous relationship with his sister at the same time. Throughout this period, he also had a relationship with his mistress named Katherine Trompin, though it's a little difficult to discern the exact relationship, he met her one night whilst out drinking and seduced her with his "fair and flattering speech". Katherine was a well known and well liked woman from Bedburg. She was tall and slender and her beauty was described as:

"so fair of face and comely of personage, that she resembled rather some heavenly Helfin than any mortal creature, so far her beauty exceeded the choicest sort of women".

Naturally, one does not acquire such looks without some sort of trickery and the document later suspects that she was in fact a "wicked spirit in the similitude and likeness of a woman" sent to him by the devil.

As time passed however, Peter's lust for blood grew insatiable and he became transfixed on the act of killing. He stopped selecting victims for their characteristics which stood out to him or attracted him and started killing for the simple pleasure he took from it. This grew to the point where, despite being a kind father to his son whom he deeply loved, he later attacked him whilst in wolf form. The whole grisly affair was reported as such,

"so far his delight in murder exceeded the joy he took in his son, that thirsting after his blood, on a time he enticed him into the fields, and from thence into a forest hard by, where, making excuse to stay about the necessaries of nature, while the young man went forward, incontinent in the shape and likeness of a wolf he encountered his own son and there most cruelly slew him, which done, he presently ate the brains out of his head as a most savory and dainty delicious mean to staunch his greedy appetite"

The original document stops counting bodies at this point, but rather goes on to say that he killed "many" and offers us an example of how he progressed as a murderer, when one day he came across a group of three people in a forest clearing of which he knew, two young men from Bedburg who were accompanying a young woman. Crouching by a bush, he called the name of one of the men, and when they walked over to see who was calling his name, Peter quietly killed him outright. When the second came to look for his friend, he promptly dispatched him too and then chased the lone woman down, raped and murdered her. The bodies of the men were found in the woods by a patrol in later days, though the woman was never found and was presumed to have been eaten.

After twenty five years however, Peters deeds were not going unnoticed and whilst none suspected him of any wrongdoing, it became harder and harder for him to kill whenever he pleased, as most locals had begun to travel armed or with bodyguards, all afraid of the monster that lie in the forest and that by this point, had become legend. Around this time, as security tightened and fear gripped the villagers to walk alone, Peter suffered his only documented close call, when upon storming into a group of unaware children, he grabbed one young girl and unable to sink his teeth into her throat due to the virtue of her high and stiff collar, she let out a scream that startled the nearby cattle, who, apparently "by the will of God" stampede towards Peter, forcing him to drop the child and run for his life. This young girl is the only documented survivor of an attack by Peter.

Time was running out for Peter by now and his misdeeds had run on for too long. In a desperate attempt to alleviate the village of Bedburg from fear, a small force of men were enlisted to hunt the wolf using dogs, who rather quickly entrapped the beast in the forest. Seeing there was no advantage for him in his predicament, Peter slipped out of the belt, transforming to his human form in front of their eyes. The men, all amazed at what they had witnessed, but knowing Peter well, escorted him to his home, whereby they called upon the local magistrate to arrest him. He was put to the rack, a form of torture in which a subjects ankles and wrists are tied on each corner of a frame and then through turning a crank, the whole body slowly pulled and stretched, inducing excruciating pain for anyone unlucky enough to experience such an interrogation. In fear, Peter quickly confessed his entire life story, from his encounter with the devil, his taking ownership of the belt and its magical properties to a long list of victims names that he had murdered during his reign of terror.

In the telling of his story, he admitted to casting the belt aside before his apprehension, however when men were sent to look for it, nothing could be found. This was supposed:

"that it was gone to the Devil from whence it came, so that it was not to be found. For the Devil, having brought the wretch to all the shame he could, left him to endure the torments which his deeds deserved."

Trial

On the 28th October, 1589, Peter Stumpp faced trial for the murders of countless men, women, children and cattle in and around Bedburg. He was found guilty almost immediately and as hinted at in the previous passage, Peter was indeed sentenced to "endure the torments which his deeds deserved."

On the 31st of October, in a square of Bedburg and in the presence of many peers and princes of Germany, Peter Stumpp was placed on a device known as a "breaking wheel", a large cart-wheel, where he was tied and bound. With red-hot pincers, his skin was torn from his bones, his arms and legs were then broken with wooden hatchets, mercifully he was at last killed outright through beheading and finally his body burnt. Deemed as accessory to murder, his daughter Sybil and mistress Katherine were also found guilty, however suffered slightly less, their method of execution was to be thrown onto the burning body of Peter and burnt to ashes.

In celebration for the downfall of his reign of terror over the village, a macabre shrine was erected, using the breaking wheel as the centrepiece upon which an engraving of a wolf was placed on top of a pole, along with Peter's head. The whole thing was encircled with 16 pieces of wood a foot in length, symbolising the victims of Peter whose names were known.

The document of the life of Peter Stumpp is finished with a telling passage,

"This, Gentle Reader, have I set down the true discourse of this wicked man Stub Peeter, which I desire to be a warning to all sorcerers and witches, which unlawfully follow their own devilish imagination to the utter ruin and destruction of their souls eternally, from which wicked and damnable practice, I beseech God keep all good men, and from the cruelty of their wicked hearts. Amen."

Werewolves in European Lore

Werewolves have appeared in literature as far back as the ancient Greeks, when King Lycaon tested Zeus' omniscience by feeding him the cooked remains of his own son. Zeus was not best pleased with this human meal and in turn transformed King Lycaon into a wolf, whilst returning his son to life, presumably uncooked.

Throughout the medieval period, werewolves were rarely mentioned and it's believed that there was no real folklore surrounding such creatures, however in the literature of the time, some "wolf men" were depicted as a human trapped inside the body of a literal wolf, though they were often gentle and only hunted with purpose, attacking whoever had cursed them into the bestial form, which was often their wives. As time passed however, this attitude and the beliefs themselves shifted, mostly due to outside forces and by the 14th Century and increasing until the 16th Century, werewolves were written of in religious texts as servants to the devil and wicked forms of black magic associated with witches.

As this shift in perception was underway, werewolves also took on a metaphorical role in folk tales. Wolves were a plentiful and much hated animal in Europe throughout the middle ages. They were notoriously difficult to hunt and inedible if you did happen to kill one. They carried rabies, ate livestock and cattle and most thought them dangerous to humans and in some cases, especially in rural areas, they were. In old allegorical texts, the wolf was seen as a greedy savage that led to the werewolf being used as a general term in law to refer to someone as an outlaw and in clerical texts as a derogatory term for someone who refused to gel within a community and participate in the mutual responsibilities of rural life.

Perhaps inevitably, an animal with such a bad reputation would be grafted into the folklore as a fearsome beast with dark associations and would also pave the way for the later persecutions when witch trials became a regular feature.

Werewolf Trials

Werewolf trials evolved throughout Europe parallel to the infamous witch trials and much like the witch trials, hinged on the need to blame somebody for the many socio-political turmoils of the period. As the biblical depiction of Satan grew in popularity, so did the persecution of "sorcery" as the perception changed from being a pagan heresy to a demonic practice.

The very first documented witch trial in Valais actually included werewolf trials and as you move East across Europe, werewolf trials became more and more commonplace. In France and Germany, there were relatively few with our good friend Stumpp being one of the most infamous accounts, but in Baltic countries they were far more commonplace, in Estonia for example, they were even more common than the witch trials themselves.

Germany in the 16th Century

As far as Germany goes, the case of Peter Stumpp is sensationalist in the extreme. From the way in which the victims were killed, to the stories of incest and cannibalism to the final act of his execution, there is never a moment in the tale which is not deeply horrifying, even in today's climate one would consider it a fringe case of brutality, but in 16th Century Germany, it was not only brutal, but caustically heretical.

During the time of the murders, Germany was highly religious, recovering from plague and under the influence of the Holy Roman Empire, though it creaked at the seams and support waned. In 1587, Protestantism was still being pushed at a state level to be made the official religion by law as part of the wider Protestant Reformation, however Italian and Spanish mercenaries and soldiers, who happened to be recent occupiers of Bedburg castle, were heavily invested in restoring the Catholic faith as part of the wider context of the Cologne War. All of this religious division had devastated the local area around Cologne and laid the groundwork for the coming 'thirty years war' which saw 8 million dead. This atmosphere of violence, fear, uncertainty and division served as the backdrop to which our tale of Bedburg and Peter Stumpp was set.

It is clear that wolves were feared and hated within communities of the 16th century and werewolves seemed to take the next logical step for many by adding sorcery and black magic to the mix, but can such a beast truly exist or was it simply hysteria, helped along by religion and social fears?

Theories

The first place we should look for evidence is the source material, with such a turbulent setting, how can we be sure that any of the details laid out concerning "the damnable life and death of one Stubbe Peeter" are true at all? There are several theories of what happened in 1590, each allotting a certain degree of truth to the claims. As far as the document itself claims, every word is true, sworn by a litany of witnesses, it states:

"Witnesses that this is true: Tyse Artyne. William Brewar. Adolf Staedt. George Bores. With divers[e] others that have seen the same."

Further, there is an account by one Master Tice Artine, a London based brewer and who was apparently loosely related to the surviving young girl attacked by peter:

"An that this thing is true, Master Tice Artine, a brewer dwelling at Puddlewharfe in London, being a man of that country born, and one of good reputation and account, is able to justify, who is near kinsman to this child, and hath from thence twice received letters concerning the same; and for that the first letter did rather drive him into wondering at the act then yielding credit thereunto, he had shortly after, at request of his writing, another letter sent him, whereby he was more fully satisfied; and divers other persons of great credit in London hath in like sort received letters from their friends to the like effect."

To look any further for proof would be impossible, however, there are records of Death and it's generally accepted that the story has, in the least, elements of historical truth. As to why it happened, we do not have to look far to find the many theories.

Religious Influence

One theory alludes to the concept that religion played a role in the trial and execution of Peter Stumpp. When considering this theory, the symbolism and theological metaphors within the text allude to the religiosity of the time. There are numerous direct religious passages, one early example in the story of Peter Stumpp is as follows,

"Those whom the Lord doth leave to follow the imagination of their own hearts, despising his proffered grace, in the end through the hardness of heart and contempt of his fatherly mercy, they enter the right path to perdition and destruction of body and soul forever"

The language used for the victims often likens them to sheep or lambs and when Peter killed livestock, it is only the sheep and lambs which are named directly, the rest are lumped together as simply "other cattle". It's important to remember that this leaflet was meant primarily as entertainment and therefore this emotive language with a religious bent was most probably assumed to bring about the greatest impact for the time, playing to an audience.

Use of language aside, the main crux of this theory lies with Peter's recent conversion to protestantism. Some claim that it was the work of the local Catholic lord, newly instated through the Cologne war, who used Peter as an example to other would-be protestants in a thinly veiled political trial.

This theory varies the level of Peter's guilt as a factor for his execution, some stating that Peter committed the crimes either as a wolf or a man and the whole affair played well into the religious angle, proving to be a convenience that had to be made an example of. There are others, however, that extend the religious theory even further, proclaiming that Peter was entirely innocent and that he was simply in the wrong place at the wrong time. As terrifying and painful an experience as the rack was, some believe that peter would have admitted to the crimes freely either through hope of a lighter sentence or through fear of the coming agony of the torture he was about to endure, stating anything that he himself had known or heard about the murders. There are some that even suggest the murders were not murders at all and that over the period of 25 years, it's plausible to believe that they were simple wolf attacks.

The text itself speaks quite well of Peter until of course, he begins to murder and rape the locals, going so far as to call him well known and respected as an elder of the village. He had, after all, managed to earn a decent living in the village and attract a mistress whose beauty was so great, it was presumed she was sent by the devil himself. It's not uncommon for a murderer to be both brutal killer and charming socialite together, however the brutality of Peters crimes and the claims of incest certainly leaves room to wonder how much was rumour and how much was truth.

Mental Illness & Physical Disability

One other common theory for Stumpp's behaviour is that rather than a werewolf, Peter was simply mentally ill. Mental illness is poorly understood today, in the 16th Century most variations of mental illness were put down simply as "madness" in various forms. Peters' long list of possible problems could have been depression, epilepsy, psychosis, any number of dissociative disorders and most interestingly, clinical lycanthropy, a medical delusion whereby the sufferer actually believes themselves to be able to transform into an animal. Even in 1584, Clinical Lycanthropy was put forward as a possibility for the existence of werewolves by Reginald Scot is his published work "The discoverie of witchcraft".

Each of the above can take us down any number of paths as to the outcome, with once again varying levels of guilt on Peter's part. Was he delusional and simply admitting to crimes he had not committed? Or had he committed the crimes under the delusion he was a beast? If it was psychosis, once again the same questions can be asked. One other possibility is that as misunderstood as mental illness was no doubt by the general populace, was he simply outcast and made an example of? This last line of thought makes sense to a degree, but seems doubtful in peter Stumpps case, being that he was well known and well liked within the village, but it's a possibility none the less and it could be possible that he had made certain enemies among the villagers, which would account for the rumours of his incestuous relationships. This same line of thinking can be enlisted when considering Peter's physical disability in regards to his lack of left hand also.

Serial Killer

A theory which does not excuse Peter nor believe him to be innocent states that he was a brutal serial killer. Werewolves were often depicted in wood blocks from Germany as simple men, crouched on all fours and the idea that werewolves were gripped by a cyclical blood lust worked its way into folklore and sits at his heart. A serial killer's brutal outbursts can be seen as an explanation for such behaviour.

In the 16th Century, it could be entirely plausible that most people found it difficult to attribute such acts to people, with such a distance from any form of recognised normalcy within such behaviour, people seek to place the perpetrator as an "outsider" or an "other". I will refrain from pointing out in detail how we still do the same today, however in the medieval and early modern ages, jumping to the supernatural was a simple way to achieve this and is not without precedent. Many historical serial killers in history have long been dubbed as Vampires.

If this was the case however, then why the story of the black magic and the belt? If Peter wanted to admit to his crimes, why did he need to make such a fanciful explanation?

Werewolf

Of course, we are left with the theory that Peter Stumpp was simply an actual werewolf, it's safe to say however, that there is little to no evidence in support of this theory. The problem is, there is little to no evidence for any other theory concerning Peter Stumpp. Over the years there have been reported sightings of werewolf-like creatures and there have been skulls found throughout the years that have been put forward as evidence for their existence, one example being the skull found by Trayche Draganov on his farm in Novo Selo, Macedonia. This theory hinges on where your beliefs in the supernatural lie, for many it is no more and no less plausible than any other explanation given for the crimes of Peter Stumpp.

Conclusions

In the end, we cannot ignore the fact that there was no real evidence that Peter Stumpp was a murderer, except for his confession which was made under extremely difficult circumstances. Perhaps he was ill, perhaps he was truly a vicious serial killer. Religion and politics may well have played its part, or perhaps he was, despite all our over complicated explanations, just a man who had made a pact with the devil and was able to transform into a murderous beast. In reality, it seems likely that the brutal killings of Peter Stumpp are a wild mix of all of the common theories.

And there is also the case of the mysterious belt, where did it disappear to, if it indeed existed in the first place? Though Peter told at his trial how he had thrown it aside during his capture, and presumably his captors knew the area relatively well, nothing was ever found. It's all very easy to dismiss its existence outright, but why then had it made its way into the story in the first place?

Whether or not Peter Stumpp was true and to what degree, the author of The Damnable Life and Death of Stumpp Peter is absolutely certain of one thing in regards to werewolves:

"Of all others that ever lived, none was comparable unto this Hell hound, whose tyranny and cruelty did well declare he was of his father the devil, who was a murderer from the beginning."

Episode 17 - The Pimlico Poisoning

In the early hours of New Year's morning, 1886, Adelaide Blanche Bartlett roused her landlord in Pimlico, London with a few simple words: "come down, I think Mr Bartlett is dead". She had awoken suddenly, sitting at the foot of her bed where she had dozed off earlier that night to find the feet of her husband, Thomas Edwin Bartlett, stone cold. During the following days, a postmortem was conducted and evidence found of a large quantity of Chloroform in the stomach of the deceased, however, there were no signs of how it had been ingested. There were no burns, nor were there any sores or other signs of irritation that would usually line the mouth and throat from drinking such a caustic poison.

In the words of Sir Charles Russell, the Attorney General who oversaw the inquest, "How came the Chloroform there?"

Thomas Edwin Bartlett

Thomas Edwin Bartlett was born in London in 1845. He was the son of a builder and had built a small chain of grocery shops up around Herne Hill, South London. By the age of 29, he was the co-owner of six shops and lived a financially comfortable life. He was a strong and well built man with a relatively imposing physical frame.

In 1875, he met Adelaide De La Tremoille, a young 19 year old French woman who was staying at his younger brother's house and was immediately taken with her. He quickly made his intentions clear to her and without discussing with his family, the pair were married at the Parish Church of Croydon on April 9th, 1875.

Adelaide Blanche Bartlett

Adelaide Blanche Bartlett, born Adelaide De La Tremoille was born in Orleans, France in 1855. 11 years younger than her husband Edwin, she was 19 years old at the time of the marriage. It was heavily rumoured that her father was a man of great wealth and possibly even titled, Comte De Tours D'escury, essentially a count of Torraine. Many propose she was an illegitimate child with an English mother, which accounts for her having been sent to live with a family, presumed to be her aunt and uncle in England at a young age. Details of how or why she became acquainted with Edwin's brother are not talked about in any of the cases materials, however, it was during her time there she met Edwin and seemingly agreed to marriage with no hesitation.

After the couple were married, Adelaide professed her will to gain a complete education, as her own had been fractured and had suffered due to her earlier upheaval from France to England. Edwin approved and she spent the first year of marriage attending a boarding school in Stoke Newington, visiting Edwin during the holidays. After the completion of schooling there, she then spent a further 18 months at a Convent school in Belgium, before returning to London to live as a family in 1877.

Strange Relations

So begins a strange relationship between husband and wife. From the outset and for reasons never discussed, Edwin and Adelaide agreed that their marriage should be platonic.

After the death of his mother, Edwin's father moved in with the couple above one of Edwin's shops, however their cohabitation did not sail so smoothly. Edwin's father had held a distrust of Adelaide from the outset and later, when asked about the couple's marriage, he stated:

"I was not asked whether I thought she was suitable or not. I did not particularly disapprove of it. I certainly did not much approve of it, but I did not disapprove of it."

And apparently this was not without reason, for he had accused Adelaide of having an affair with Edwin's brother. Considering the circumstances the couple had met in, this might not have been so far off the mark, however Adelaide took so great offence she moved back to her Aunt's house for a short period and finally, after much coercion from Edwin, his father apologised and retracted his statement in front of a solicitor before peace returned to the household. One can imagine that it was fragile however and by his own words, in a later statement, Edwins father said of the apology:

"I signed an apology, but I knew it to be false. I knew it to be the truth of what I said at the time. When I signed it, it was to make peace with my son."

Despite this however, they lived "mostly on friendly terms together". In 1881, despite their marriage being platonic, Adelaide fell pregnant. She said that her willingness to have a baby outrode the importance of their platonic agreement and stated they had sex only once, so I guess you could call them pretty lucky in that department. Regardless, Adelaide fell pregnant and their nurse, Annie Walker moved in one month before the baby was born. Tragedy befell the family however, when upon giving birth, the baby was stillborn, something which greatly affected Adelaide, who swore to never have another child in her life. During the labour Annie Walker insisted she needed the aid of a doctor, however, Edwin insisted that he "didn't want another man interfering with his wife" and disallowed it until the last minute, by which point it was already too late for the baby.

Shortly after the difficult problems with the stillborn birth of their child the couple moved out from the space above the shop to live apart from Edwin's father and spent the some time hopping from house to house, living above another of Edwin's shops for a time, a cottage and finally, in 1883, they moved to Merton Abbey, close by to Wimbledon, where they began attending a local church in Putney and met the Reverend George Dyson, a man who would gain quite an interesting relationship with the couple.

Reverend George Dyson

Reverend George Dyson was born in 1854 and had gained a BA degree at Dublin University before taking up residence as minister in a Wesleyan church, a branch of Protestant Christians that followed Wesleyan Theology, today, evolving through splinters and unifications, into the methodist church. The New York Times described him as

"A pale serious looking clergyman, with close cut little whiskers and a heavy black moustache".

At 27 years old, he was only one year older than Adelaide and in his duties as minister, visited Edwin and Adelaide in their home on occasion. Edwin took an immediate liking to Dyson and so too did Adelaide. The trio appeared to develop something of an unusual relationship.

After their first few meetings, Edwin made a request to Dyson for him to visit more frequently, he asked if the Reverend, with his degree and Holy teachings, take Adelaide under his wing and tutor her in Latin, History, Geography and Mathematics. This however, was not all that was requested of the Reverend and early on in their relationship, Edwin apparently requested that if he should die, he expected the Reverend to Marry Adelaide, a bizarre request to make of anyone. Later, Dyson would admit to having kissed Adelaide in front of Edwin who "seemed to quite enjoy it" and Alice Fulcher, the couple's maid, testified somewhat amusingly that she had several times walked in on Adelaide and the Reverend in "Positions unusual for tutor and pupil".

Despite this, to all outside sources, including Edwin's father, the couple appeared to live a happy life together as a married couple. Reverend George Dyson visited 2-3 days per week and when Edwin and Adelaide went on holiday for a month to Dover, he visited them twice, on both occasions all of his expenses were paid by Edwin himself.

In 1855, the couple moved to an apartment in Pimlico, a relatively well-to-do area in the City of Westminster, Central London and Edwin bought Dyson a season ticket for the train so that he could continue his "tutoring". He also wrote Dyson a letter concerning their relationship, it read:

"Dear George - Permit me to say I feel great pleasure in this addressing you for the first time. To me it is a privilege to think that I am allowed to feel towards you as a brother and hope our friendship may ripen as time goes on, without anything arising to mar its future brightness. Would that I could find words to express thankfulness to you for the very beautiful, loving letter you sent Adelaide today. It would have done anyone good to see her overflowing with joy as she read it when walking along the street, and afterward as she read it to me. I felt my heart going out to you. I long to tell you how proud I feel at the thought that I should soon be able to clasp the hand of the man who could from his heart pen such noble thoughts. Who can help loving you? I feel I must say to you two words, "thank you", and my desire to do so is my excuse for troubling you with this. Looking forward to the future with joyfulness, I am yours affectionately, Edwin."

I think most would agree, that this is a peculiar letter and it's made nonetheless strange when considered that the letter sent to Adelaide and talked of by Edwin was a verse of poetry, written by Dyson, to Adelaide and was concentrating on his love for her.

Edwin had enquired with the Reverend on several occasions what the bibles position on Polygamy was and often spoke lightly of the concept of having two wives, one who would be a loving partner and one who would undertake the "duties of a wife", Dyson however, chalked it up to Edwin's eccentricities, as he was apparently quite a peculiar character. His own doctor had at one time considered him insane and pressed him on several subjects to determine whether or not he may be mentally ill. In his doctor's words, Edwin was:

"One of the most extraordinary men I had ever dealt with - Though a very pleasant and nice man."

Around the Autumn of 1885, Edwin re-drafted his will. Adelaide had been unhappy concerning a stipulation included within the original document that if he were to die, she should not remarry. This was a common caveat at the time and so was not unusual to have been included, however, upon re-writing the document, Edwin removed the clause and at the same time, named Dyson as his executor.

And so the strange trio's relationship continued for several months, however, as the winter fell upon London, things moved from somewhat peculiar to darkly suspicious.

December 1885

On the 8th of December 1855, Edwin left work early feeling ill. He later wrote to his partner to excuse himself from work the following day. Aside from his other peculiarities, Edwin was seemingly also something of a hypochondriac. The Reverend noted that as long as he had known Edwin, he had clutched at his side compulsively, as if in pain and he frequently complained of illness and ailments. He thought he was suffering from tapeworms, syphilis and also, as the days in December ticked by, an unnamed terminal illness, despite the doctors repeated insistence that he was suffering from nothing of which he could not recover fully. He also had had severe problems with rotting teeth in the past and had visited a dentist who decided the best course of action was to shear off the rotten teeth at the gumline and fit a denture. Now however, he suffered severe pain from the roots and had taken to rubbing them with chlorodyne to keep the infection and pain away.

Edwin's long term Doctor, Alfred Leach diagnosed Edwin with Dysentery and Gastritis, though it also appeared as if he suffered depression and insomnia also. He took to sleeping on the couch in the drawing room and Adelaide, who nursed him throughout December, slept at his feet. Though she felt some concern as to how Edwin's friends thought of her as a bad nurse, the doctor remarked that night after night she would sleep at the foot of the bed, despite her own welfare.

As Christmas came around, Edwin's health improved. He visited a new dentist who had seen fit to remove his rotten teeth and his overall health benefitted from it. He was so much better in fact, that Doctor Leach saw fit to stop his frequent visits and suggested that the couple take a seaside break to gain some fresh sea air, a popular Victorian remedy.

Throughout his illness, just how fractured the relationship between Adelaide and Edwin's father had begun to show. She sent him a series of letters, essentially placing him at arm's length and in not so many words, told him not to visit. They read,

"The doctor was very angry that I had permitted Edwin to see visitors last night, as it caused his head to be so bad and he says no one is to be admitted unless he gives permission. Edwin is slightly better this morning. I will write to you every day and let you know how Edwin is. I can see myself how necessary it is that he should be kept calm."

The second letter, sent two days later went on,

"Edwin is up; He seems to have stood his tooth drawing very well. Please do not come all this distance, it is not right to have visitors in a sick room, and I don't feel it right to leave Edwin so long alone while I was downstairs talking to you. When he wishes to see you, I will write and let you know - Yours, Adelaide.

And a third states it quite plainly,

"I hear that you are a little disturbed because Edwin has been too ill to see you. I wish, if possible, to be friends with you, but you must place yourself on the same footing as other persons - that is to say, you are welcome here when I invite you, and at no other time. I wish you to understand that I have neither forgotten nor forgiven the past."

This series of letters would be blunt already, but considering the time of year and that these were dated between the 24th and 27th December, Christmas time, we can see just how little love there existed between the pair.

On the night of 27th December, during one of his usual visits, Adelaide and the Reverend went for an evening walk. She asked him if he could buy her some Chloroform, the better to help Edwin sleep on occasion that he had trouble. She mentioned she had asked the doctor at first, however he had seemed reluctant on account that she was not an experienced chemist and cited that it would not be the first time a bottle of Chloroform would be knocked over in bed, gassing the couple. She claimed the nurse, Annie Walker had bought it before, however she had left for America and so could not rightly ask her anymore. The Reverend gave full statement concerning their conversation:

"She told me she wanted some chloroform, and that Annie Walker had brought the Chloroform to her before. She said she wanted it to soothe her husband, to give him sleep, and asked me if I could get some for her. I told her I would and I did."

The reverend casually bought four small bottles of Chloroform from four different chemists, all within walking distance from his church and from chemists which all attended his services and knew him well, telling them he needed it to remove grease stains. He combined the bottles into one large bottle and on the 29th December, passed it to Adelaide.

On the 31st December, New Years Eve, Edwin returned home from the Dentist, he told Adelaide that the Dentist had diagnosed him with Necrosis of the gums, though despite this, in good spirits he sat down to eat dinner, made arrangements of a large Haddock to be cooked for his breakfast and retired to the drawing room to sleep. Adelaide joined him after talking with the maid until late into the night and sat at her usual spot at the foot of the bed. She awoke at around 4am with a pain in her arm from cramp and upon noticing that Edwins feet were cold and he was not moving, checked his vital signs for life. Edwin was dead.

The Unusual Death of Thomas Edwin Bartlett

Adelaide's first instinct upon discovering Edwin lying lifeless on the couch was to attempt to rouse him using Brandy, she poured almost a half-pint of brandy down his throat and when that failed to gain any reaction from her husband, she sent for Doctor Leach and then rushed upstairs to the landlord of the house. Mr Frederick Horace Doggett, who also happened to be the district's registrar for Birth and Deaths. She knocked at his door and told him "Come down, I think Mr Bartlett is dead."

Upon entering the room, both Doctor Leach and Doggett took note of the surroundings. There was an unlabelled bottle upside down in a glass tumbler on the mantelpiece alongside a wine glass with dark fluid, assumed to be brandy and a small tincture of Chlorodyne, which Adelaide had told the Doctor Edwin had used on his gums earlier that night. They gave the time of death to have been three hours prior, however, they could not find anything wrong with the body to immediately give away a cause of death and when a second doctor, John Gardner Dudley arrived, he remarked"

"He has no business being there, a strong man like that."

The doctors first thought was that he had possibly taken some sort of poison and enquired to Adelaide upon this being a possibility. She replied that she thought it to be impossible, stating,

"I could not suppose he had got hold of any poison; That he had no poison and could not have got it, or had it, without my knowledge."

The possibility of poison had not seemed far from the mark of Edwin's father also, who, upon his arrival, immediately walked over to his son and,

"leaned over him and kissed him passionately, and smelled his corpse for Prussic Acid."

Due to its colourlessness and highly poisonous properties, Prussic Acid, or Hydrogen Cyanide, was a common instrument used in a number of poisonings throughout the 1800's. Later it was tested by the US as a chemical weapon during the first world war and was a key component of Zyklon B, which should I hope, need no introduction for it's horrific use in the Nazi concentration camps. On this occasion however, Mr Bartlett smelt nothing, though ever suspicious of Adelaide, he was careful to state that he had kissed his son's forehead, not his mouth, so there was still a possibility.

The doctors conferred that a post mortem should take place to gain some idea on the cause of death and scheduled it for the following day, the 2nd of January. Adelaide was aghast and pleaded with the doctors to get on with the job immediately, but for the doctors to be present that Dr Leach wished for, it would have to wait.

Postmortem

The postmortem took place the following day on the 2nd of January by four doctors. No natural cause of death could be found and the heart, liver and lungs all seemed to be healthy. In fact, there was little to be found by the doctors at all. That is until, upon opening his stomach, a strong odour of Chloroform filled the room. It was so strong that the doctors remarked it was like opening a fresh bottle of the poison. They also found slight irritation of the tissue and drops of liquid Chloroform both in his stomach and lower intestine, suggesting a large quantity of the poison had been ingested. Furthermore, it was noted that there was a slight inflammation on the lower part of the stomach, which would only have occurred if the drinker had been lying on his back to allow the irritant to have rested on that particular area of the stomach. Doctor Leach also found that when he had discovered the body, there was a peculiar whitening of the tongue, however by the time of the postmortem, the whitening had passed and it had returned to a normal colour. Later the mad bastard would drink Chloroform himself to "test a hypothesis" and found that drinking Chloroform did indeed have the very same effect on his own tongue, which passed after a few hours.

After the postmortem, the doctors reported to Edwin's family that they could find no immediate cause of death, however the contents of the stomach were suspicious and had been preserved for further examination. Nothing of the specifics concerning Chloroform were mentioned.

In the early days of January, Doctor Leach himself felt that Edwin may have possibly ingested the Chlorodyne rather than simply rubbed it on his gums and spoke of it several times during his visits to Adelaide, though on each occasion, she insisted that Edwin did not drink the Chlorodyne, only used it to rub onto his gums. Nevertheless, her possession of the bottle of Chloroform appears to have weighed heavy on her mind, since on the 6th of January, the first day she was permitted to collect her things from the scene and the day before the inquest, she took a train and discarded the bottle out of the window.

On January the 26th, Doctor Leach visited Adelaide to tell her that the coroner was ready to create it's report on the findings of the stomach and told her that it was good news, that she had appeared worried in the uncertainty and that they would be announcing the case for Chloroform. This was good news, as far as Doctor Leach was concerned in that it was likely to remove Adelaide from suspicion. He told her:

"that should put your mind at rest; but had it been one of the secret poisons given in small amounts, and which could be administered without the patient knowing it, you would have most certainly been very seriously accused of having poisoned him by some people."

However, to the contrary, Adelaide merely replied:

"I am afraid, Doctor, it is too true. I wish anything but Chloroform had been found."

Adelaide then went on to give the Doctor a full rundown of her married life with Edwin, that from the outset they had agreed a platonic relationship and that Edwin had been a kind man and they saw to each other with utmost affection. She then explained Edwins strange insistence that she meet other men and often invited men to their house:

"He thought me clever, he wished to make me more clever, and the more admiration and I gained from these male acquaintances the more delighted did he appear. Their attention to me seemed to give him pleasure."

"We became acquainted with Mr Dyson, my husband threw us together. He requested us, in his presence, to kiss and he seemed to enjoy it. He had given me to Mr Dyson."

She claimed however, that in December, as his health improved, so too did his libido and he now wished to resume his "marital rights" as they delicately and chauvinistically put it in the 1800s. Adelaide had taken disagreement to this, due to her already being practically fiancee'd with The Reverend Dyson and this, apparently was the true reason she wanted for the Chloroform. She planned to use it to put off her husband's sexual advances and furthermore, she explained this to Edwin on the night of his death, actually showing him the bottle of Chloroform and explaining her intention to use it if he were to make any sexual advances. The doctor asked her "Was not your husband very cross with you, or alarmed?" To which she replied:

"No, he was not cross; we talked amicably and seriously and he turned round on his side and pretended to sleep."

That was their final conversation, when she woke next, Edwin was dead.

In February, the coroner's inquest began, Dyson gave testimony of having bought the Chloroform for Adelaide, who was arrested under suspicion of wilful murder, whilst Dyson himself was arrested as accessory to murder.

Trial

The trial gained no small amount of public attention and on it's opening day on the 13th April, 1886, the first of six days of trial began surrounded by much media fanfare. At this stage, probably accounting to her foreigner status more than any other, Adelaide was not looked on well by the public and everyone presumed that she would be found guilty with no shadow of doubt.

At the trial, Adelaide was not permitted to give sworn evidence on her own behalf, as by law, defendants were not given the choice of testifying until much later, with the Civil Evidence Act of 1898. Instead, Adelaides defence lawyer,

Edward Clarke, who was a leading member of the bar and had recently gained huge notoriety defending high profile prisoners in court, maintained on her behalf that Edwin had committed suicide and highlighted evidence that would suggest said verdict.

The Crown Prosecution on the other hand, put forward three possibilities to the jury, that of suicide, murder and accidental death.

In the first act, the jury was asked to excuse Dyson from guilt by the prosecution, which they presently did so. This was unusual, however it gave the prosecutors advantage, as it now allowed Dyson himself to testify against Adelaide.

Dyson promptly gave testimony that throughout January, the pair had had many conversations concerning the Chloroform he had purchased and expressed that he had wanted to give his full account of the purchase to the police at the time, however had not done so due to Adelaide's insistence to keep quiet. He originally asked her what she had done with the Chloroform before any suspicion of the chemical had been aroused, and she replied,
"I have never used it, the bottle lies there full and uncorked. This is a very critical time for me, and you mustn't worry me with questions. Put away from your mind the fact that you ever gave me Chloroform."

The Reverend was clearly troubled by it, however, and two days later, asked her again, whereby she apparently seemed very frustrated, stamped her foot and shouted to him "Oh damn the Chloroform!" insisting that if he did not incriminate himself, she would not incriminate him. He stopped questioning her after a final outburst, when she yelled at him:

"Why don't you charge me outright for administering Chloroform to my husband?"

Naturally, the very next thing the Reverend did was exactly the opposite to avoid incrimination. He took it upon himself to discard the four small empty bottles that he had originally purchased by throwing them into a ditch in Wandsworth Common on his way to church one morning.

Appearing to nail the coffin home, Annie Walker, the nurse who Adelaide had told Reverend Dyson had purchased her Chloroform on occasion before and who was apparently now in America testified that she had never brought Chloroform, nor had she ever visited America, in fact, she had never left England in her life.

Despite all this looking very damning for Adelaide, the doctors testified as to the difficulty of killing someone with Chloroform. Doctor Leach also gave testimony to their relationship, stating that throughout Edwin's illness, Adelaide had been incredibly helpful in nursing him:

"She was most affectionate - In fact, I could not wish for a better nurse."

Their relationship was also described in detail, including the bizarre peculiarities of the odd love triangle, however at the same time, it was insisted that their relationship was not damaged at all by these circumstances:

"As far as the evidence which we have to offer to you on the part of the crown, and of course we shall put before you all the evidence we have, whether it makes for or against the prisoner at the bar, does not point to the existence of any quarrel between husband and wife. They seemed to have lived, so far as ordinary observers could see and judge, upon fairly good terms."

As if Edwin was not already eccentric enough, Doctor Leach also testified to the court that towards the end of December, he had had a conversation with Edwin concerning "mesmerism". Edwin, in the presence of Adelaide, had asked the doctor if he thought such things could be possible and if he could offer any advice. He told the doctor:

"I am doing such strange things, against my common sense; In fact both my wife and I are both doing so!"

Despite the doctor finding the conversation more than a little strange and Adelaide's chafing, Leach probed Edwin on the matter, concerned for his rationality and mental well-being and asked him if he found the idea of being under control of another to be troubling, however, on the contrary, Edwin simply replied that he liked it and Adelaide chimed in that "He was a dear friend to both of us." which would strongly suggest that Edwin might have been having a change of heart towards his dear friend George Dyson and their complicated agreement between himself, The Reverend and Adelaide.

All four doctors further testified to the difficulty of killing someone with Chloroform. The defence called no witnesses, however, at the end of the trial, Edward Clarke gave a six hour long closing speech, highlighting suicide and drawing particular attention to a lack of motive within the case.

The jury were out for only a short time and when court reconvened to hear the verdict, it was given as such,

"Although we think grave suspicion is attached to the prisoner, we do not think there is sufficient evidence to show how or by whom the chloroform was administered."

Adelaide was found Not Guilty.

Theories

As a case that is grounded in normality, the theories behind the death of Thomas Edwin Bartlett are quite simple, that of murder, accident or suicide. It is the individual motives for each where speculation is able to run rampant. No single theory answers all the questions and many simply demand more.

Murder

By many, murder has always been the first and foremost line of suspicion. Adelaide herself had remarked to Doctor Leach earlier in December, before Edwin's death,

"If Mr Bartlett doesn't get better soon his friends will accuse me of poisoning him."

Indeed, there is much to be suspicious of. Why had she thrown away the bottle of Chloroform if it really had been unused and unopened? And why had she seemed so highly strung when it was mentioned by the Reverend?

The Reverend also seemed to suffer an element of guilt, suggesting that perhaps he also suspected Adelaide to a degree. In January, their relationship appeared strained and at this time, he returned a watch to Adelaide that Edwin had left to him along with a reasonable chunk of money that had been given to him for expenses for visiting Adelaide by Edwin.

On the other hand however, she appeared to co-operate in many aspects of the case. As we heard during the trial, the Doctor remarked how she had cared most affectionately for Edwin throughout his illness and to all outside onlookers, their relationship was perfectly stable. Furthermore, all of the doctors testified as to the difficulty of using Chloroform for murder, stating that only about 30% of subjects die from ingesting the liquid poison and though in these cases, all were receiving medical care at the time, most deaths had taken between 48 hours to a week to die. It had only been observed that only in a very small portion of cases, the subjects had died quickly.

It was also remarked on the amount that would be needed to kill, suggesting around Three quarters of an ounce might be enough. Though Adelaide certainly had enough of the poison, how then had she managed to coerce Edwin into ingesting it? And how exactly had she done so without leaving any burns around the mouth?

The main theory suggests that she would have had to first use the Chloroform on a handkerchief or similar to lull Edwin into an anaesthetised stupor, before pouring it down his throat. Doctor Murray, one of the doctors who undertook the postmortem testified at the trial that,

"If the insensibility was profound, there would be no difficulty that I can see. It could be poured down."

However, in order for this to have been effective, the condition of Edwin would have had to have maintained a fine balance between stupor and his ability to retain muscle reactions, allowing him to swallow. Chloroform being a rather volatile substance, this was no easy task, even for anaesthetists of the time. Chloroform was routinely used as shampoo throughout the Victorian era and clients were told to eat well before visiting the salon and would be seen to by an open window, such was the unpredictability of it's efficiency.

On the subject of motive, most presume that despite outward appearances, Adelaide was unhappy with the current situation and would simply have been happier with Edwin "out of the picture" so to speak, where she would be free to marry the Reverend. Whether or not that's enough is a matter of mystery.

Suicide

The second theory concerning Edwin's death is that of Suicide. The defense pushed the line hard throughout the trial and in Edward Clarke's six hour long closing speech. Most of it emphasised Edwin's lack of grasp on reality with his own health, and chiefly that he seemed to be somewhat obsessed with the ideas he was suffering from a terminal illness. Edward Clarke stated that Edwin, afraid he was dying and having knowledge of the Chloroform, filled the wine glass full of the poison, drank it whilst Adelaide was not in the room and Adelaide had used the same glass to fill with brandy upon finding him dead, thus disguising the smell.

If this were truly the case however, why then had Edwin ordered breakfast? He was also apparently in good spirits and his health had been steadily returning throughout the end of December. If we are to believe Adelaide's words, he had even renewed his sexual advances towards her. Though some say that her outright disallowing of said advances could also have been motive enough for him to kill himself.

We can also look at his conversation with the Doctor concerning Mesmerism with renewed suspicion in the light of a suicide. Was Edwin now regretting an earlier decision to include the Reverend so deeply within his marriage?

Accidental Death

There is one other line of thought concerning the Death of Edwin, that of accidental death, though even at the time, it was considered as only an outside possibility. It is posited by some that Edwin, after waking and in a drowsy state, could have reached for the bottle of Chloroform on the mantelpiece thinking it was some other medicine and drank it mistakenly. However, would he not have realised his mistake quite quickly and if that was the case, why would he have quietly laid back down and died? It seems quite unlikely that Edwin would not have woken Adelaide, either intentionally or through his sheer panic of having ingested a wine glass full of poison.

After the Trial

After the trial was concluded and Adelaide was found not guilty, both herself and the Reverend George Dyson withdrew from the public eye. What became of the pair only exists in rumours, however most agree that the couple never met again.

Adelaide was heavily rumoured to have emigrated to the US, where she lived quietly until her death in 1933. There are little other details available as to her life, she simply vanished from trace.

The Reverend has been the subject of much more exciting rumours and one states that after the trial, he too emigrated to the US, taking up residence in New York City, where he married a wealthy young woman, who he promptly murdered for her estate. Given his character and all we know about him through the trial notes, this seems highly unlikely however.

Another rumour which seems much more probable, if a little less intriguing, suggests that he emigrated to Australia and took up position in a church there, living a quiet and peaceful life until his later death. This can be backed up to a certain extent through the church records, which show a British man named Dyson doing exactly that.

Conclusions

One statement which altogether makes the case more murky, was given by Doctor Leach when he was asked about Adelaide's state upon finding her husband to be dead. He stated:

"She seemed not only grieved, but very much alarmed, very much scared."

As for the Reverend, it seems apparent that he was naive in the extreme and there are many that presume he was manipulated by Adelaide into both buying the Chloroform and keeping quiet about it after the fact.

Edwin's father certainly did not trust Adelaide, though it could be said they had a difficult past, he even questioned the veracity of the will and had the witnesses called upon in court to testify that Edwin himself had in fact signed the document.

Even if we are to discount theories and motives for a moment, the Pimlico Poisoning case still leaves us with it's biggest mystery, chiefly, how on earth was the chloroform ingested without causing any traces of passing through his system? We are drawn back to the original question from the trial, "How came the Chloroform there?". This is a question that could provide answers, but ultimately leaves us with only more speculation and guesswork, probably for the rest of time.

In the days after the trial, Sir James Paget, a renowned surgeon responsible for laying the foundations of scientific medical pathology, wrote publicly in a piece for a medical journal:

"Now that she has been acquitted for murder and cannot be tried again, she should tell us in the interest of science how she did it!"

Episode 18 - The Second Life of Omm Sety

A young girl frantically wound in and out of the large stone statues of ancient Egyptian kings and queens. She stopped to kiss their feet and called them "my people" in a heavy egyptian accent, scolding passers by for not removing their shoes in the presence of the gods.

The scene was proving to be a little awkward for her parents, as the girl was British born, 4 year old Dorothy Eady, the statues were in the British museum and the year was 1908.

The Early Life & Death of Dorothy Eady

Dorothy Eady was born in Blackheath in London, England in 1904 to a relatively modest, but comfortable family. Her father, Reuben Ernest Eady worked as a master tailor, whilst her mother, Caroline Mary Eady stayed home to look after Dorothy. They lived an unremarkable and peaceful few years, it was the turn of the new century, and they were able to enjoy all the comforts of Edwardian life in a prosperous Britain.

At the age of three, disaster struck however, when Dorothy tripped and fell down a full flight of stairs whilst playing at home. The doctor was called to the scene, however, after testing for vital signs via placing a mirror and feather by her mouth, there was no hope as far as he could see and he pronounced Dorothy dead. Her parents were distraught as the doctor carried her to her bed and laid her down, before returning to his surgery to enlist the aid of a nurse to prepare Dorothy's body to be taken to the funeral home. Upon his return an hour later however, much to his shock, as he walked into Dorothy's room, he found the young girl, perfectly alive. She was sitting up in bed and playing, chirping happily away to herself and upon inspection appeared to have suffered no real injury. Dorothy's parents, disturbed by the chain of events, chased the doctor out of the house, all the while knocking back his concerned protestations that to the best of his knowledge, the girl had most certainly been dead when he had last seen her. As strange as this situation was, this was just the start of a series of strange events concerning their young daughter for the Eady family.

Shortly after the accident, Dorothy began breaking down into tears. She would sit hidden under the dining table and cry to herself for hours and when asked what was wrong, would tell her parents simply "I want to go home". Despite telling her over and over again that she already was home, the behaviour went on, all the while Dorothy insisted despite her parents efforts to comfort her. On one occasion, her mother finally decided to ask "Dorothy, if this is not our home, where is?" to which Dorothy replied "I don't know, but I want to go there".

It was also this period of her young childhood that Dorothy began having recurring dreams of a large building with vast stone columns and wide open gardens, a lotus pool nestled among exotic Jasmine, Oleander, Mimosa, Dwarf Chrysanthemums and mandrakes. Dorothy did not recognise any of these details at the time however, only that the dream would come night after night. At times, Dorothy unsettled her parents, when she spoke with a heavy accent, foreign to her own, slipping in and out seemingly unaware to Dorothy herself. This was dangerous territory for anyone, where trips to mental asylums or workhouses had been an easy answer for troubled children, but at only 3 years old, Dorothy was fortunate to be too young and her parents merely tried to console her when she showed signs of being upset and frustrated.

When Dorothy was four years old, her parents, unable to find anyone to look after her, took her along with them on an outing to the British Museum. Dorothy was, as expected by her parents, difficult work in the museum. As every normal young child of four years of age, she showed little sign of any interest in the exhibits, and towed around behind them as they did their best to keep her amused. As they entered the egyptian exhibits however, Dorothy suddenly and, much to her parents' surprise, became wildly enthused at the surrounding works of art. She ran quickly in and out, weaving through the large statues of the Egyptian gods and bent down to kiss their feet and spoke angrily at other visitors for wearing their shoes in the presence of the gods. Somewhat embarrassed at their child's behaviour, they pulled Dorothy away and as they did so, she spotted a mummy in a display case. Dorothy fell silent immediately, walked over the glass tomb and sat down, refusing to move and staring blankly at the preserved face of the Ancient Egyptian. Her mother and father, bemused but at least relieved that their daughter was causing no more commotion, left her alone, as she would not respond when they spoke to her and would not budge from the floor in front of the case. Half an hour later, they returned to collect Dorothy and when exasperated at trying to get her to move, her mother scooped her up from the ground. Enraged, Dorothy yelled out:

"Leave me... These are my people!"

Her mother later stated that her voice was "like that of a strange old woman rather than that of a child" and was so startled, she actually dropped her daughter to the floor. After more commotion, they managed to drag Dorothy away from the museum, kicking and screaming. It was to be another three years however, before any of the events at the British Museum would begin to make a small amount of sense to the family.

Finding Home

In 1911, Dorothy was now seven years old. Originally her behaviour was thought to be a passing phase, the struggles of raising a small child, by her parents, however, her peculiar outbursts had remained a constant. One day, whilst passing a bookshop on his way home from work, Reuben stopped in and picked up an edition of "The Children's Encyclopedia" by Arthur Mee, a popular, serialised encyclopedia that ran from 1908 to 1964. In this particular edition, there was an article on the Rosetta Stone which enthralled Dorothy. Her parents commented how the volume was constantly to be found open at the article and often with a magnifying glass lying next to it, which Dorothy used to try to read the writing from the images on the page. When her mother asked her why she was trying to read the etched words, as they were not in English, Dorothy replied:

"I know it. I've forgotten it, but perhaps I might remember it."

Shortly after, Dorothy finally made a discovery that would put an end to years of frustration. Whilst reading a magazine of her father's, Dorothy came across a photograph of The temple of Seti the First. An ancient Egyptian temple built for the pharaoh Seti, the son of Ramesses I, in Abydos, the capital of Upper Egypt, 7 miles West of the Nile. From the moment she spotted the picture, a wave of satisfying understanding flooded over her. She quickly sprung up and rushed to tell her parents of her discovery. "This" she pointed to the photograph "Is my home!". However, things were not quite right in the photo, Dorothy immediately pointed out that the gardens were missing, and included details such as the trees and vast Lotus Gardens that existed thousands of years before the ruin was rediscovered. The same happened later when she discovered another photograph, this time of Seti himself, mummified, but recognisable to Dorothy as a man she had known well. Again, her parents dismissed her insistences in exasperated tones, but still Dorothy adamantly told them that she had known him well and he had been "A nice and kind man". Whilst still utterly puzzling for her parents, Dorothy at last had an answer as to why she had felt such a draw to Egypt since she was three years old. Her story was still incomplete, but the fog was rising in her mind and she gave herself to learning as much as she could of her "homeland".

The next few years were no easier for Dorothy, despite her newly made discovery. She was still acting 'oddly' according to what her parents expected of her. She refused to wear shoes and would walk barefoot at every opportunity, begrudging the times that her parents enforced footwear onto her. At her Sunday school, she told her teacher that Christianity was nothing but a pale imitation of the Ancient Egyptian religion, which ended in the first of many home visits from her teachers and Pastors over the next several years. She would often visit the Catholic church because she enjoyed the ceremony of Mass, the traditions of burning incense was something she was particularly fond of, however, when confronted by the priest on whether or not she was in fact a Catholic at all, as he thought he knew her parents, who were in fact protestants. She explained matter-of-factly that she was not, however, Catholicism reminded her "of the old religion" and explained once again, to an astounded priest the virtues of Ancient Egyptian religion. The very next day, the priest wound up visiting her home to lecture her parents on the dangers of Dorothy's philosophies and asked that she keep away from his church until they had successfully steered her from the path to hell.

When she was expelled from her school in Dulwich for throwing a hymn book at a teacher after being scolded for refusing to sing a hymn that included the line "Curse the swart Egyptians", her parents decided on extreme measures. They sat Dorothy down and threatened her, quite gravely, that if she continued such behaviour, they would send her away to a convent school in Belgium. Dorothy simply replied that that would be fine, as she would simply run away and in fact, it would be easier for her to travel to Egypt from Belgium than from England. This soon put a halt on such ideas from her parents.

As she grew older, Dorothy found school tiring and from the age of 10, began to skip classes frequently, instead choosing to spend her time among the Egyptian exhibits in the British Museum. It was here that she met Ernest Wallis Budge, a respected Egyptologist and keeper of Egyptian and Assyrian Antiquities at the British Museum. He taught Dorothy how to read Ancient

Egyptian hieroglyphics, setting her phrases from "The book of the dead" to translate, checking them with his own work. Dorothy learnt at a pace which surprised Wallis and eventually, after Dorothy had committed several hundred of the pictographs to memory, he asked her how she was able to learn so much, so quickly. Dorothy stated simply that:

"I had known it all before, Now it is simply coming back to me."

This was an enjoyable period for Dorothy, with every glyph learnt, she felt she was coming one step closer to an understanding that had slipped her grasp for so many years, however, just as she turned 12 years old, shortly after the first world war broke out and bombing raids became more frequent on London, the Museum was closed and Dorothy was sent to Sussex, to live on her Aunt's farm. As headstrong as always, Dorothy rode one of the farm horses miles every day to the coastal town of Eastbourne, where she would sit in the library, reading everything on Egypt that she could and once again, found peace in the solitude of a life 3000 years in the past.

Seti the First

In 1918, Dorothy returned to London, now aged 14 years old. What happens next is best explained in her own words. One night whilst sleeping, she experienced an event which would give her the next clue she had waited so long for:

"I half woke up, feeling a weight on my chest. Then I fully woke up, and I saw this face bending over me with both hands on the neck of my night dress. I recognised the face from the photo I had seen years before of the Mummy Seti. I was astonished and shocked and I cried out, and yet I was overjoyed."

"I can remember it as if it was yesterday, but still it's difficult to explain. It was the feeling of something you have waited for that has come home at last."

After this, Dorothy began having a recurring dream of standing in a dark room, thick with the smell of incense as a decorated and stately looking man questioned her aggressively and beat her. She would wake up screaming, her mother often rushing in to comfort her, night after night. The dream meant little to Dorothy, but she knew that it yielded an important part of a memory she had lost and had spent her life so far seeking. Her parents however, thought very differently of the situation and unsurprisingly for the time, committed her for psychological evaluations at the local mental hospital on several occasions, however all of her stays were brief and never found any reason for concern, promptly discharging her.

Wilderness Years

Once Dorothy turned 16, she was no longer forced by law to attend school. She promptly took this offer and instead intensified a curriculum of self study on all matters of Egypt that she had previously been following alone for the past several years. Her father however, was keen to follow his own journey of self-discovery and had recently quit his job as a master tailor to pursue his hunch that moving pictures would be a lucrative business in the coming years. The family took to touring around England and Dorothy would visit the library in every city they stayed in to find new books she hadn't read previously. Eventually, they settled in Plymouth, where her father built a large cinema, complete with pipe organ. The Eady's lived in the flat above the cinema and Dorothy would sing to the pipe organ for the audiences on the nights no films were played. As it turned out, Reuben had made an astute observation and the cinema made them a comfortable living, raising them economically.

Dorothy had very little love for the Cinema however, and enlisted in art school. As she grew to a young adult, her philosophies matured and she began investigating the concepts of reincarnation, partaking in a local group dedicated to sharing their own past life stories, as well as several spiritualist groups. When she recounted the tale of her past, the groups theorised that it was unlikely that she had been reincarnated and were more prone to believe that as she had died, falling down the stairs at three years old, her soul had opened her up to possession, which was surely the true answer to everything that she had experienced of past memories filtering back to her like sunlight through a dark curtain for so many years. Dorothy thought all this was pure guff and so, once again, consoled herself with books and returned to studying alone.

And so, the years passed, until finally in 1931, aged 27, Dorothy moved to London against her parents wishes and took a job writing articles for an Egyptian public relations magazine. This was still a volatile period between Britain and Egypt, though formerly the British Empire had declared Egyptian independence from the Empire in 1922, they still occupied the country and controlled much of the affairs of the Egyptian government and Dorothy wrote articles for the magazine promoting Independence for Egypt. Whilst writing for this magazine, she met Imam Abdul Meguid, though the very next day after their chance meeting, overwatching a session in the house of commons, Imam returned to Egypt. Despite this, they continued to correspond regularly, writing letters back and forth for a year, when finally, in 1933, Imam wrote to Dorothy asking for her hand in marriage, which she accepted.

Aged 29 years old, Dorothy stepped off the boat, knelt down and kissed the ground. She had finally returned home.

Omm Sety

Unfortunately, Dorothy's marriage to Imam was not as smooth sailing as she had hoped. His family was well off and didn't take kindly to her headstrong attitude towards life. Dorothy, never one to keep the fractured details of her past life secret, also irked them, it was simply not how one should conduct themselves in Egypt as far as they were concerned and this caused further friction with her new family. Still, she fell pregnant and gave birth to a son named Sety, which placated them to a degree.

It was not long after her arrival in Egypt that Dorothy would finally come to understand all of her faded memories of her past life in intimate detail.

During the nights, Dorothy's new husband would frequently awake at night, only to see Dorothy standing by the writing bureau, frantically scribbling notes onto paper under the moonlight. In later years, Dorothy spoke of these occurrences:

"Most of the time when I was writing, I was rather unconscious, as though I were under a strange spell - neither asleep nor awake. I was being dictated to. The gentleman who was narrating my story - his name was Hor-Ra - Really took his time. He would tell me just a few words, then be absent for a fortnight or so, then come again - always at night - and relate to me a couple of other lines or episodes and after that his voice would just die away. It was as though this Hor-Ra were bored to death, as if he were fulfilling a mission that filled him with loathing. Every night when he came, I felt as though something were shaking me in order to wake me, just as in a dream. When I was writing the bits and pieces of the story I felt I was hearing a soft voice without being able to see anybody."

"When I was being dictated to, I felt as if I could understand every word, but later on, when I started to decipher the scribblings, I found they were quite difficult to understand. In fact, in the mornings when I woke up, everything seemed so vague, so uncertain, that if I hadn't been absolutely sure it wasn't my own handwriting, I would have said it was somebody else's. The bits and pieces were there, and when finally Hor-Ra stopped coming, I started to piece together what looked to me like a big jigsaw puzzle."

This lasted for almost an entire year, in which time Dorothy wrote over seventy pages of fractured hieroglyphic text. For the whole period, she had kept the few fragments she had picked up from Hor-Ra that she could make sense of a secret from her husband Imam, who had grown increasingly concerned about his new wife's behaviour. With Hor-Ra's tale complete, however, Dorothy worked on translating, with every new segment she would transcribe, the story of her past life became ever more clear. After almost thirty years, she finally began to understand the meaning behind all of her strange dreams, all of the tears she had shed as a child and of those frustrating years she had spent, grasping for answers in the dark.

Bentreshyt

Hor-ra's story told of how Dorothy had spent her previous life as a young woman named Bentreshyt. She had been born in Abydos to common parents, her mother a vegetable seller and her father a military man who was stationed in a Barracks away from the family home. At two years old, her mother had passed away and her father, unable to care for the child, took her to an ancient temple at Kom El Sultan, to the North of a large construction site which was shortly to become the Temple of Seti the First. Here she lived under the tutelage of the High Priest, a man named Antef who she described as,

"His shaven head, his immaculate clothes and his imposing figure commanded respect. He was the prototype of the Egyptian aristocrat - A very distinguished but frightening person indeed."

At 12 years old, she made her vows to remain at the temple as a virgin priestess. The temple performed plays and Bentreshyt studied "The Drama of the Resurrection and Death of Osiris" under the hard supervision of Antef. One evening, whilst singing in the garden of the temple, she happened upon Pharaoh Seti the First himself, who was visiting the shrine during a visit to oversee the construction of the Temple of Seti. The pair were to hit it off and Seti took a liking to Bentreshyt and during his time staying in Abydos which he extended for as long as possible to spend as much time with the girl as he could, they had something of an illicit affair. After his calling away however, Bentreshyt became aware that she was pregnant with the pharaoh's child, which was complicated on several levels. For the king it presented obvious complications, but for Bentreshyt, who was a sworn virgin priestess in the temple of Osiris, this was also a dangerous position to find oneself in.

Word managed to spread of the pregnancy through the temple and when Antef became aware, he took Bentreshyt down to the heart of the tomb and questioned her, beating her to find out who the father was. She refused to give a name but finally, as the high priest forced her palm onto the statue of Osiris, Bentreshyt succumbed to her faith and named the king. The crimes for her part, she was bluntly informed, were to be punishable by death as tradition commanded. This presented yet further problems for all parties involved, however, as a death sentence in ancient Egypt could only be enforced after a trial, a process which would make the secret of the pharaoh's involvement impossible to conceal. Realising the bleak situation she now faced, Bentreshyt commited suicide in order to save the face of the man she had fallen in love with.

As she finished translating the story, Dorothy fell into peace, within the seventy pages of hieroglyphics, the answers to her past life were finally hers.

The Later Years of Omm Sety

In 1935, Dorothy's fierce independence and bizarre eccentricities had taken their toll on her marriage and when Imam moved to Iraq to teach English, the couple divorced. Dorothy took custody of their son and Dorothy moved to a town nearby the Giza pyramids. She took a job with Egyptologist Selim Hassan, working as his secretary and draughtswoman. She observed ancient Egyptian religion and spent nights sleeping in the Great pyramids and until 1956, when the Pyramid research project was terminated, she assisted and worked with many prominent scholars and Egyptologists, both translating works and writing her own papers, becoming a respected scholar in her own right.

In 1957 she finally returned to Abydos and took on the name of Omm Sety. During a visit to the Temple of Sety, which she describes as "like walking into somewhere I'd lived before", the chief of antiquities was visiting at the same time. He had heard of Omm Sety before, as had most in the area, as she was well known for both her unsettling knowledge of ancient Egypt and her eccentricities. He was keen to test Omm Sety, and took her to the temple, in complete darkness they instructed her to walk to various parts of the temple and call out when she thought she was in the correct places. After six attempts to find fault with her knowledge of the temple, all failing, he gave up, thoroughly bemused. At the time of this visit, no articles on the layout of the temple had been published, in fact, even the excavators themselves hadn't catalogued the entire temple.

It was also during this time that the gardens she had told her parents were missing from a photograph of the temple were excavated. The gardens were exactly as she had described almost fifty years prior as a young girl who had never set foot in Egypt.

In 1964, Omm Sety turned sixty years old and was forced by law into retirement, however, this she felt was quite unsuitable and the Department of Antiquities allowed an exception for her to keep working until 1969, when she finally took retirement and worked part time as a consultant and tourist guide for the Antiquities Department at the Temple of Seti until 1972. During this time, she claimed she knew the location of the undiscovered tomb of Nefertiti, though was reluctant to give precise details. She did however give a rough location "close to the tomb of Tutankhamun", which ran counter to the opinion of every other scholar of the time. However, in 2015 and using modern scanning technology, this theory is now gaining acceptance and looking to be very much correct.

During her life in Egypt, she had assisted a vast list of respected Egyptologists in their works and cemented herself as a respected scholar and writer in her own right. In 1972, she suffered a heart attack and decided to take retirement for real this time. She lived the rest of her days in Abydos, observing the rights, traditions and systems of ancient egyptian religion until her death on the 21st April 1981.

Reincarnation

To those of us in the West, many believe that reincarnation is a fringe belief, however in the majority of Eastern religions and philosophies, it is a topic which is absolutely common belief and in most, a key concept, only raising eyebrows in atheistic circles. It dates back as far as the Greeks and several ancient religions held some belief in rebirth.

Despite most Western religions holding linear belief systems, that is that we are born, live and die and continue to live on in an afterlife, a 2009 poll showed that 24% of American Christians have professed a belief in reincarnation and a similar poll from 1989 showed that 31% of European Catholics have likewise professed a belief in rebirth to some degree.

It has been the subject of both serious, religious and non-clerical led academic study and yet still we find that to most it exists in the realm of the paranormal or new-age. For the believer, Psychiatrist Professor Ian Stevenson spent 40 years case filing more than 2500 children who had claimed to have past life memories. His studies found correlations between the children's stories with real people in history and further correlations were found whereby birthmarks and defects could be matched with wounds from previous lives identified from autopsy photographs and medical records.

There have been several documented cases of Xenoglossy, the phenomena whereby a person is able to speak or write a second language they have never studied previously and even more cases of children leading people to make discoveries of events, murderers and locations that would have been impossible for them to have known in any normal sense, such was the case of a young Druze boy who led police to a neighbouring village, where upon walking through the residents, he pointed out his own murderer. The man confessed to the crime and the boy later led police to dig up the murder weapon.

Conversely, critics point to anecdotal evidence being used as empirical data and claim that in many cases, our own cultural conditioning leads to spontaneous past life memories. Cryptomnesia has also been cited as responsible for cases of past life memories, a condition where past memories are forgotten and when they return to the subject, they are believed to be new memories.

Oftentimes, past lives are heavily romanticised which has obvious psychological assumptions and in cases in the East, where Caste systems operate, scams are not uncommon.

Whether one believes or does not believe is neither here nor there, however there exists failings in the academic arguments both for and against reincarnation. In many cases, basic psychological factors play an important role in the debunking of cases, but how then can we explain away the cases where correlations can be found between memories and the present? If cultural conditioning and belief systems play no role, why then, do we not all have such memories of past lives? Despite reincarnation being a phenomena that many view as rooted in the paranormal or spiritual, it is rather unique in that it has had such extensive, credible academic study and yet, the mystery endures.

Specifically in the case of Dorothy Eady, as a young child, is it not unusual to have an understanding of some of the concepts of an ancient tradition that she demonstrated? Even for someone who is a bright, fast learner, learning to read ancient hieroglyphics at only ten years old, in the time she had to learn is an impressive feat. In her later years, how did she know the things she did of the locations of the tombs and gardens and how did she have the knowledge of the temple of Seti that she appeared to hold, before any publications on the temple had been released?

Conclusions

The life of Dorothy Eady is fascinating even if you are to discount all of her claims of reincarnation. However, as a case specifically concerning the phenomena, it is one of the most well documented cases and even to a sceptic, provides intrigue and mystery. It is one thing to hold a passing phase as a child, but entirely another to live an entire lifetime dedicated to a quest to uncover memories of a past life with the dedication that she showed.

Professor James Peter Allen, an American Egyptologist working at Brown university said of Omm Sety:

"I don't know of an American archeologist in Egypt who doesn't respect her,"

"Sometimes you weren't sure whether Omm Sety wasn't pulling your leg. Not that she was a phoney in what she said or believed – she was absolutely not a con artist – but she knew that some people looked on her as a crackpot, so she kind of fed into that notion and let you go either way with it...She believed enough to make it spooky, and it made you doubt your own sense of reality sometimes."

On the topic of Omm Sety, Sir William Golding, author of Lord of the Flies, wrote of Egyptologists he had met during his travels in the 1980s:

"All were as well disposed to the Mystery as any child could have wished. When the question arose of a dear lady who believed herself to have been a priestess of a particular temple, they did not dismiss her as a crackpot but agreed that she had something."

Episode 19 - Joshua Maddux: The Boy In The Chimney

In May of 2008, 18 year old Joshua Maddux bid his sister farewell and left his house to take a walk. A nature lover and free spirit, this was nothing unusual, however, when he didn't return, things took a strange twist. The search for Josh continued for seven long years but remained unfruitful.

In 2015, less than a mile away, Chuck Murphy was demolishing his old wood cabin to make way for a property development. The cabin hadn't been used in years and inside was damp, the stuffy space smelt badly of rot. As they tore down the chimney, they made a grim discovery. Crammed inside the brickwork lay the mummified body of Joshua Maddux.

Joshua Maddux

Joshua Maddux lived in Woodland Park, a small city with a population of around 7,500, nestling among the natural beauty of the Pike National Forest in Teller County, Colorado. Josh was 6 feet tall, 150 Lbs and apparently something of a creative mind and a free spirit. He had a carefree attitude to life, grew his hair long, loved music, played the guitar and spent much of his free time writing. At school, he was a bright student and was seemingly well liked and well known. His mother and father were divorced and Josh lived with his father Mike and two sisters Kate and Ruth.

On the 8th of May, 2008, he left the house, telling his sister Kate that he was going out for a walk. He loved nature and often went out hiking alone, so his sister thought little of the farewell but when he failed to return later that evening, worry settled in. Having always been such a free spirit, at first the worry was only a small nagging in the back of their minds, however, as the days passed and Josh had still not returned, his father took the sudden disappearance more seriously and on the 13th May, called the police to report Josh missing.

"I got up one morning" He said, "and Josh was there, then he just never came home. The next day he still didn't come home. I called his friends, nobody had seen him. Nobody knows where he is."

The searches were spread far and wide, scouring the neighbourhood and wider parkland area, days turned to weeks and weeks turned to months yet still no clue as to his disappearance had been uncovered. Hope of finding Josh began to fade and his sister Kate spoke of how she had always hoped that he had simply skipped town to go play music or start a different life and held onto the hope of such an eventuality. In a post online, she wrote of her brother's disappearance,

"'Since Josh was 18, it has been reasonable to assume he may have decided to leave town to start a new life. As one of his two older sisters, I have always chosen to believe that this was the case. I have expected Josh to return home to my father's house at any time with a wife and small children so that they can meet their grandparents and two aunts. Josh has always been known for his musical and literary talent, so maybe we would find him playing music with a band on tour, or catch him writing successful novels under a pen name so that he could keep his preferred lifestyle of solitude in the woods."

They had no reason to believe that Josh had gotten involved in any trouble and he had not given them any worry or concern about his mental health, although two years prior to his disappearance, on June the 1st 2006, a week before his high school graduation, Josh's Older brother, Zachary, had committed suicide. His father spoke about the tragic death of his son and how it had affected Josh,

"I buried his older brother two years before and it was so difficult on Josh. When his brother died, it pushed him over the edge. It was a big shock for the family and a big shock for Josh. He thought highly of his older brother."

Despite this difficult period however, his family noted that Josh had been doing well and was happy around the time he disappeared. The police had no reason to suspect any criminal activity and so listed him as a missing person. The searches continued and the missing persons file remained open. His father Mike retained ownership of the family home after they moved, in case Josh would ever return, as that would be the only place he would have known to go, but news of Josh remained elusive. That was, until 2015, when a local builder by the name of Chuck Murphy made a grim discovery.

The Body in the Chimney

In 2015, Chuck Murphy, a builder from nearby Colorado Springs, was demolishing his old wood cabin. The cabin sat on a large patch of land, surrounded by tall pines. The cabin hadn't been used for over ten years and had fallen into a state of disrepair. Chuck had made the decision to tear down the building to make way for a property development and in August, the time had come to begin demolishing the decaying building.

He had originally purchased the cabin in the 1950's. It had formerly been the Homestead of Thunderhead Ranch, a locally infamous drinking and gambling complex owned by 'Big Bert' Bergstroms. Bergstroms had come to America from Sweden in 1912 and run the thunderhead Inn as a dining and drinking Establishment after the end of prohibition. On the side however, he used the ranch as an illegal gambling den and was rumoured to offer prostitution. He was arrested by the FBI, but the jury, who one would assume enjoyed a little of what Bert offered, promptly found him not guilty.

In more recent times, Chuck's brother had lived in the cabin until 2005, but since moving out, it had become a storage facility and Chuck had rarely visited the property. Animals had been a problem and inside it carried an uninviting stench. As they dismantled the chimney and reached the interior, Chuck made the horrifying discovery of the body of a young man, cramped into a fetal position with his legs above his head. He called the police who arrived with the County coroner who, with the help of a forensic odontologist used dental records to positively identify the corpse to be that of Joshua Maddux, less than a mile from his family home.

Accidental Death

The Maddux family were stunned when the news of the discovery of Josh's body was delivered. His sister Kate said,
"The situation doesn't make any sense at all. We were really expecting him to be anywhere else in the world and he was actually very close. The only thing we can figure is he was being an 18-year-old kid, checking out a cabin -- it had already been abandoned for a long time -- and a horrible accident happened."

Al Born, the Teller County coroner undertook an autopsy and found no evidence of any drugs in Josh's system. Speaking to the press, he stated,

"The hard tissue showed no signs of trauma. There were no broken bones, no knife marks. There were no bullet holes. There are so far no answers to a number of things. It is very confusing."

The cabin sat on Meadowlark Lane, only two blocks from the Maddux family home, yet the searches had overlooked the building. There had not been any sign of life from the old structure, it was simply concealed from suspicion due to its own banality. Chuck Murphy, the cabin owner himself, had rarely visited, however, on the occasions that he had to check in, he himself had not noticed anything unusual about the property. The cabin itself stood centrally in a large plot of land, surrounded by tall pines, offset from the roadside by around fifty feet. Police suggested that with no adjacent homes, if Josh had cried for help, no one would have been able to hear him regardless.

"It was not an instant death. How he died is only a matter of speculation, but we know he did not starve to death because that takes many weeks. So then you go down the chain and you have dehydration, which can take just a few days and the other thing would be hypothermia, which could take a day or two. We have no evidence to say which one came first."

Eventually, on the 28th September 2015, after failing to find any rational cause, Born made a ruling of "Accidental Death". Born suggested that Josh had climbed down the chimney and become lodged within the brickwork. He concluded the most likely cause for death was Hypothermia, as the temperature around the time of his disappearance had dropped to -6 Celsius at its coldest. Chuck Murphy, however, found this conclusion to be far from satisfactory.

Discrepancies

Immediately following the ruling, Chuck questioned the Coroner's conclusion of accidental death. Born had stated that Josh's position in the chimney "appeared to have been a voluntary act in order to gain access", however when he heard that, Chuck made a testimony stating that this would in fact, have been impossible. The chimney had been built twenty years previous and during its construction, had been fitted with a steel rebar, a large, thick wire mesh hung from steel hooks used to keep animals and debris from becoming lodged inside the chimney or from entering the cabin itself. Murphy spoke openly about the rebar, stating that,

"It was a heavy wire grate, a wire mesh, I installed it across the chimney about one row of bricks from the top. We didn't want trouble with raccoons and things getting into the chimney."

This led to a subtle and public back and forth between the builder and coroner, with Born replying that the grate could have been rusted or corroded and further stated:

"Nobody saw the metal mesh, we didn't see it in any of our photos. It may have disappeared."

However, Born said that during the demolition, all metal work had been collected and stashed into the back of a truck to be taken for scrap, which would explain why the mesh was not clearly identified by the coroner as it wasn't anywhere near the chimney, if it was still on the site at all at the time of the visit by the coroner. Conceding to Murphy, Born reopened the case three days after his initial conclusion. It was not only the rebar that caused doubt however, there were, in fact, several other pieces of information which failed to make any sense to Murphy and had led him to doubt the coroner's report. The dots just weren't connecting.

There was, for one thing, the mysterious shifting of a large wooden breakfast bar that had been torn from a wall in the kitchen and dragged over to block the Chimney from inside the cabin. This fact was probably the very reason that Chuck himself had not noticed anything unusual about the chimney in the first place. However, the question remained that if the Breakfast bar had been torn from the wall, then who had done it and why?

Josh's body had also been found in a fetal position, with his legs above his head, and disjointed from his torso. In order to have gotten into such a position, he would have had to have entered the chimney head first. This was a fairly unusual position and Born had earlier commented that he thought it would have taken two people to position him in such a way.

There was also one final question that lingered with Chuck and it concerned no small detail. When Josh's body had been found, he had removed all of his clothing, he had been found wearing only a thin thermal shirt. This would already strike one as unusual, however, his clothes had actually been found inside the cabin, folded up next to the fireplace. This, fact hadn't escaped Born however, he was well aware of the clothing and remarked about them:

"This one really taxed our brains. We found his clothing just outside the firebox. He only had on a thermal t-shirt. We don't know why he took his clothes off, took his shoes and socks off, and why he went outside, climbed on the roof and went down the chimney. It was not linear thinking."

He quickly concluded that given his options, that of cause of death being accidental death, murder or undetermined causes, he finally concluded that:

We've come up with the most plausible explanation and it will remain an accident. He did come down the chimney, that's our conclusion."

Murphys rebuttal was now less than subtle, he stated simply:

"There's no way that guy crawled inside that chimney with that steel webbing. He didn't come down the chimney.".

Murphy remained convinced that the death of Joshua Maddux had been no accident. As it happened, Al Born had mentioned that several calls had been made to both the police and Coroners office, suggesting leads and naming suspects that had bragged of killing Josh.

There was one main suspect, though he remained unnamed, he was now spending time in a Texas jail and had previous time in Seattle and Portland prisons with a long list of violent criminal behaviour. The tips had told Born of how he was, apparently the last man to have been seen with Josh, but Born could not place him at the crime scene. When speaking of the man, he said: "They can't give me times and specifics and we can't generate stuff that goes back seven years."

He also doubted that the man would have been able to have positioned Josh in the chimney in such a position alone. And that, as far as Born was concerned, was the end of that suspect and line of thinking. However, there was to be a more modern twist just around the corner.

Reddit

As it turned out, there was a post on Reddit in 2015, which reads as if it was made most likely from one of the very people who had called in to the Coroner suspecting the previously spoken of man. The post gave a name to the suspect, which leads to many new facts, an abbreviated version of the post tells his side of the story:

I went to highschool with this skinny dorky hippy named Andy who played guitar in a band. I was never good friends with him or anything, but a year or so after I graduated one of my good friends, Josh, started hanging out with him and then went missing.

Turns out that in addition to becoming a lot scarier looking, Andy had indeed headed down to New Mexico, where he found himself shooting the shit with the caretaker of a disabled guy, and got invited over to their apartment.

Caretaker gets in the shower, and when he comes back out, the disabled guy is stabbed to death and Andy's gone. When Andy got arrested, he also claimed to have killed a woman in Taos and stuffed her body in a barrel.

The cops had indeed found a woman stuffed in a barrel in Taos, but already had somebody in custody for it and decided to stick with that guy instead. Years later, I found out that the caretaker had died in a bar fight, and without him the cops didn't have much in the way of evidence somehow, so that case against Andy was dropped, too.

Several of us went to the cops saying "Yo, Josh Who Went Missing was last seen with Andy Who's A Murderer, maybe you should check that out?" Despite a fair amount of pestering, nothing ever really came of it, and by nothing I mean that the police mostly didn't even return our calls, and once accidentally cancelled the bulletin on Josh because "He's alive and well and living in the next town over!" (he wasn't)

He was actually in the chimney of an abandoned cabin like two blocks from his parents' house. The coroner said the body had been there for about seven years, and ruled the death accidental, concluding that Josh had probably climbed down the chimney in an attempt to break into the house and gotten stuck. Which, given the age of the corpse, doesn't seem overly ridiculous.

Except for the fact that in addition to Josh having last been seen with Andy-immediately-before-his-stabbing-spree, people called in to report having heard rumors that Andy was bragging about having "Put Josh in a hole."

Somebody had ripped a heavy bar off the wall in the kitchen and propped it against the fireplace. Or the fact that Josh's stuff was already inside the cabin, meaning (a) he'd already broken in and would have had to lock himself out to have to go for the chimney, and (b) he might have noticed that either the flu or the big bar would have prevented him from getting in through the fireplace. Or the fact that when he was found, Josh's knees were above his head, which sounds to me like he would have had to go in head-first (disclaimer: not an expert at fucking all). Or maybe the fact that Josh was barefoot and naked from the waist down.

This is just my opinion, but I don't care who you are: you don't try to climb head first into a chimney via a hole rusted through a metal grate with your dick hanging out.

As far as I can tell, nobody even bothered to call Andy to ask if he knew anything. (By the way, from what I hear, Andy's still out and about doing his thing when he's not in the mental hospital).

All I'm saying is: I wish they had done some police shit. Open an investigation. Try to track down some leads. Interview some of the folks who've been calling in tips for the last seven years. Maybe check for some semen or something. I don't know. Don't just say "accidental", dust off your hands, and call it a day."

As it happens, "Andy"does in fact exist. He was also a music lover, he played in a band and apparently lived quite a free lifestyle himself. It is not unthinkable, one might suggest, that Andy and Josh may very well have known of each other.

Andrew Richard Newman

Andy's full name was Andrew Richard Newman. He was arrested on suspicion of a fatal stabbing in New Mexico that went exactly as the Reddit post had described. During high school he played guitar in a band named "The Baumers" and was also well known and seemingly, well liked. In an article about his arrest for the New Mexico stabbing, there are several replies from users who had gone to school with him that describe him as "intelligent" and a "very smart guy". Although he seems to have left the state and traveled nomadically around the country after graduating high school, he kept in contact with many of his old friends. One would believe that it is not at all a grand stretch of imagination to place Andy and Josh together. They shared similar interests and similar outlooks on life. If that is the case however, the post on Reddit sums it up quite well with the line:

"All I'm saying is: I wish they had done some police shit. Open an investigation. Try to track down some leads. Interview some of the folks who've been calling in tips for the last seven years".

Conclusions

The case of Joshua Maddux is utterly perplexing for several reasons. It seems fairly safe to presume that Chuck Murphy is to be believed concerning the rebar in the chimney, after all, what possible reason would he have to lie about the existence of it in the first place?

However, when one starts to consider the other outlying factors, the clothes by the fireplace, the breakfast bar dragged to cover the fireplace and the numerous tip offs concerning "Andy", the biggest mystery is perhaps, why on earth was Andy not in the very least, pulled in for questioning?

In a follow up post on the same Reddit thread, the user who posted the original post stated that he believed Andy to now be housed in a mental hospital somewhere. Whether or not the case will ever be reopened or further investigated remains to be seen, though in the past two years, it remains dark and the official conclusions of the County Coroner stand.

Episode 20 - Krampus & Co.

Dating back to 1823, the American Christmas Elf is an immediately recognisable character in modern, Anglo-American Christmas traditions. They are a short, enthusiastic little helper, who makes toys, takes care of the Reindeer and checks on children's behaviour. The Christmas elf carries very little threat and aligns with the benevolent nature of Santa Claus himself.

In a more distant past, tangled among European Folklore where the Elves' roots are firmly buried in the frozen winter ground, their origins are far from friendly little cherubs making wooden trains however.

The Christmas Elf

Elves have a long tradition in Folklore dating back over a thousand years. Largely independent of Christmas, it wasn't until 1823, with the publication of the classic Christmas poem, attributed to Clement Clarke Moore, "A visit from St. Nicholas" more commonly known today as "The night before Christmas" that the mention of Elves in relation to Christmas and the Anglo-American version of the Santa Claus figure was born. In the poem, Santa Claus himself is actually mentioned as a "jolly old elf".

"He had a broad face, and a little round belly
That shook when he laugh'd, like a bowl full of jelly:
He was chubby and plump, a right jolly old elf,
And I laugh'd when I saw him in spite of myself;"

In 1857, this was extended when Harper's Weekly, an American political publication printed a poem called "The wonders of Santa Claus" that referred to his helpers as elves who would make toys and fill the stockings of children on Christmas Eve night. Disney released a short film in 1932 called Santa's Workshop that had the elves helping out prepping Santa for his journey delivering presents as well as doing tasks around the workshop. This is more or less, a depiction of Santa's Elves that still holds true today and has gone mostly unchanged in popular media and entertainment for almost a hundred years.

The concept of "Santa's little helper" is not entirely modern, however and long before he was depicted as a rosy cheeked man full of cheer, with a white beard and red costume, Santa had help of a different kind.

Saint Nick & His Band of Merry Men

Prior to the insertion of Christianity, the tradition of a gift-bringer during Winter festivals was widespread throughout Europe. In Germanic Paganism, the midwinter festival of Yule had Wodan, or Odin, the leader of the wild hunt, a ghostly visage of a supernatural horde of huntsmen depicted in Folk Mythologies throughout Northern Europe that would tear across the land on midwinter nights.

Odin was often depicted as an old man, wearing a cloak. He had only one eye and a long white beard. He led the hunt on a white, eight legged horse named Sleipnir and wielded Gungnir, a legendary mythological spear. He was feared and loved in folklore. The wild hunt was said to bring raucous scenes to villages and as he rode past in the sky on Sleipnir, Odin would leave gifts of fruit and sweets in childrens boots along with weapons for the adult men.

There are some scholars who claim Odin was the original inception of the gift bringing figure we have today, though it is debated, alongside the theory that Sleipnir shows some parallels with Santa's sleigh or perhaps the magical reindeer. Though again, these links are debated. The history itself is mired in folklore and varies so much that making any solid links between the two would be a very difficult task.

Although having some earlier presence in Europe, it wasn't until later, after the widespread introduction of Catholicism, that a more prominent version of the modern Santa Claus emerged throughout Europe and took the primary position for a midwinter festival. Among several other things, Saint Nicholas was the patron saint of Children and was celebrated on St Nicholas' Day, the 6th of December. Gifts were given in celebration and thanks for the miracles he had worked throughout his life, such as bringing back from the dead three children who had been murdered by a butcher and saving a young family of child prostitutes. He was celebrated for his benevolence and good cheer and in recognition of his miracles and status as a protector. After the Protestant Reformation, Christmas Day was worked into the annual calendar to bring the midwinter festival to focus more on the birth of Jesus, however, the traditions of Saint Nicholas Day remained and many of the traditions merged with Christmas Day and Saint Nicholas as a gift bringer was one such tradition that shifted to the newer holiday, though his life as a saint was diminished to a sideline, in favour of the nativity tale.

Saint Nicholas, much like Santa Claus today, did not work alone. Just like the Santa Claus figure of today, he too judged the behaviour of children and gifted to them accordingly, and just like with the elves today, he too had a band of helpers. Throughout Europe, there are folk tales of several figures who helped him to judge whether or not children had been good or bad. Some are widely known, whilst others are regional variations and some are more forgiving than others, though they all hold a similar role, that of the judge and jury and as a child in 17th Century Europe, you'd best hope you have behaved well.

Knecht Ruprecht

First appearing in Germany during the 17th Century, Knecht Ruprecht, or "Farmhand Rupert" is one of Saint Nicholas' most widely known helpers. In some countries he was working alone as both benefactor and punisher, whilst in others, he acted as an assistant to Saint Nicholas, doling out punishment to naughty children.

He was depicted as an old man who walked with a limp. He wore tatty and torn robes of black or dark brown and carried a bag of ashes and a long wooden staff. He would approach parents to ask if their children had been good or not, often asking if they had been praying. If the children had been good and had diligently prayed throughout the year, he would give them gifts of fruits, nuts and gingerbread, however, if the children had neglected their religious duties, he would beat them with the bag of ashes. In some stories he gave them gifts of coal, sticks or stones and in Austria, there were tales that he would take the worst offenders into the darkness of the winter woods and beat them with Birch sticks before stuffing them into a hessian sack and tossing them into the river, never to be seen again.

Belsnickel

In Southern Germany, the character of belsnickel is a common associate of Saint Nicholas. There are some scholars who believe him to be a regional variant of Knecht Ruprecht, however, unlike Knecht Ruprecht, Belsnickel operated solo rather than working alongside Saint Nicholas. His name is derived from "Belzen" the German word for "Wallop" and "Nickel", a diminutive form of Nicholas.

Belsnickel was also depicted as wearing tatty robes and walking with a limp. He wore fur clothing, carried a large stick and painted his face or wore a mask. He watched children throughout the year, monitoring their behaviour for Saint Nicholas and on the night of Saint Nicholas Day, shortly after children went to bed, he would knock on their windows to enter their rooms. If the children were deemed by Belsnickel to have been good, he would leave them gifts of snacks and cake which he carried in his pockets, however, if the children were judged to have had bad behaviour throughout the year, he would beat them with his stick. That's if they were lucky. Some stories told of how he would drag the bad children out of their rooms and off into the forest, where they would never be seen again.

Interestingly, due to German migration to the USA, Belsnickel has some folk history in Pennsylvania and Indiana, where celebrations still told stories of his work and legends of his judgements were still told to some children right up until modern times.

Perchta

Perchta was one of Saint Nicholas' more troubling associates. Originally, she was a Pagan goddess, depicted in two forms as both a pale, young woman of immense beauty and an haggard old lady. In her haggard form, she wore black robes, torn and roadworn and had a hooked nose. Some scholars date Perchta's activities during midwinter as far back as the 10th Century and her presence still holds a central role in celebrations today in Austria and many other Southern European countries.

Perchta roamed the land during midwinter, followed by either a band of tiny demons or sometimes, unbaptised babies. Throughout the twelve days of Christmas, she would enter the houses of families and ask the children and young servants if they had been good and worked hard throughout the year. If they had been good, she would lay a silver coin in their boots and no doubt a sigh of relief in their hearts, as if they had been deemed to have been bad, Perchta would slit open their stomachs, remove their innards and stuff them with straw and pebbles.

There are still many more of Saint Nicholas' little helpers. Most are all variations of the previous, doling out punishments to naughty children and working alongside the benevolent saint. There is one, however, whose name is perhaps a little more famous in modern times, even outside of traditional folklore. That of the Krampus.

Krampus

Deriving from "Krampen" the german word for claw, Krampus was a horned, demon-like figure, walking upright on two legs, with the lower half of his body taking on goat-like appearance, complete with cloven hooves. His body is often depicted covered in dark fur and he often had a tail. He had large fangs and a long tongue and was, for all intents and purposes very close to the classical depiction of a devil figure, though he also held many similarities with earlier folk creatures, such as fauns from Roman mythology and Satyrs from the Greeks. By the 17th Century, Krampus was fully integrated into the midwinter festivals and a staple by the side of Saint Nicholas.

One of the scarier elements of the Krampus character are the chains he carried with him, dragging them behind him as he walked into towns and villages, at times thrashing them about to let the children know Krampus was coming.

He was always depicted as carrying bundles of Birch sticks and often with a wicker basket strapped to his back. These were, in typical fashion, the tools of which Krampus used to punish the bad children.

Krampus also differed from the previous associates of Saint Nicholas in that he had a night dedicated solely to him. The 5th of December, one day before Saint Nicholas Day, was the festival known as Krampusnacht. On Krampusnacht, the horned helper appeared to take care of the bad children, leaving the good for Saint Nicholas the next night. As night fell, children would clean their boots and place them in the porch or by the front door of their houses and in softer versions of the tale, Krampus would roam the streets, simply placing birch sticks within the boots of the children he had judged as having misbehaved, though in other versions, he would use the Birch sticks to beat the children. In more extreme folk tales, Krampus used his wicker basket to scoop up the children and transport them away, either into the woods or down to his chambers in the underworld, where he would chain and beat them, lost forever.

The Nightmare Before Christmas

Throughout history, across physical borders and spiritual eras, we see time and again similar depictions of these characters that closely resemble one another. In Iceland there are the yule lads, whose depictions over time have varied from a gang of young pranksters to demonic monsters that eat children, though their role as both judge and gift bringer to children over the Christmas period has remained the same. Iceland too has the myth of the Yule cat, a feline stalker who visited children on Christmas eve and would bring either gifts or punishment, depending on their work rate throughout the year, a criteria which was symbolised by the state of their clothing, as only the well dressed children or workers with new clothes would have been the ones who had worked hard during the cotton harvest in the run up to Midwinter with a successful harvest being rewarded with clothes made from said cotton.

In some areas of France, there was Hans Trapp, a man who disguised himself as a scarecrow to capture poorly behaved children who was struck down by God and now returned on Christmas Eve to punish poorly behaved children. France also retains the legend of Pere Fouttard, the very butcher who killed the children Saint Nicholas was said to have brought back to life. After the miracle was performed, Pere Fouttard was brought into the service of Saint Nicholas to punish naughty Children on Christmas Eve.

Despite the at times extreme depictions of Saint Nicholas's helpers, they are not necessarily evil spirits or demons themselves. Saint Nicholas himself was a benevolent character, he brought happiness and positivity and so, these helpers represented the darker sides of the festivals to allow Nicholas to maintain his benevolent figure. Krampus and Co. were necessary punishers, working together, they were manifestations of a duality as a manner of teaching people right from wrong, good from bad and fostering a fear to keep children in line with the societal expectations of the times. We still use a similar, yet much softened version of the same folklore in modern society, if you misbehave Santa won't bring gifts and in some cases will only bring coal, for example. Over time the folklore of the winter gift bringer has become much more mild, though the end result is the same.

Nowadays, Krampus and various other companions of Saint Nicholas are still celebrated today, though again, their presence is much softened. They have become mythological figures in old folk tales and characters to dress up as and celebrate the Winter Solstice or the holiday season in a time for cheer and as a reaction to the commercialism of Christmas itself. Midwinter remains a period of the year when the dark surrounds us and we look to celebrations and festivities to see us through and bring us together.

About The Author

I'm Ben, a hair stylist with an academic background in History and Social Sciences. As a teenager, I was a fan of The X-Files, The Twilight Zone and The Outer Limits and later, all manner of the fringe elements of society.

I live with my cat, Nyanme Turbo and my dog, Captain Bigglesworth, in Brighton where I was born and raised, nestled up against the rolling hills of the South Downs of England. Aside from Dark Histories and cutting hair, I also write fiction from time to time, play what could loosely be described as music, fumble through a second language and keep fish.

darkhistories.com

Dark Histories: Season One

Printed in Great Britain
by Amazon